Developing Excellence in Teaching and Learning in Higher Education through Observation

Offering interdisciplinary, evidence-informed discussion and practical resources for using observation as a tool of educational inquiry to enhance understanding and the quality of teaching and learning in higher education, this book draws on forward-thinking, contemporary research.

Illustrated with real examples and case studies of collaborative observation from a range of subject areas, it provides a conceptual and practical guide for harnessing observation to better understand the relationship between teaching and learning.

This is a must-read book for all those interested and involved in using observation to understand, develop and improve the quality of teaching and learning in higher education.

Matt O'Leary is Professor of Education and Director of CSPACE Education Research Centre at Birmingham City University, UK. He is internationally renowned for his extensive body of work on the use of observation in understanding and improving teaching and learning across education sectors.

Vanessa Cui is a Senior Research Fellow at Birmingham City University CSPACE Education Research Centre. Her research focuses on higher education learning and teaching policy and practices, with a special interest in the students' involvement in quality development activities and staff and student collaborations in learning and teaching.

Developing Excellence in Teaching and Learning in Higher Education through Observation

MATT O'LEARY AND VANESSA CUI

LONDON AND NEW YORK

Designed cover image: © Getty Images

First published 2023
by Routledge
4 Park Square, Milton Park, Abingdon, Oxon OX14 4RN

and by Routledge
605 Third Avenue, New York, NY 10158

Routledge is an imprint of the Taylor & Francis Group, an informa business

© 2023 Matt O'Leary and Vanessa Cui

The right of Matt O'Leary and Vanessa Cui to be identified as authors of this work has been asserted in accordance with sections 77 and 78 of the Copyright, Designs and Patents Act 1988.

All rights reserved. No part of this book may be reprinted or reproduced or utilised in any form or by any electronic, mechanical, or other means, now known or hereafter invented, including photocopying and recording, or in any information storage or retrieval system, without permission in writing from the publishers.

Trademark notice: Product or corporate names may be trademarks or registered trademarks, and are used only for identification and explanation without intent to infringe.

British Library Cataloguing-in-Publication Data
A catalogue record for this book is available from the British Library

ISBN: 978-0-367-35808-2 (hbk)
ISBN: 978-0-367-35810-5 (pbk)
ISBN: 978-0-429-34190-8 (ebk)

DOI: 10.4324/9780429341908

Typeset in Dante and Avenir
by SPi Technologies India Pvt Ltd (Straive)

Contents

List of illustrations vii
Acknowledgements ix

1 Introduction 1

2 Contextualising the importance of teaching and learning in higher education 9

3 Understanding teaching and learning in higher education 31

4 Developing a scholarly approach to higher education teaching and learning 52

5 A review of the role of observation in teaching and learning 73

6 Designing and implementing a collegial peer observation scheme 100

7 Developing observation and coaching skills 138

8 Collaborative observation between students and staff as a catalyst for meaningful improvement 158

9 Unseen observation: an alternative approach to thinking
  about academics' professional learning   198

10 Concluding comments   217

   Index   *220*

Illustrations

Figures

Figure 5.1	An overview of the 7 stages of the unseen observation cycle	80
Figure 6.1	Cycle of Peer Observation (CoPO)	109
Figure 8.1	Cycle of Collaborative Observation (CoCO)	165
Figure 8.2	Students' ideas on what it means to 'observe' something	182
Figure 8.3	Students' suggestions on what can/cannot be observed in an educational environment	183
Figure 8.4	CoCO annotated with student observer activities	185
Figure 8.5	Radiotherapy CoCO Cycle 1 tutor observation notes excerpt	188
Figure 8.6	Radiotherapy CoCO Cycle 1 student observer reflection excerpt	189
Figure 9.1	An overview of the 7 stages of the unseen observation cycle	202

Tables

Table 3.1	Features of Higher Education Teaching and Learning	33
Table 4.1	Existential, Critical and Communitarian Perspectives on Authenticity in Teaching	58
Table 6.1	Some Thinking Prompts for Self-Reflection on Teaching and Learning	121

Table 6.2	Examples of Stage 1 Observee Self-Reflections	123
Table 6.3	Examples of Stage 6 Self-Reflections by Observers and Observees	131
Table 7.1	Words Commonly Associated with Observation	149
Table 7.2	Reflective Questions on Observation and the Role of the Observer	150
Table 7.3	Observer Reflections on Their Role	151
Table 7.4	Defining Teaching and Learning	151
Table 7.5	Coaching Task 1	154
Table 7.6	Coaching Task 2	154

Boxes

Box 6.1	Example A – Extract Of Observation Notes	126
Box 6.2	Example B – Extract Of Observation Notes	128

Acknowledgements

This book is dedicated to all those colleagues, staff and students in higher education who have participated in our research and ongoing work in developing teaching and learning in higher education over the last decade. Your participation in and support for our research has been invaluable. We would especially like to thank our colleagues and students in the Faculty of Health, Education and Life Sciences at Birmingham City University. You have been instrumental in developing our thinking and actively contributing to the project work that has provided much of the inspiration and the substance for the writing of this book.

We would like to thank Routledge for commissioning this book and the support we have received from the editorial team throughout the publishing process. We would also like to thank our external reviewers for their helpful comments on our initial book proposal.

Finally, we save extra special thanks for our families. We would never have been able to complete this book without you. Thanks for putting up with us shutting ourselves away all those evenings, weekends and holidays to focus on writing. Thanks for the endless cups of tea and food you brought us. And most of all, thanks for your love, support and continuous encouragement. We dedicate this book to Kate, Lola, Ella, Tom and Ffion.

Introduction   1

This book focuses on the improvement of teaching and learning in higher education (HE) through the use of observation. Historically, peer-based models of observation have been the dominant model in the HE sector, ranging from informal, ad hoc approaches to more formal, institutionally regulated models. Despite the differences between models, what unites them is the way in which observation has been predominantly conceptualised and used as a method of assessment. This is where this book differs. It takes a conscious and deliberate stance to sever the link between observation and assessment by choosing not to use observation for assessment purposes. The rationale for this is both evidence-based and strategic as we identify assessment as the single most significant barrier to making the best use of observation to understand and improve the quality of teaching and learning. Instead, the approaches that we put forward in this book reposition observation in the domain of educational inquiry. Drawing on over two decades of ground-breaking research, this book reconceptualises and reconfigures observation as a tool of inquiry for HE academic staff and students to explore, inquire and reflect on their teaching and learning collegially and collaboratively.

So, why a book on observation specifically for the HE sector and why now? As we explore in the first half of the book, observation is a powerful tool that is used across education sectors globally. It has played a key role in ongoing quality enhancement and assurance work across educational institutions for many decades and continues to do so. It has maintained a long-standing role in assessing teaching and learning as well as developing teachers' knowledge and skills, and this is unlikely to change in the near

DOI: 10.4324/9780429341908-1

future. It has also been a key focus for policy makers, government agencies and educational providers as part of an ongoing agenda for continuous improvement in the standards of teaching and learning. While modern HE has traditionally prioritised research over teaching and learning, policy developments have looked to redress this imbalance, with the result that teaching and learning has emerged as an area of growing interest and investment in HE internationally in recent decades. A key focus of recent activity has been on improving the quality of teaching, with observation playing a pivotal role for new and experienced HE staff alike. These policy developments and the wider global interest in understanding and improving teaching and learning in HE provide an important backdrop for locating this book. As part of this growing interest and investment in teaching and learning in HE, observation has become an increasingly integral element of institutional policies aimed at developing and evidencing the quality of teaching and learning and supporting the pedagogic upskilling of its workforce. However, to date there has been a significant gap in literature that critically examine the conceptual, theoretical and practical understanding and application of observation as policy and practice in the context of HE.

Observation remains an under-researched area of empirical inquiry with very few specialist books available, particularly in HE. Owing to the dearth of publications and HE-based studies, the HE sector has often drawn on observation work from schools and colleges to inform its development. Whilst teaching and learning in schools and colleges may share some similarities with HE, there are also very distinctive elements to the nature of teaching and learning in HE and how it operates, not to mention the differing roles and expectations of academic teaching staff and students. Thus, there is a clear need for a book that provides a guide to the praxis of observation and one which is tailored to those working in HE. Furthermore, one of the consistent findings to emerge from our applied research into observation in recent years is that it has the potential to add significant value to the ongoing drive for understanding teaching and learning in HE. One of the important contributions of this book is to provide the reader with guidance as to how higher education institutions (HEIs) can best tap into this potential to bring about richer, more meaningful teaching and learning experiences for both academic staff and students.

The inspiration for this book came from an initial frustration and dissatisfaction with engrained policies and practices in HE that purport to enhance the quality of teaching and learning but actually do very little to move forward understanding across the sector and even less to improve it. As we argue throughout the book, many of these teaching and learning policies and practices are the products of an engrained neoliberal narrative that has dominated HE policy thinking and decision-making in recent decades. While there are parts of the book where we are critical of what we perceive as the epistemological and methodological shortcomings underpinning this neoliberal policy thinking, we were also mindful of the limitations of simply critiquing the status quo without attempting to change it. With this in mind, we were determined that this book should make a meaningful contribution to filling some of the gaps left by sector and institutional policy and practice by putting forward a counter narrative that presents credible, evidence-based alternatives.

It is important to say a little about some of the key influences on the thinking behind the book and the wider context in which it was written. Conceptually and theoretically, the book includes a range of international research and scholarly work relating to teaching and learning in HE. For example, one of the ongoing frames of reference that we draw on in many of the chapters relates to the international literature on the Scholarship of Teaching and Learning (SoTL). Together with particular education policy reforms, we identify the emergence and development of SoTL as a key factor in the interest and focus on teaching and learning in HE globally. We acknowledge that much of the education policy discussion and the applied practice examples that we include in the book are predominantly situated in the UK HE sector, where both authors are based and where much of our empirical research has been carried out. While we recognise that there are context-specific factors, conditions and issues that may be particular to the UK HE context, we firmly believe that the substantive content of this book transcends international contexts and will be of relevance to all those working in the sector. The critically reflexive insights into observation policies and practices discussed in the book are applicable to a range of teaching and learning contexts internationally, thus extending its appeal and relevance beyond the UK HE sector. Added to this, although it might be argued that the book goes some way to capturing the recent upsurge in interest of the use of observation in HE as a result of recent policy and practice developments, its focus and content transcend any time limits as they have emerged in spite of rather than because of any recent trends in education policy. What this means is that the book is not temporally bound.

In terms of the wider backdrop to when this book was written, it would be remiss not to mention the COVID-19 pandemic in this introduction and its impact on teaching and learning in HE. We were part-way through the writing of the book when the pandemic occurred. It cannot be denied that the pandemic has left an indelible mark on the educational landscape that is likely to be felt for years to come, though the extent of its impact is still unknown. When governments across the world announced national lockdowns in the Spring of 2020, educational institutions were forced to prepare for a rapid transition from face-to-face teaching to online provision. Variations in resources, support systems and the digital literacy of teachers and students, among other factors, all played a part in determining these alternative online teaching and learning experiences. With the 'new normal' quickly established, it was not long before attention was turned to how best to support teachers to adapt and maximise the effectiveness of their practice in this new environment, especially given that the overwhelming majority had limited experience of teaching and learning in online spaces.

One of the consequences of the pivot to virtual teaching and learning was that it placed academic teaching staff in a position where they were forced to think differently about their roles and those of their students, as well as the way in which they prepared for and delivered their teaching online. Arguably, the pandemic gave rise to an opportunity for teachers to reconceptualise their teaching, their students' learning and the interrelationship between the two. While it is not within the scope of this book to explore these developments in any depth, we reflect on the impact of the experiences of the pandemic on teaching and learning practices and the implications for future practice.

An overview of the book and a statement of its aims

Developing Teaching and Learning in Higher Education through Observation has two interconnected aims. The first is to enable readers to acquire a detailed and situated understanding of how observation can be used as a lens for exploring the complex relationship between teaching and learning in HE. Following on from this, the second is to equip readers with structured frameworks and practical resources for developing and applying observation in HE contexts as a means of collaborative inquiry to understand and improve teaching and learning.

While there is a range of publications on the topic of observation, many of these tend to adopt a 'toolkit' approach, largely conceptualising observation as a mechanistic tool for assessing teaching performance. They also lack a theoretical underpinning to them. One of the unique strengths of this book is its conceptual and theoretical groundings. At the centre of the book's original contribution is its critically reflexive approach to reconceptualising and reconfiguring observation from a tool of assessment and transforming it into a powerful platform for collaborative and collegial inquiry.

Drawing on forward-thinking, contemporary research, this book provides the reader with a holistic insight into how to use observation as a vehicle for researching, understanding and improving teaching and learning. It includes authentic examples of collegial observation practices from a range of subject areas, along with case studies of collaborative observation work between staff and students. It unearths some of the complexities surrounding HE teaching and provides a conceptual and practical guide for harnessing observation to better understand the relationship between teaching and learning. For example, Chapters 6–9 provide detailed accounts of three tried-and-tested models of collaborative observation between academic staff and between students and staff, along with how to implement these approaches with a bank of resources and activities to support their use.

The book is targeted at a wide readership, especially those involved in teaching and learning in HE e.g. lecturers, readers, professors, teaching fellows, professional services, academic support staff and managers responsible for teaching and learning. It will be of particular interest to those undertaking initial and continuing qualifications and professional development programmes in HE (e.g. PG Cert in Learning and Teaching in HE, HEA/Advance HE fellowship applications, Graduate Certificate in Tertiary Teaching, SEDA accredited programmes). It will also appeal to teacher educators and students of education (e.g. Initial Teacher Training, Education Studies and postgraduate education research). Furthermore, the book is likely to appeal to education researchers and research students (undergraduate and postgraduate), especially those students researching HE pedagogy, their own practice and observation in the HE context.

Organisation of the book and chapter summary

This book can be broadly divided into two parts. Chapters 2–5 provide the reader with a clear illustration of the conceptual and theoretical positions we adopt. These chapters offer the reader clear reference points to the conceptual and theoretical work we cite throughout the second half of the book (i.e. Chapters 6–9). As we already mentioned, Chapters 6–9 offer three models of collaborative observation models which we developed, implemented and researched in recent years. Each of these chapters provides a comprehensive insight into the application of our conceptual and theoretical thinking in practice, together with research evidence from the projects in which these observation models were situated. They also include practical guides on how to use these models and the accompanying resources that we developed during the course of these projects (e.g. observation training, coaching training).

Chapter 2 starts by contextualising the emergence of interest in teaching and learning in HE, identifying some of the significant policy developments that have crystallised this interest. We offer our critical analysis of these policy reforms and their impact and implications on developments in teaching and learning across the HE sector. Chapter 3 interrogates what teaching and learning mean in the context of HE. It provides a critical discussion of two key conceptual underpinnings of our work. Firstly, the idea that teaching and learning are part of complex, dynamic and interdependent relationships that comprise multiple elements (students, teachers, resources, environment etc.). Secondly, the idea that teaching and learning are socially situated, intellectual activities that require the creation of knowledge and meaning situated in such complex contexts accordingly to be able to enhance understanding and bring about subsequent improvements. Chapter 3 also builds on the idea of a Scholarship of Teaching and Learning discussed in the previous chapter by exploring what this means in an applied sense and the implications for academic staff and their students. Chapter 4 discusses some of the theoretical perspectives that influenced our thinking when we created our models for developing teaching and learning through observation. We put forward our theory on developing a scholarly approach to teaching and learning in HE. Running through our theorisation of this scholarly approach are the core concepts of authenticity, intersubjectivity and critical engagement in HE teaching and learning. In addition, we discuss the key conceptual underpinning of our work that is based on the premise that students and academic staff are members of a shared academic community. Chapter 5 provides a review of the use of observation as a method and its differing role in relation to teaching and learning in different educational contexts. It undertakes a critical examination of extant research and publications relating to observation across education sectors internationally, identifying key themes and issues to compare and contrast its main use(s) and impact on those involved.

Chapter 6 provides an illustrative case study of the design and implementation of a Collegial Peer Observation Scheme. It discusses the conceptualisation, theoretical underpinnings, implementation and evaluation of the scheme. Drawing on a substantive, longitudinal evidence base of research data, the chapter also examines the attitudes, perceptions and experiences of academic staff involved in this scheme to date. The insights shared in this chapter from our research demonstrate the complexity of teaching and learning in contemporary HE. They also uncover new opportunities for using observation as a catalyst to develop collegial understanding of effective teaching and learning. Chapter 7 focuses on the 'act' or 'skill' of observing as well as managing the dialogic interaction in an observation cycle by the use of coaching questions. Drawing on relevant theory and research, it offers the reader two integral sets of skills and training resources to prepare for engaging in an inquiry-based approach to observation. This chapter includes a range of practical tasks and resources developed to facilitate observer development. Chapter 8 shares the creation and development of an innovative staff-student collaborative observation model. It includes analysis of research evidence, a case study and practical resources from a longitudinal project involving five undergraduate programmes that participated in two years of systematic staff-student collaborative observations. We also discuss an emerging concept which we call 'classroom consciousness', which involves academic staff and students improving teaching and learning through developing reciprocal, contextualised awareness and understanding of their pedagogical practices. Chapter 9 discusses the cutting-edge practice of unseen observation as an alternative, peer-based model of observation to support academics' professional learning. Drawing on the concept of intersubjectivity to theorise unseen observation, the principles, purpose and practical application of this model are discussed, along with its benefits and challenges. We argue that unseen observation offers a structured approach for stimulating and channelling opportunities for academics to engage in honest introspection, participatory sensemaking and reflexive dialogue of their practice. As it is a new development in observation practice, it calls for further research to test out the application and impact of unseen observation in HE. Finally, Chapter 10 concludes by drawing together some of the key themes and messages to emerge throughout the book. Looking ahead, it reflects on the implications for continuing to develop a scholarly approach to teaching and learning in HE through observation, along with the possibilities for future areas of research and scholarly work in this area.

A final note about nomenclature

Finally, it is worth us providing a little detail about some of the nomenclature used in the book and the rationale for our decision-making in the choice of the terms used throughout the book. Firstly, we have chosen to use the terms 'higher education' (HE) and 'higher education institutions' (HEIs) instead of 'university' and 'universities'. This is because in the UK and globally, higher education is not the exclusive domain of universities but is provided by many different types of educational institutions. We therefore wanted our discussion about teaching and learning in HE to fully represent all of these institutions, as we feel that the overarching missions of HE teaching and learning are shared by all these different providers as well as their staff and students.

Secondly, we use the term 'pedagogy' to describe the methods and practices of teaching and learning. We are, of course, aware of the provenance of the term and how it has traditionally been associated with the teaching of school-aged children. However, in contemporary educational research and educational studies globally, we feel 'pedagogy' carries with it a global currency and intelligibility, together with capturing a broader understanding of teaching and learning practices. Besides, other alternative terms associated with describing adult or higher education teaching and learning such as 'andragogy' are arguably not commonly used by international scholars. Thus, after much deliberation, we decided to use the term 'pedagogy' consistently throughout this book.

Finally, we use both 'academics' and 'academic teaching staff' throughout the book to refer to those HE staff who undertake a teaching role. We are mindful of how, in the UK for example, there has been an increase in 'teaching-only' positions and contracts over the last decade, with some failing to recognise or classify these staff as academics and instead positioning them as 'teaching-only'. We strongly oppose what we see as a movement of deprofessionalisation and do not want to exacerbate such a problematic divide in the academic community. While there is a tradition of 'research-only' positions in HE, we feel very strongly that staff who are responsible for teaching and learning should always have the recognition of an academic dimension to their role.

Contextualising the importance of teaching and learning in higher education

2

The rise of the scholarship of teaching and learning in higher education

Over thirty years ago, Boyer's (1990) report *Scholarship Reconsidered: Priorities of the Professoriate* was a catalyst for inspiring the emergence of the 'Scholarship of Teaching and Learning' (SoTL) as a concept and what has since come to be considered an academic movement in its own right, driven by a desire to raise the status of teaching and learning in HE. Boyer's report proposed four key areas of focus for scholarship, one of which was the Scholarship of Teaching, which stressed the importance of developing a deep understanding of disciplinary knowledge together with pedagogic knowledge, which, when combined, would help to critically inform teaching practices, reminiscent of Shulman's (1986) concept of pedagogic content knowledge. It was only towards the end of the 1990s that 'learning' was added to the Scholarship of Teaching to create the now commonly used acronym SoTL to refer to what has become an international movement as well as a concept and area of inquiry (Canning and Masika 2022).

Looking back on a report that is now over thirty years old, some of the issues Boyer covered almost seem ahead of their time. There are three aspects that are particularly worth highlighting as they are relevant to the focus of some of our discussion in this chapter and subsequent chapters. Firstly, one of the golden threads running through Boyer's argument centres on what he perceived as the divisive stratification between teaching and research in the US HE sector. At that time, the common perception was

DOI: 10.4324/9780429341908-2

that research was more valued as a marker of academic success than teaching, as evidenced by the fact that research and academic publications were the 'primary means by which most professors achieve academic success' (1990, xii). Boyer argued that it was time to move away from such narrow and binary conceptualisations of the work of academics in HE and to define in more creative ways 'what it means to be a scholar' with a 'renewed commitment' (1990, xii) to teaching as well as research. Arguably, the stratification between the value of research vs. teaching in the context of academic success is as pressing an issue in the 2020s as it was when Boyer was writing in the 1990s. However, as we shall discuss in this and subsequent chapters, there have been developments in HE internationally and in the UK that have sought to address this dichotomy, some of which have occurred as a result of government policy.

Secondly, another example of Boyer's forward thinking relates to his identification of the importance of student voice in the US HE sector, particularly in relation to discussions about teaching and the student learning experience. With hindsight, his observations seemed to pave the way to greater student influence on the quality of teaching and learning in the current HE environment. As he comments in the preface of the report: 'Especially significant is the fact that students themselves increasingly have raised concerns about the priority assigned to teaching on the campus' (Boyer 1990, xi).

Thirdly, Boyer was critical of how universities had become too concerned with measuring themselves 'far too frequently by external status rather than by values determined by their own distinctive mission' (xxiii). He lamented the growth of ever-more complex administrative structures, disciplines and departments becoming increasingly divided and disconnected from one another, resulting in a fragmented curriculum. The fragmentation of the curriculum and the division of academic disciplines and departments is epitomised by the process of modularisation and the way in which the knowledge and skills associated with different subjects are compartmentalised into discrete modules. The end result is that subjects become artificially atomised, with content packaged into distinct units, largely to satisfy the demands of an assessment-driven agenda. These modules are then subjected to a system of standardisation, from the writing of module guides which require explicit description of learning outcomes, assessment briefs, teaching/learning activities etc. to the time allocated for delivery of these modules.

Since Boyer's seminal report, SoTL has grown considerably as both a concept and an international movement. In relation to the former, opinions differ as to the definitions of SoTL. Some argue that it has become an umbrella concept that comprises a variety of activities and practices rather than a distinct area of inquiry (e.g. Levander, Forsberg and Elmgren 2019). Yet there are those who embrace the diverse focus of SoTL as scholarly work on teaching and learning that maps across disciplines and educational levels (ISSOTL website n.d.). In relation to SoTL as a movement, it has its own international association known as the International Society for the Scholarship of Teaching and Learning (ISSOTL), which was founded in 2004. ISSOTL hosts a large international conference annually and also has its own journal, *Teaching and Learning Inquiry*. Kreber (2013, p. 107) argues that SoTL 'involves adopting a critically reflective and inquiring approach towards teaching, including reflecting on the practices, wider goals, social purposes and present policies of higher education'. Kreber's assertion that SoTL should be underpinned by critical reflection, incorporating an understanding of the way in which teaching and learning interacts with and is influenced by wider social agendas and policies, serves as an important reminder for the need to situate teaching and learning in the socio-political context in which they occur. In the UK context, HE policy has increasingly had a more noticeable impact in shaping the practices of teaching and learning since the mid-1990s. In order to understand this relationship between policy and practice and its impact on teaching and learning, the next section of this chapter now turns its attention to charting some of those policies that have left their mark on the UK HE sector.

Higher education policy in England

Professionalising teaching

The 1990s saw a significant increase in the volume of interest in teaching in the HE sector internationally, largely as a response to Boyer's seminal work and the emergence of the SoTL movement. In the case of England, the emergence of the SoTL movement in HE also coincided with major policy reforms such as the Further and Higher Education Act of 1992 (HMSO 1992), which resulted in a new group of universities (now commonly referred to as the 'post-1992s'), which had formally been polytechnics under the control of local education authorities. The original focus of many polytechnics was applied education for professional work, particularly in STEM subjects such as engineering, applied science and life sciences. However, soon after they formed in the 1960s, many developed faculties in other disciplines such as humanities, law, journalism and other professional practice occupations. The Further and Higher Education Act of 1992 empowered former polytechnics with independent university status, broadening their educational scope and allowing them to award their own degrees. Added to this, the 1992 Act gave rise to an increase in further education (FE) colleges offering HE courses, often in collaboration with these 'post-1992' universities. One of the shared characteristics of these 'new universities' and FE colleges that distinguished them from other more established universities was a focus on teaching for professional practice, with research featuring as a peripheral pursuit in many of the new universities. This proliferation of new HE providers led to a rapid expansion of the sector, which in turn resulted in increased competition. It was in the light of these developments that scholarship and expertise in teaching started to emerge as an important characteristic of HE providers.

One particular policy outcome of the 1992 Act was the establishment of Teaching Quality Assessment (TQA), introduced by the university funding councils in response to their obligations under the 1992 Act. This was the first time that a national level teaching quality assessment framework and exercise was used for HE teaching. While this particular assessment ended in 1995, it paved the way for subsequent HE teaching quality initiatives and methodologies.

The 1997 National Committee of Inquiry into Higher Education Report (NCIHE), also known as the Dearing Report, marked the second significant policy reform and intervention in HE in the UK in recent history. The report, entitled *Higher Education in the Learning Society*, paid substantial attention to teaching and learning in HE for the twenty-first century. Under its central recommendation of widening participation in HE, it suggested a whole host of practices and initiatives that would act as the key drivers to enable the UK to realise its ambition of becoming a world-leading knowledge economy for the twenty-first century, with HE at the centre. One particular powerful idea from the Dearing Report was that HE teaching could become a profession. It recommended that,

> Institutions of higher education begin immediately to develop or seek access to programmes for teacher training of their staff, if they do not have them, and that all institutions seek national accreditation of such programmes from the Institute for Learning and Teaching in Higher Education.
>
> (NCIHE 1997, p. 126)

Following the Dearing Report, the Institute for Learning and Teaching in HE (ILT) was founded in 2000. In 2004, following the proposal in the White Paper, *The Future of Higher Education* (Department for Education and

Skills 2003), the ILT was merged with the Learning and Teaching Support Network and the National Coordination Team for the Teaching Quality Enhancement Fund, resulting in the formation of the Higher Education Academy (HEA).

The Dearing Report also introduced the new Quality Assurance Agency[1] to replace the quality audit and assessment responsibilities previously carried out by the HE Quality Council and the Funding Councils. This continued the HE quality assessment reform brought about by the 1992 Act to bring quality inspections of different kinds of HE providers (i.e. pre-92 universities, post-92 universities, college-based HE and other providers) under the same framework and carried out by a single body. The rationale for this reform was to ensure consistency in assessment criteria and judgements made about HE quality. This included other elements such as the student experience, along with the quality of course provision.

Accelerated policy interventions on teaching and learning

The 2010s arguably marked a key turning point for HE policy in terms of increasing public awareness of and interest in the sector. Prior to 2010, HE policies were rarely found in political party manifestos. While there had been a series of major policies implemented by previous governments, the extent to which such policies triggered national debates was relatively limited. In relation to teaching and learning, policy reforms introduced after 2010 were to have significant impact and implications for the sector, though this did not occur overnight. The 2011 White Paper *Students at the Heart of the System* (BIS 2011) significantly increased student contribution to HE funding and put student choice as a central driver of the new system. It followed the *Independent Review of Higher Education Funding and Student Finance* (also known as the Browne Review 2010) in 2009–2010 where drastic changes to the funding model of English HE were proposed. In a nutshell, the Browne Review recommended removing the fee cap on the tuition fees that universities could charge students (at the time it was £3,290). It also recommended that the government provide upfront loans to cover tuition fees and other student costs[2] (including part-time students) and that students pay back the loans after graduation when they were earning more than £21,000. The 2011 White Paper incorporated many of the recommendations from the Browne Review, though it proposed a minimum and maximum fees threshold, with the minimum amount (or a 'basic amount' as it is described in the policy paper) of £6,000 a year[3] for undergraduate courses and a maximum cap of £9,000 per year, which was later increased to £9,250.

Many identify the 2011 White Paper as the key turning point when the English HE sector became firmly established as a market-driven system with its 'vision' captured by the pithy phase in the White Paper, 'better informed students will take their custom to the places offering good value for money' (p. 32). The government at the time claimed that the new system would put students at 'the heart of the system' but as consumers in a marketplace rather than as participants in an educational relationship. Introduced in 2011, this new policy embodied the discourse of marketisation by persuading students to pay only for what they thought was worth having and that universities would have to provide this. Later in this chapter, we will examine the impact of this marketised conceptualisation of students, the notion of student voice and the implications for teaching and learning.

The 2016 White Paper, *Higher Education: Teaching Excellence, Social Mobility and Student Choice* (BIS 2016) marked another defining moment for HE teaching and learning. It introduced the Teaching Excellence Framework (TEF) and established the Office for Students (OfS) as the new regulator for all HE providers, replacing HEFCE's role in regulating and funding taught provision in HE. In 2017, the introduction of the HE and Research Act[4] provided a legislative basis for the TEF and the OfS. One of its key aims was purportedly to strengthen student choice as a central driver in the HE market. This first iteration of the TEF used a set of core metrics to measure and assess the quality of teaching. These included:

- 'Teaching Quality' (student engagement, valuing teaching, rigour and stretch, and feedback)
- 'Learning Environment' (resources, scholarship, research and professional practice, personalised learning)
- 'Student Outcomes and Learning Gain' (employment and further study, employability and transferrable skills, positive outcomes for all).

Following its introduction in 2017 (DfE 2017), HE providers were assessed against these metrics and awarded either a *gold*, *silver* or *bronze* ranking, with the rankings subsequently announced in the public domain as a market indicator for prospective students to use to inform their choice of provider and programme of study. Originally, there were plans to link the TEF outcomes with fees and to introduce an additional layer of subject-level TEF assessment. However, the TEF paused its assessment from 2019 to 2022 due to the COVID-19 global pandemic and a consultation on the framework, followed by the independent review of the TEF in 2019. At the time of writing, the maximum tuition fee that HE providers in England can charge for a full-time undergraduate course remains at £9,250 per year, although those without a TEF award can only charge a maximum of £9,000 per year. That said, as part of the updated 2022 TEF, government guidelines state that any providers who are awarded the new ranking of 'requires improvement' rather than a gold, silver or bronze may only charge up to £6,000 for a full-time course if they do not have an OfS access and participation plan in place, or up to £9,000 if they have an OfS access and participation plan in place.

Policy impact and implications on teaching and learning

Since the end of Second World War, the UK government has taken an increasingly interventionist stance to policy making in HE. According to Shattock,

> One interpretation of the whole period from 1945 to 2011 could be that it represents a long march from a fully subsidised higher education system to a substantially privatised one; another could be that the long march has been from an age participation rate of around 3 per cent to one around 43 per cent; and another might reflect the growth of universities themselves from small inward-looking institutions to large international organisations.
>
> (2012, p. 7)

Nevertheless, HE policy reforms from 1945 to the present have resulted in the strengthening of the government's hold over HE, while continuing a policy agenda that has prioritised marketisation, internationalisation and diversification of the sector as the key drivers.

Shattock (2012) has argued that UK HE policy making has never followed a rational model but has been the product of a complex interplay of context, ideologies, ministers and bureaucracies. The Treasury has traditionally been the key decision-maker in approving major public policies, while other sector policy bodies and key stakeholders have played their role in shaping policy creation. Shattock's *Making Policy in British Higher Education* (2012) provides a longitudinal account of the making and implementation of HE policy between 1945 and 2011. While it is not in this book's scope to undertake a detailed analysis of the policy-making process per se, there are important points of reference to consider when developing our understanding of HE policy reforms and their impact on teaching and learning in recent decades.

Neoliberalising teaching and learning

The dominant ideology underpinning HE policy reforms in the UK, particularly in England, is defined by some as 'neoliberalism' (e.g. Ball 2012; Davies 2017). According to Davies (2017), neoliberalism is 'an attempt to replace political judgment with economic evaluation' (p. 5) and 'the rendering of the economy, state and society as explicit and quantified as possible' (p. 10). Davies' definition evokes memories of the ideology of Thatcherism popularised during the 1980s and encapsulated in a slogan that was commonly referred to at the time as the 'three E's' i.e. economy, efficiency and effectiveness, which were employed as the guiding rationale for the Conservative government's neoliberal agenda for the privatisation and marketisation of public sector institutions. As Davies alludes to in his definition of neoliberalism above, these terms were removed from the realm of political discourse and subsequently repackaged in an ideology of so-called neutrality, which meant that they were conceptualised and discussed as being 'technical' rather than political or ideological issues.

In a similar vein, Ball (2012, p. 29) maintains that 'neoliberalism involves the transformation of social relations into calculabilities and exchanges, that is into the market form, and thus the commodification of educational practice – e.g. in economies of student worth, through performance-related pay, performance management'. What Ball and Davies' explanations of neoliberalism reveal is the overriding ideological influence of the market as a conceptual lens through which to understand, organise and valorise educational practice. Every action, interaction and behaviour is one that is mediated as a market transaction with economic value that is subject to a process of quantification.

How neoliberalism operates in and on HEIs in the context of teaching and learning is through a range of what Ball refers to as 'practices and technologies' (2012, p. 29). Arguably the most recognisable of these practices in HE, itself closely aligned to the ideology of neoliberalism, is that of 'managerialism' [sometimes also known as new public management (NPM)]. Like neoliberalism, managerialism is underpinned by an allegiance to the ideals of the free market and the imperatives of efficiency, calculability, control and accountability with a reliance on quantitative methods. Wallace and Hoyle (2005, p. 9) state that:

> [Managerialism] is underpinned by an ideology which assumes that all aspects of organisational life can and should be controlled. In other words, that ambiguity can and should be radically reduced or eliminated.

There are numerous examples in HE where innovations intended to change/improve teaching and learning practices and cultures have been appropriated by a managerialist agenda. As a result, the purposes and applications of these innovations have been primarily used to serve the interests of a quality assurance and performance management agenda instead of teaching and learning. One example of such innovations is the modularisation of the curriculum.

The early intentions of modular curriculum design and delivery when it was introduced in the 1960s (see Goldschmid and Goldschmid 1973; Theodossin 1981; van Eijl 1986) was to allow students to proceed at their own rate and choose their own learning mode. In other words, modularisation was meant to facilitate a personalised mode of learning (Goldschmid and Goldschmid 1973). This was to address the inflexibility of traditional linear programme structures and to respond to the demands of new conceptual models of the university as 'multiversity' (Kerr 1963). This idea of giving students choices was very appealing to a number of disciplines internationally. It was believed that such approaches to teaching and learning would increase student motivation, as they were given the autonomy to choose what they would like to learn and when they would like to do so, and were also offered greater opportunities for mastery as students could choose to take on particular pathways in a particular discipline or subject area. For teachers, the independent nature of modular units meant that each module could be used intact in different courses and the development of content and pedagogy for their modules could become more specialised.

However, as subsequent research revealed (e.g. Morris 2000; Robertson 1996), the main reasons for the introduction of modularisation across many programmes in the UK were to satisfy the personal ambitions of managers, to respond to pressures from external regulatory agencies, and a desire to emulate initiatives undertaken by competitor institutions. Such findings echo Boyer's observation and critique of the growth of ever-more complex administrative structures and the fragmentation of the curriculum and the divisions of disciplines and departments.

Early literature on modularisation (see Goldschmid and Goldschmid 1973) highlighted that managing and resourcing a modular system required some special points of attention. Medium- to long-term planning was crucial to its success and managers and administrators needed the power to coordinate and control this complex system effectively. However, what seemed to have been overlooked in the discussions about modularisation was how well students and staff were informed and prepared for this new mode of teaching and learning. While research suggests students seem to value greater choice and flexibility, there have been very limited studies that have explored the guidance and support students need to navigate their way through programmes to be able to make informed choices and engage with such complex ways of learning. Decades since its early introduction, the original intentions of learner-centred flexible approaches to HE teaching and learning are rarely mentioned in discussions about modularisation. Instead, it has become a managerialist tool for managing timetables, resources, staff time and funding streams.

Measurement, measurement, measurement

Nowadays, the practice of managerialism in HE takes on a number of forms, including performance management and quality assurance systems such as appraisals or performance reviews, target setting, course audits, monitoring of student progression and attainment, workload allocation models etc. These are all examples of a form of metagovernance (Ball 2012). In other words, different means of governing or controlling what HEIs and their staff do by establishing and organising the conditions for governing the quality of those activities. But managerialism is arguably one of three interrelated levers responsible for generating these 'conditions' of metagovernance that co-exist, the other two of which are performativity and marketisation.

Ball (2003, p. 215) has described performativity as a culture that 'requires individual practitioners to organise themselves as a response to targets, indicators and evaluations, to set aside personal beliefs and commitments and live an existence of calculation'. In short, performativity 'operates within a framework of judgement' (Ball 2012, p. 31) and is concerned with measuring and evaluating quality, productivity and performance. One situated example of this in HE in the UK would be the TEF.

As described above, the TEF uses a set of core metrics to measure and assess the quality of teaching and the outcomes of the TEF assessment are ranked in *gold*, *silver* and *bronze* across HE providers, though the revamped version of the TEF in 2022 has also introduced a *requires improvement* ranking. The measurements of the core metrics are proxies that largely focus on the quantifiable inputs and outcomes of teaching and learning. For example, one particular area of the TEF core metrics uses data on graduate employment outcomes (graduate-level jobs, and earnings in the short term and long term) and progression to further study to assess the outcome of student learning and evaluate the employment market value of the overall quality of teaching and learning.

Despite criticisms of the TEF by students and academic staff across the English HE sector, it was made into a legal requirement for English HE providers as the quality assessment framework replacing the previous QAA framework, which operated largely on a peer-to-peer evaluation model. Failing to pass the TEF assessment could result in institutions losing their status, but it also allows new providers to enter the market. The ranking that an institution receives also has far-reaching implications for the way in which providers are able to market themselves to prospective students and its student body. Interestingly, when the TEF assessment outcome was announced, students from several institutions which received a bronze rating publicly condemned the inappropriateness and inaccuracies of the TEF assessment in relation to teaching and learning experiences and quality at their institutions.

The implementation of the TEF at an institutional level has arguably strengthened performative approaches to managing and evaluating teaching and learning quality. Following its introduction, we conducted a large-scale research study involving over 6,000 HE staff from 154 university and 143 college-based HE providers (O'Leary, Cui and French 2019). Findings from our research clearly revealed how the TEF had led to a significant increase in audit-driven activities among HE providers relating specifically to satisfying the TEF metrics. Institutional approaches reported by staff have mainly focused on initiatives and activities that directly collect data/information for TEF submissions, changing environment/practices with a focus on addressing TEF core themes/metrics. To this end, institutions' behaviours serve to legitimise the TEF policy. A strong criticism of many institutions' approaches to implementing the TEF is their failure to appreciate the extent to which teaching, its development and delivery, is a collective rather than an individual activity.

Where changes to institutional-level policies and/or procedures were reported in our research, many of them related to the ratcheting up of monitoring mechanisms and accountability procedures involving both staff and students, driven principally by the student experience and student outcomes. There was very little evidence of any substantive and meaningful impact on the everyday teaching and learning cultures and practices of staff and students. In other words, energies were focused on measuring performance rather than any tangible impact on actually improving teaching and learning. Among some of the most frequently cited changes were: 1) a steep rise in the reliance on learning analytics; 2) increased programme evaluations; 3) increased student evaluations; 4) performance-management-led observations; 5) standardisation of templates for student assessments and student evaluations across programmes; 6) requirement for academic staff (new and existing) to gain teaching qualifications such as the PG Cert in HE Learning and Teaching and/or other accreditation such as HEA fellowship (latterly known as Advance HE fellowship).

The operationalisation of the TEF within institutions is mainly top-down and instructional rather than inclusive and discursive. The majority of staff, especially those most involved in teaching, are excluded from the TEF process and its related activities. This contradicts one of the central aims of the TEF stated by Sir Michael Barber that it should 'be a catalyst for improvement of, and innovation in, the quality of teaching … [to] generate informed dialogue about teaching quality both within institutions and between them' (2017). Our research found very limited evidence that any such dialogue occurred within HEIs. In fact, our findings reinforced the position that the operationalisation of the TEF by HEIs exacerbated the 'hyperrealism' of teaching excellence (Canning 2019), with institutions implementing strategies, initiatives and activities that are mainly directed at satisfying TEF metrics, whilst most of those in teaching and learning roles remain sidelined as passive recipients of institutional diktats. Across the sector, evidence of active and meaningful staff involvement in TEF-related activities has been very limited. If the implementation of institution-wide teaching excellence policy continues like this, it could be argued the dissonance between the TEF narrative of HE teaching and the everyday experiences of teaching and learning by students and staff will become even greater.

Students and their voice

HE policy reforms in England have chosen to frame the sector explicitly in economic terms with policy discourses emphasising students as consumers. This is a particular dimension of the marketisation of HE that we wish to explore in this chapter as we consider it an essential element of understanding and interrogating the impact and implications of policy on teaching and learning. The conceptualisation and discourse of students as consumers plays a key part in the marketisation and privatisation of HE. It is underpinned by a set of interrelated suppositions where students come to see HE as a right based on the increasingly private nature of their contribution, with the value of HE equated to the costs of participating (Tomlinson 2017). Throughout the 2016 White Paper and publications from the OfS, 'value for money' is repeatedly emphasised as a key driver for determining quality in HE participation. Two interlinked conceptualisations of 'value' articulated in the White Paper are: 1) the economic value of the degree to the labour market, measured by graduate employment metrics; and 2) the value of the investment made by students in their HE courses. The core metrics, which include student satisfaction evaluations, are intended to capture institutional outcomes across a range of performance criteria in order to inform prospective students, thus creating a market of differentiated 'quality'. In other words, it makes explicit the link between what students pay in and what they perceive to get out of their HE experience in return, reinforcing students' status as revenue providers, consumers and evaluators of the sector.

Viewed through the current policy lens of economisation and marketisation, teaching becomes a service and/or commodity produced for students to consume and subsequently evaluate through large-scale instruments such as the National Student Survey (NSS), which is a national survey directed at all final year undergraduate students annually in the UK to gather their 'opinions on the quality of their course' (HEFCE 2017). The NSS prescribes a list of items as key indicators of the quality of the services provided by the institution for students to evaluate their HE experience. Based on this student-consumer model and the 'value for money' ethos, such types of evaluations focus on the (in)congruence between student expectations of teaching and their perceptions of teaching on their course. Advocates of the marketisation of HE would argue that by increasing competition between HEIs for students, this forces them to prioritise improvements in the quality of teaching, as each HEI seeks to gain a market advantage over its competitors in order to attract more students.

In a marketised system, institutions need to enhance their market competitiveness, which can often lead to the creation of institutional policies and initiatives that serve to reinforce the student-consumer ethos. An example of this at an institutional level is how the student voice agenda has spawned a predominant culture of student evaluation (O'Leary, Cui and French 2019). From module evaluations, to end of year evaluations and the NSS, all these have become integral to institutions collecting student feedback. The quality of teaching is regarded as one of several key criteria used to determine the effectiveness of an institution's services and products in helping students achieve their desired outcomes. Implicit in these evaluations is the assumption that students are best placed to make judgements about teaching and what they want to get from HE. However, such metrics are problematic when used to inform our understanding of teaching and learning and policy decision-making within institutions. Used as a quality enhancement tool to evaluate staff performance on an annual basis, the value of such evaluations is questionable in terms of their contribution to informing situated understanding of teaching and learning practices.

For some, as long as the institution provides the right environment, there is an assumption that learning will take care of itself. This position foregrounds teaching as the most critical factor in achieving desirable learning outcomes. Though 'student voice' does appear in evaluations of teaching, it is enshrined in a process model of communication (Fiske 1990) in which students' views on teaching are disseminated to staff, sometimes directly, sometimes via management and/or professional services. Students may be consulted about their perceptions of teaching with the purported aim of raising standards of teaching quality, rather than for any sense of active membership of their course community as learners. Gourlay (2015) refers to this form of student engagement as 'the tyranny of participation', where only public and observable forms of behaviours are viewed as legitimate engagement behaviour.

In terms of learning, institutions also evaluate successful forms of learning and learning outcomes through the widespread incorporation of institutional and programme-level evaluation and performance data, through student attainment, progression and retention (Ransome 2011). Macfarlane (2015) calls this a form of 'student performativity' and questions its intrinsic educational value. Green (2011) has also critiqued such student metrics, questioning how much they meaningfully enhance situated understanding of teaching and learning and/or bring about subsequent improvements.

It is important to emphasise that students are conceptualised in many other ways beyond that of consumer. For example, others have written about them as 'academic apprentices' (Bourdieu and Passeron 1979) and 'critical agents' (Barnett 1997). In the context of teaching and learning, students simultaneously see themselves as consumers, academic apprentices, professional apprentices, 'Guinea pigs' of policy reform, critical agents and learners (see Cui 2014; Tomlinson 2017). While some of these conceptualisations may seem contradictory and even conflicting, some align well for producing meaningful teaching and learning, in particular when situated learning is prioritised (Cui 2014; Tomlinson 2017).

The rise of teaching and learning

While the HE sector undergoes neoliberal policy reforms and endures the complex impact and implications brought about by marketisation, performativity and managerialism, policies since the 1990s have made explicit attempts to raise the status of teaching and learning in HE, improve teaching and learning quality and make teaching and learning a core business of the sector.

The 1992 FE and HE Act attempted to introduce and recognise new forms of knowledge production in HE through giving polytechnics and college-based HE providers university status. This reoriented the relationship between teaching, learning and research at sectoral level. It also introduced new teaching and learning priorities to the sector, as demanded by the massification and diversification of institutions, student bodies and the purposes of HE in the wider society. The introduction of national-level quality assurance bodies and frameworks was another attempt to legitimise the importance of teaching comparing to research.[5]

The policy position adopted by the New Labour government from the late 1990s played a significant part in shaping sector-wide initiatives and practices. Two noteworthy examples are the creation and development of the Higher Education Academy (HEA) fellowship scheme and the Centres of Excellence in Teaching and Learning (CETL) initiative in the mid-2000s.

CETLs were created to recognise and reward excellence in teaching practice across English HEIs. This initiative was funded by the then HEFCE as part of a broader move to enhance the status of teaching and learning in HE, recognising that pre-existing esteem and reward systems within HE providers were often more likely to recognise excellence in research than teaching. With this in mind, the CETLs were therefore introduced as 'a major initiative designed both to reward and promote excellence in teaching and learning across the higher education curriculum' (Gosling and Hannan 2007, p. 634). As well as being accredited with CETL status, successful institutions were also awarded funding which they were expected to invest in further developing their teaching practice so as to improve the overall quality of teaching and the student learning experience. Funds were awarded to a selection of 73 HE providers (69 from England and 4 from Northern Ireland) following an open bidding process. The CETL initiative remains the largest single funding initiative in teaching and learning to date in the sector in England, with a total of £315 million invested from 2005 to 2010. The initiative concluded in 2010, although initially it was intended to run as a regular competition which placed the CETL funding as parallel to quality-related (QR) research funding.

Evaluation on the initial impact and the long-term impact of the CETL initiative and each CETL's contribution to sector-wide and institutional level teaching and learning paints a very mixed picture. Nevertheless, the initiative brought legitimacy and enhanced status to teaching and learning through the access it provided to specialist staff and expert methods, with work grounded in pedagogic research. The CETLs were diverse in terms of the types of institutions, the disciplinary/subject areas and the pedagogical focus of each CETL. In many cases, individual CETLs provided an increase in opportunities for staff to develop their practice, share with others and be informed by, and contribute to, pedagogic research. To date, the legacy of some CETLs continues to have an impact on teaching and learning in their institutions and relevant communities (e.g. the *Centre for Excellence in Professional Training and Education* at Surrey University, *Embedding, Enhancing and Integrating Employability* at Sheffield Hallam University). This impact has largely been attributed to individuals in key positions who can influence institution level initiatives and activities.

While the CETL initiative focused on institutional-level recognition of 'teaching excellence', the HEA fellowship scheme was created to offer individual staff with teaching responsibilities a pathway of professionalising and continue developing their teaching knowledge and practice. Following the Dearing Report's recommendation on professionalising HE teaching, the UK Professional Standards Framework (UKPSF) for teaching and supporting learning was developed by the HEA in 2004. The framework has been used to accredit training schemes for HE teachers such as the Postgraduate Certificate in HE Teaching and Learning. Following the 2003 White Paper, all new HE teaching staff were required to achieve a qualification based on the UKPSF. What was the HEA, now known as Advance HE, the body responsible for the UKPSF, subsequently developed its professional recognition scheme to encourage excellence in teaching. Interestingly, since its introduction, the HEA fellowship scheme has become a proxy indicator for HEIs to demonstrate levels of professionalisation and quality among its teaching staff, even though it is not a teaching qualification, nor it is mandatory for staff teaching in HE. As discussed before, since the introduction of the TEF, many institutions have started to require academic staff to gain HEA/Advance HE fellowship status.

As of November 2021, there were over 150,000 fellows registered worldwide (Advance HE website n.d.). van der Sluis (2021) suggests that the number of academic staff with a HEA/Advance HE fellowship grew from a fifth to over half from 2011 to 2018. These fellowships have increasingly come to be regarded by some organisations as an important proxy for the recognition of teaching competence and effectiveness. Yet the extent to which they can be considered a valid and/or reliable indicator of teaching quality is contested in terms of the assessment validity of these fellowships and what they purport to measure. Recent research 'raises questions about the credibility and validity of the HEA fellowships', with some of the study's participants referring to it as a 'form-filling' and 'box-ticking exercise' (van der Sluis 2021, p. 10). The fellowships are essentially a desk-based, paper exercise that largely depend on the self-narratives and supporting evidence provided by the applicants themselves. Individual applicants are required to complete a written application that demonstrates how they have achieved each of the descriptors for their respective level, along with a supporting statement(s) from other HE professionals. These applications are then evaluated by a group of accredited assessors who decide whether the evidence presented in the application successfully meets the established criteria, with the final decision ratified by a confirmation panel. Thus, the decision to award fellowship is ostensibly based on the ability of the applicant to present a convincing written case of their professional practice, knowledge, skills and values. It could be argued that the process is as much about the applicant's proficiency in literary expression as it is about demonstrating tangible evidence of excellence in teaching.

From an assessment perspective, there are also question marks concerning the validity and reliability of the process. Validity refers to the notion of an assessment actually assessing what it purports to assess. Reliability refers to the consistency and replicability of the assessment results. Thus, in relation to the fellowship scheme, the most obvious question concerning validity centres on the extent to which a written form of assessment can be regarded as a suitable and credible representation of one's teaching expertise. Furthermore, given that the HEA/Advance HE fellowship scheme was originally created with a focus on learning and teaching and the accreditation of HE teachers, it is interesting to note that the most senior level of recognition (principal fellow) is saved for those who invariably occupy the roles of senior leadership and management in HE. What is clear about this fellowship scheme is that it enshrines a hierarchy of excellence in which strategic leadership is valued more highly over teaching, at least in terms of its recognition and accompanying status. Furthermore, as recent research exploring academics' perspectives on the fellowship scheme has revealed, it is commonly perceived as an exercise 'serving managerial priorities and not necessarily educational ones' (van der Sluis 2021, p. 11).

While the HEA/Advance HE fellowship may have been conceived and created with the best intentions of raising the profile and ensuring greater recognition of teaching and learning in the sector, it has increasingly been appropriated as a competency-based, tick-box exercise with many HEIs adopting a blanket policy to push all academic staff to acquire their fellowship in light of the TEF. The extent to which participation in the process and the award of fellowship status to individuals captures teaching excellence or indeed has a tangible impact on the quality of learning and teaching and the student learning experience in the institution as a whole remains unclear. Another contributory factor to this may be the individualistic conceptualisation of teaching encapsulated in the scheme. As a recent report from the British Academy has recommended, perhaps the way forward for AdvanceHE to make a more meaningful and sustainable contribution to advancing the quality of teaching and learning in HE would be for it and its fellows to 'encourage the development of a culture of greater reflective practice and of pedagogical practices which enhance the relationship between teaching and research' (British Academy 2022, p. 5).

One of the clear findings to emerge from evaluating the impact and implications of HE policy reforms on teaching and learning is the lack of support and recognition for the role that collaboration plays in teaching and learning. Attempts to recognise and reward so-called teaching excellence have mainly focused on the achievements of individual staff members or individual centres/teams/departments. Initiatives and exercises like the HEA/Advance HE fellowships, CETLs and the TEF may very well have been conceived and created with the intentions of raising the profile and ensuring greater recognition of teaching and learning in the sector. The reality is, however, that they have increasingly been appropriated as or used as proxy measurements to legitimise and enable marketised competition which has little real meaning to teaching and learning practices and experiences. In short, teaching excellence has become a commodity which is currently used to compete for student admission, funding, awards and status. Although the focus of these policies has often been on raising the status of teaching, their starting point has been one that largely views teaching from a deficit position in which it is considered inferior to research both in terms of importance and its overall standing in the sector. This is illustrated by the observation of David Willetts (then the Minister of State for Universities and Science) before the introduction of the TEF that 'teaching was by far the weakest aspect of English higher education' (Gill 2015).

While policy reforms since the 1990s have undoubtedly made explicit attempts to raise the status of teaching and learning in HE, the neoliberal vision and its accompanying values and technologies have created and strengthened cultures and practices of marketisation that facilitate competition across the HE sector. They also encourage institutions to take up managerialist approaches to managing, monitoring and evaluating teaching and learning. As discussed in the implementation of practices such as modularisation or policies like the TEF, the external pressure to compete with other institutions while conforming to the policy demands and market norms has driven many institutions to put in place 'metagovernance' practices and technologies (Ball 2012). Such practices and technologies are largely geared towards satisfying the demands of policy makers and the market rather than feeding into a cycle of continuous improvement. An unintended consequence of this is the competing priorities to satisfy external demands have become a distraction to any meaningful pedagogical work and relationships.

Concluding remarks

Since the 1980s, policy interventions in HE in England have brought about unprecedented changes and impact on the sector. Collectively, these policy reforms have fundamentally changed the purposes of HE, its relationship with the state and its government, its funding structure, and the relationships and responsibilities of its students, staff and the communities it serves. Our review in this chapter on the changes to the English HE system and its impact and implications to learning and teaching makes a case in point.

National policies have certainly played a powerful role in recent decades in shaping and changing HE teaching and learning, but policies are alive and can be viewed in a state of becoming (Ball 2006). Seeing policies through this lens, the texts, discourses and technicalities of policy and policy implementation are neither fixed, rigid rules nor instructions. Sometimes policy is created with deliberate ambiguity; sometimes there are gaps and spaces in policy implementation for responses to interpret and re-interpret policy reflexively. We have seen the ongoing reviews, responses and changes to the TEF since its introduction in 2016. As Ball (2006) argues, policies do not normally tell us what to do, they create circumstances in which the range of options available in deciding what to do are narrowed or changed or particular goals or outcomes are set. What this means is that key stakeholders such as students, staff and HE institutions can and ought to create spaces, actions and discourses that translate the abstract policy texts into meaningful, interactive and sustainable practices.

In the following chapters of this book, we will discuss the critical, reflexive interactions academics and students take when engaging with policy on HE teaching and learning. We draw on a number of theoretical and conceptual underpinnings, such as the idea that teaching and learning are socially situated practices (e.g. Kreber 2002, 2013; Lave 1993), improving teaching and learning builds on intersubjective understanding of learning and teaching (e.g. Bowden and Marton 2004), to help academics, students and institutions bridge the long-standing gap between policy and practice in terms of enhancing the quality of teaching and learning. A particular body of work we draw on throughout this book is the international literature on the Scholarship of Teaching and Learning (SoTL). As we have explained towards the start of this chapter, Boyer's observation and analysis on the scholarship of teaching over 30 years ago inspired the emergence of the SoTL concept and movement. We intend to contribute to this body of work in our book by offering several examples of research-informed classroom observation practices in HE to illustrate our approaches to critical, meaningful and authentic engagement teaching and learning in the HE context.

Notes

1 In Scotland, quality assessment continued to be carried out by the Scottish HEFC.
2 Means tested grants for students from lower income families were proposed.
3 This minimum amount fees was later scraped.
4 While the 2017 Act applies to the UK, the TEF is only mandatory to English HE providers and OFS is a replacement for HEFCE.
5 Research quality assessment first took place in the UK in 1986 conducted by the University Grants Committee to determine the allocation of funding to universities. Since then the university funding councils conducted periodic assessment of research quality for the same purposes.

References

Ball, S. J., 2003. The teacher's soul and the terrors of performativity. *Journal of Education Policy* 18(2), 215–228.
Ball, S. J., 2006. *Education Policy and Social Class: The Selected Works of Stephen J. Ball*. London: Routledge.
Ball, S. J., 2012. *Global Education Inc. New Policy Networks and the Neoliberal Imaginary*. London: Routledge.
Barber, M., 2017. *Tending the Higher Education Landscape: Priorities for the Office for Students*. Birmingham: University UK. https://www.universitiesuk.ac.uk/news/Documents/sir-michael-barber-speech-uuk-june-2017.pdf.
Barnett, R., 1997. *Higher Education: A Critical Business*. Buckingham: Open University Press.
Bourdieu, P. and Passeron, J. C., 1979. *The Inheritors: French Students and their Relation with Culture*. Chicago: Chicago University Press.
Bowden, J. and Marton, F., 2004. *The University of Learning: Beyond Quality and Competence*. London: Routledge.
Boyer, E. L., 1990. *Scholarship reconsidered: Priorities of the professoriate*. Princeton: Carnegie Foundation for the Advancement of Teaching.
British Academy, 2022. *The Teaching-Research Nexus – Project Summary Report*. British Academy, June 2022.
Browne, J., 2010. *Securing a Sustainable Future for Higher Education: An Independent Review of HE Funding and Student Finance*. London: Department for Business, Innovation and Skills.
Canning, J., 2019. The UK Teaching Excellence Framework (TEF) as an illustration of Baudrillard's hyperreality. *Discourse: Studies in the Cultural Politics of Education* 40(3), 319–330.

Canning, J. and Masika, R., 2022. The scholarship of teaching and learning (SoTL): The thorn in the flesh of educational research. *Studies in Higher Education* 47(6), 1084–1096.

Cui, F., 2014. *The 'wicked' problem of employability development in HE degree programmes: Experiences, understandings and perceptions of lecturers and students.* unpublished PhD Thesis, Liverpool John Moores University: Liverpool.

Davies, W., 2017. *The Limits of Neoliberalism*. London: Sage.

Department for Business Innovation and Skills, 2011. *Students at the Heart of the System*. London: Department for Business Innovation and Skills.

Department for Business, Innovation and Skills, 2016. *Success as a Knowledge Economy: Teaching Excellence, Social Mobility and Student Choice*. London: The Stationery Office.

Department for Education, 2017. *Teaching Excellence and Student Outcomes Framework Specification*. London: Department for Education.

Department for Education and Skills, 2003. *The Future of Higher Education*. London: The Stationery Office.

Fiske, J., 1990. *Introduction to Communication Studies*. London: Routledge.

Gill, J., 2015. David Willetts interview: "What I did was in the interests of young people". *Times Higher Education*. Article published online 18th June 2015. Available at: https://www.timeshighereducation.com/david-willetts-what-i-did-was-in-the-interests-of-young-people.

Goldschmid, B. and Goldschmid. M., 1973. Modular instruction in higher education: A review. *Journal of Higher Education* 2, 15–32.

Gosling, D. and Hannan. A., 2007. Responses to a policy initiative: The case of centres for excellence in teaching and learning. *Studies in Higher Education* 32(5), 633–646.

Gourlay, L., 2015. "Student Engagement" and the tyranny of participation. *Teaching in Higher Education* 20(4), 402–411.

Green, J., 2011. *Education, Professionalism and the Quest for Accountability*. New York: Routledge.

Higher Education Funding Council For England, 2017. *National Student Survey*. Last updated online 21st December 2017. http://www.hefce.ac.uk/lt/nss/.

HMSO, 1992. *Further and Higher Education Act*. London: HMSO.

Kerr, C., 1963. *The Uses of the University*. Harvard: Harvard University Press.

Kreber, C., 2002. Teaching excellence, teaching expertise, and the scholarship of teaching. *Innovative Higher Education* 27, 5–23.

Kreber, C., 2013. *Authenticity in and through Teaching in Higher Education*. London: Routledge.

Lave, J., 1993. The Practice of Learning. In Chaiklin, S. and J. Lave, (eds.) *Understanding Practice*. Cambridge: Cambridge University Press, 3–32.

Levander, S., Forsberg, E. and Elmgren, M., 2019. The meaning-making of educational proficiency in academic hiring: A blind spot in the black box. *Teaching in Higher Education* 25(5), 541–559

Macfarlane, B., 2015. Student performativity in higher education: Converting learning as a private education learning in the United Kingdom. *Higher Education Quarterly* 65(2), 206–223.

Morris, H., 2000. The origins, forms and effects of modularisation and semesterisation in Ten UK-based business schools. *Higher Education Quarterly* 54(3), 239–258.

National Committee of Inquiry into Higher Education, 1997. *Higher Education for a Learning Society*. London: HMSO.

O'Leary, M., Cui, V. and French, A., 2019. *Understanding, Recognising and Rewarding Teaching Quality in Higher Education: An Exploration of the Impact and Implications of the Teaching Excellence Framework*. London: University and Colleges Union. https://www.ucu.org.uk/media/10092/Impact-of-TEF-report-Feb-2019/pdf/ImpactofTEFreportFEb2019.

Ransome, P., 2011. Qualitative pedagogy versus instrumentalism: And antinomies of higher space into a public performance. *Higher Education Research and Development* 34(2), 338–350.

Robertson, D., 1996. The Reconciliation of Academic Disciplines and Modular Frameworks: Student Choice, Knowledge Production and the "New" Rigidities, in HEQC, (ed.) *Modular Education in the UK in Focus*. London: Higher Education Quality Council.

Shattock, M., 2012. *Making Policy in British Higher Education 1945–2011*. Maidenhead: McGraw-Hill and Open University Press.

Shulman, L.S., 1986. Those who understand: Knowledge growth in teaching. *Educational Researcher* 15(2), 4–14.

Theodossin, E., 1981. The modularization of english higher education. *Research in Education* 26, 89–103.

Tomlinson, M., 2017. Student perceptions of themselves as "consumers" of higher education. *British Journal of Sociology of Education* 38(4), 450–467.

van der Sluis. H. 2021. 'Frankly, as far as I can see, it has very little to do with teaching'. Exploring academics' perceptions of the HEA Fellowships. *Professional Development in Education*, DOI: 10.1080/19415257.2021.1876153.

van Eijl, R. J., 1986. Modular programming of curricula. *Higher Education* 15(5), 449–457.

Wallace, M. and Hoyle, E., 2005. Towards Effective Management of a Reformed Teaching Profession, paper presented at the 4th seminar of *the ESRC Teaching and Learning Research Programme Thematic Seminar Series 'Changing Teacher Roles, Identities and Professionalism'*, King's College London. http://www.kcl.ac.uk/content/1/c6/01/41/66/paper-wallace.pdf.

Understanding teaching and learning in higher education   3

Conceptualising teaching in higher education

Teaching in HE has evolved significantly in recent years and what it means to be a teacher in HE in the twenty-first century is multi-faceted and complex. It can mean different things to different people, depending on the context, purpose and level, and the role of teacher and student, among many other variables. For some, their conception of teaching can focus on a literal interpretation of the 'doing' of teaching i.e. they see themselves as 'deliverers' of knowledge and skills within a specific discipline/subject, which typically involves preparing courses, delivering lectures, seminars and tutorials, assessing students' work etc. Yet, for others, it can be a much more diverse and all-encompassing role that requires them to engage in pastorally oriented work as much as traditional academic activities. While the academic lecture undoubtedly remains a distinctive feature of the HE sector, it is important to acknowledge that teaching has moved a substantial way from the reliance on the traditional lecture as the default mode of delivery and interaction between academic staff and students. Nowadays, it is the norm for HE teaching to involve a multitude of differing interactions, scenarios, sites, media and agents, which require the teaching academic to be a multi-skilled, flexible professional who is able to juggle a diverse range of roles, responsibilities and variables at any given time. From switching from the dynamics of delivering a lecture to a large group of students in a lecture theatre to meeting with a student on a one-to-one basis in a tutorial to discuss how their challenging personal circumstances are impacting on their work, the teaching academic regularly needs to be able to adapt their practice accordingly.

DOI: 10.4324/9780429341908-3

Another way in which some teaching academics conceptualise their role as educators extends beyond the teaching of their subject specialism and encompasses a wider civic commitment and/or desire to make a tangible difference to the lives of their students in terms of their intellectual and personal development and their wider contribution to society. The 'transformative' potential of HE is a familiar concept, with HEIs seen as important players in providing life-changing opportunities for their students. It is therefore important to situate HE teaching in a wider socio-economic and policy context, which means that academics need to be aware of the way in which these contexts impact on their teaching as well as the learning experiences of their students. This is a point which will be discussed in more detail later in this chapter and explored in greater depth in Chapter 4, when discussing the notion of 'authenticity' (Kreber 2013) in the context of the Scholarship of Teaching and Learning (SoTL).

In our ongoing development work with teaching staff in our workplace as part of our cycle of peer observation (see Chapter 6 for detailed discussion), one of the topics of discussion that we regularly explore with academic staff is their understanding of teaching and how they perceive their roles as HE teachers. While commonalities always appear in these discussions, regardless of the discipline/subject specialism of academic staff, we have also been able to identify certain patterns in some of the responses that often reflect the provenance and personal philosophies of staff. For example, there are those whose primary perspective is to view teaching through a subject- and/or content-specific lens and describe its purpose in instrumentalist terms. Hence, they use words and phrases such as 'explaining', 'communicating' and 'transmitting (subject) knowledge and skills' to students when defining their understanding of the core purpose of teaching. In contrast, there are those who view it through a more relational, social lens, with the personal development and fulfilment of the student identified as the core purpose of their teaching. They use words and phrases such as 'nurturing' and 'inspiring curiosity and a passion for their subject' amongst their students. Su and Wood (2012) refer to these two differing views of teaching as a 'technical-rational' view vs. a 'virtuous practice' view. The former focuses on the skills and techniques required to demonstrate pedagogic competence. In contrast, the latter focuses on the affective factors and relationships involved. Naturally, many staff view teaching and their roles through multiple lenses, as both subject specific knowledge and pedagogic skills are indispensable elements of the teaching-learning interrelationship.

Whichever lens(es) academics choose to view their teaching through, their perspectives inevitably provide an important frame of reference for wider discussions among peers and with their students about the scholarship of teaching and learning, which is an element that is explored further in Chapter 4 when we discuss the importance of teachers reflecting on their individual teaching philosophies and producing statements/accounts that capture these philosophies.

It is fair to say that the multiplicity of the teaching academic's role is something that applies to *all* HE courses, and even more so for those vocationally oriented, practice-based courses that include work-based placements where students' learning occurs 'on the job', as well as part of their formal taught programme at university/college. Whilst roles and environments inevitably differ across subject-specific courses and institutions, there are still common features of the teaching and learning experience in HE that map across different disciplines and subjects. Table 3.1 captures some of these typical features. In short, the features listed in Table 3.1 accentuate that there is much more to teaching and learning in HE than the mere delivery of a lecture or a seminar to a group of students.

Table 3.1 Features of Higher Education Teaching and Learning

Features of Higher Education Teaching and Learning	Examples/Illustrations
Teaching 'events'	<ul><li>Lectures</li><li>Seminars/webinars</li><li>Tutorials/supervisions</li><li>Work-based placements</li><li>Conferences</li><li>Research cafés</li><li>Group study</li></ul>
Staff–student teaching dynamics	<ul><li>Large group lectures</li><li>Seminar groups</li><li>Small groups</li><li>Tutorials/supervisions</li><li>Lectures</li></ul>
Teaching 'sites'	<ul><li>On site/campus (e.g. lecture theatres, classrooms, IT suites, laboratories, studios, workshops)</li><li>Off-site (e.g. colleges, schools, community sites, work-based placements)</li><li>Digital/online (e.g. webinars, VLEs, synchronous video conferencing, social media groups)</li></ul>
Multiple educators	<ul><li>University tutors</li><li>Work-based mentors</li><li>Community educators</li><li>Professional support/learning support staff</li><li>Peer support</li></ul>

(Continued)

Table 3.1 (Continued)

Features of Higher Education Teaching and Learning	Examples/Illustrations
Teaching–learning relationships	• Academic staff-students • Professional support staff-students • Students–students • Employers–students • Staff-staff
Indirect teaching-related activities	• Course development/module writing • Planning and preparing for teaching • Assessment/commentary of students' coursework, dissertations, theses etc • Moderation of coursework • Pastoral support
Contextualising knowledge and skills	• Application of subject-specific knowledge and skills to practice-based contexts • Linking theory and practice
Updating subject knowledge through research and scholarly activity	• Engaging with the latest research in subject area • Undertaking academic research
Updating professional knowledge and skills	• Keeping abreast of pedagogical developments • Undertaking research into teaching and learning

Distinguishing teaching and learning in higher education from compulsory education

One of the most recognisable features distinguishing teaching and learning in HE from compulsory education typically relates to the 'intellectual identity' of HE and the underlying purposes of higher-level study. There is a commonly held assumption that HE study involves a particular type of engagement with knowledge which distinguishes it from that experienced in compulsory education. In general, HE students are required to engage in problematising, questioning and challenging established orthodoxies within their respective disciplines. That is not to say, of course, that such engagement does not occur in compulsory education at all but simply that it is more commonly associated with higher-level study. In some subject areas, this problematising and challenging may involve interrogating recognised bodies of knowledge and/or pushing at the boundaries of engrained conceptual domains. But it can also involve developing a greater social and political awareness of and in a particular subject. Thus there can be an element of subversion to studying in HE that is not commonly associated with compulsory education, particularly as relationships between teachers and students tend to be much more hierarchically divided in compulsory education, with the emphasis on the teacher's role as both knowledge gatekeeper and provider. In the HE context, students can find themselves going through a process of 'unlearning' in which they are encouraged to interrogate and critically reflect on established beliefs and assumptions about their subject as part of the process of becoming independent thinkers. Barnett captures this well when he says that:

> A genuine higher learning is subversive in the sense of subverting the student's taken-for-granted world ... A genuine higher education is unsettling; it is not meant to be a cosy experience. It is disturbing because, ultimately, the student comes to see that things could always be other than they are.
>
> (Barnett 1990, p. 155)

Arguably one of the key drivers as to why HE study can be seen as subversive is because as part of its civic mission, there is an expectation that it has an important role to play in promoting autonomy, particularly intellectual autonomy, among both students and staff. Intellectual autonomy is often associated with being able to engage in critical thinking, sense-making and making rational, autonomous decisions based upon your own deductive reasoning rather than uncritically accepting and aligning yourself to a particular school of thought. In recent years, the nurturing of autonomy in HE has taken on increasingly wide connotations that have resulted in an extension of its meaning and application beyond the confines of academic study. In many HEIs, the notion of autonomy is no longer used exclusively in an academic or intellectual sense, but more holistically to refer to students' personal development in a social sense, particularly in relation to undergraduate degrees. So, for example, qualities such as global citizenship, critical thinking, leadership and teamwork skills and ethical responsibility are all considered important for the well-rounded student to develop during the course of their studies. So much so that these qualities are often included as desirable graduate attributes (e.g. Wong et al. 2021).

While recent government policy and legislation such as the 2017 *Higher Education and Research Act* (HERA 2017) continues to fuel long-standing debates about the purpose of HE courses and the extent to which their effectiveness in preparing students for employment should be used as a key performance indicator, links between the content and focus of HE courses and the local and national communities they serve are now much more evident across the sector in the twenty-first century. Long gone are the days where universities can be seen as 'ivory towers' that are detached from the real world. The employability agenda has certainly played a key role in this in recent decades, to the extent that it has become increasingly common for many undergraduate degrees to include a work placement element nowadays. Government policy continues to emphasise the important role that universities have to play in fuelling the economy and how they are deemed 'central to the country's economic performance in the twenty-first century' (DBIS 2009, p. 9).

Another distinctive feature of HE teaching and learning in the UK is that it has not traditionally been subject to the same level of intervention and policy reform as that of compulsory education. In other words, it has enjoyed a greater level of autonomy in terms of both the curriculum and the pedagogy. Ever since the introduction of the National Curriculum towards the end of the 1980s and the creation of the Office for Standards in Education (OfSTED) in 1992, schoolteachers have experienced high levels of intervention by politicians, policy makers and external agencies, which have come to dominate and have a controlling effect over their work. These interventions have increasingly developed a reliance on metrics-based models of governance and regulation, driven primarily by a managerial and accountability agenda. The rationale for these repeated interventions has predominantly been linked to debates about 'quality', 'excellence' and the ongoing drive for improvement. One of the consequences of this policy approach has been a reduction in schoolteachers' professional autonomy.

Although academics in HE have traditionally enjoyed a greater deal of freedom in what and how they teach, there are aspects of their work that have been subjected to similar levels of scrutiny and surveillance as that of teachers in compulsory education, most notably in relation to research. Historically, much of the policy focus on 'quality' in the UK HE sector has been on research, with teaching traditionally 'regarded as a poor cousin to academic research' (DBIS 2015, p. 8). High-quality research and the prestige associated with it has thus long been seen as the gold standard for recognising and rewarding academic excellence, as well as having an influential impact on the recruitment of staff and students internationally (e.g. Blackmore, Blackwell and Edmondson 2016). Yet, in recent years, the quality of teaching in HE has increasingly become the subject of intense scrutiny by politicians and policy makers. As discussed in the previous chapter, the recent introduction of the Teaching Excellence Framework (TEF) represents a significant turning point for the sector as it places the quality of HE teaching firmly in the policy spotlight, with the government promising to 'reward excellent teaching with reputational and financial incentives'

(DBIS 2015, p. 8), which could potentially threaten that long-standing autonomy, albeit through reform at a distance.

Since the 1990s, successive UK governments have introduced policies that have attempted to redress the imbalanced focus between research and teaching in HE. In the 2010s, it was decided that for teaching to be considered of equal value to research, then an equivalent system to the Research Excellence Framework (REF) needed to be established to enable the monitoring and measurement of the quality of teaching across HE providers by means of a standardised framework. As further justification, the government argued that the TEF would help to identify, encourage and reward excellence in teaching and as such become a key lever in driving up standards across the sector (DBIS 2016), especially given that teaching had been criticised as 'by far the weakest aspect of English higher education' by a former Minister of State for Universities and Science, David Willetts (Gill 2015). Whilst HEIs have previously been judged predominantly on the quality and impact of their research outputs, recent policy developments such as the TEF mean that teaching quality in HE is now increasingly becoming more formally scrutinised and in turn subjected to a range of performance metrics similar to those that have become firmly embedded in schools and colleges. Like other policy instruments that purport to capture and measure a contested, multifaceted phenomenon such as 'quality', the TEF depends on a reductionist approach that is driven by a narrow set of metrics that act as proxy indicators of 'quality'. In short, the TEF is arguably the latest development in a long line of reductive, metrics-driven approaches attempting to capture the complexity of educational processes in an oversimplified framework, which in turn mean that the true nature of teaching is not identified. It is to a discussion of the complexity of teaching and learning that this chapter now turns its attention.

Teaching and learning as complex systems

Earlier in this chapter, Table 3.1 presented a list of some of the common features of the teaching and learning experience in HE. It is important to acknowledge that by itemising these features, there is always the danger of inadvertently reducing the complexity of the interrelationship between teaching and learning. That is certainly not our intention in the features we have listed in Table 3.1. On the contrary, part of our rationale for trying to break down some of the core constituents is to help the reader to realise what a multi-layered, complex process it is. Of course, none of these constituents operate in isolation; rather, they are part of a wider combinatorial system in which they regularly interact with each other and are typically at play, often simultaneously, in any teaching-learning scenario. We would argue that it is only by understanding the different constituents involved and how they interact with each other that we are able to develop a holistic understanding of the complex, nuanced interrelationship between teaching and learning. The same argument also applies to conceptualising the Scholarship of Teaching and Learning (SoTL), to which we will return later following our discussion of complexity.

The complexity of teaching is such that teachers need to continue to develop their understanding of their professional practice over a period of many years. In the words of Shulman (2004, p. 258), 'classroom teaching is perhaps the most complex, most challenging, and most demanding, subtle, nuanced, and frightening activity that our species has ever invented'. Understanding the complexity surrounding the interplay of the subject matter, course curriculum, assessment, learning and teaching is central to the role of all teachers. For example, it includes knowing when to revisit previously covered content, when to challenge students, when to encourage them, and when to stand back from the process of learning, amongst many other skills and dispositions. Some of these skills and dispositions are illustrative of a teacher's professional wisdom (Shulman 2004) or professional capital (Hargreaves and Fullan 2012) and can be studied through the medium of observation, as we explore in some of the subsequent chapters of this book. Yet others are more difficult to observe directly and require alternative methods such as collective reflection and discussion to gain an insight into them and how they shape professional practice.

So, what is the relevance of using complexity theory to think and talk about teaching and learning? Complexity theory provides a useful lens through which to view and conceptualise the interrelationship between teaching and learning, as it helps us not only to recognise the multiple variables involved but also to gain a deeper understanding of the interactions between these interrelated variables. For those new to teaching in HE, the experience can seem daunting and even overwhelming at times. From undertaking peer observations or shadowing experienced colleagues, to planning and delivering your first taught sessions, the range of knowledge and skills required to make sense of and assimilate can seem infinite and confusing. However, as novice academics begin to acquire experience, they also start to make sense of teaching, identifying patterns of how different elements combine and the effect of combining these elements. As a result, they start to develop strategies that help them to piece together a conceptual framework, which enables them to break down the totality of teaching into manageable chunks and ultimately to make sense of its complexity.

In essence, this is what Biesta (2010) refers to as 'complexity reduction' i.e. where the system is assimilated in simpler terms through the use of personal frameworks of understanding.

Complexity theory argues that many natural and social systems cannot be captured and represented in sequential, linear relationships, as they comprise complex processes that are not only difficult to predict but equally do not lend themselves to reductive analysis or simplistic representation. In addition, one of the distinct features of complex systems is that they are 'open' (Cilliers 1998). What this means is that their boundaries are permeable, with interactions extending beyond the confines of the sites or spaces in which they occur (e.g. seminar rooms, lecture theatres, virtual workspaces) and invariably involving the wider environment. It is therefore unsurprising that teaching and learning interactions share many of the characteristics associated with complex systems. For example, the permeable boundaries of a complex system are all too apparent in teaching-learning scenarios, either in person or virtually. The boundaries of real or virtual classrooms, for instance, extend beyond their spatial and temporal constituents. In addition, a multitude of external factors can potentially impact on students' engagement with learning, as they can equally impact on educators' teaching.

The application of complexity theory as a lens through which to view teaching and learning has grown considerably in recent years (e.g. Davis and Sumara 2006; Mason 2008; Morrison 2002). Complexity theory sees natural and social systems as comprising of a network of complex processes and relationships. Such systems are often referred to as *complex adaptive systems*. To understand such systems, appropriate conceptual frameworks need to be used which appreciate this complexity. Richardson, Cilliers and Lissack (2007, p. 26) describe complex adaptive systems as follows:

> A complex (adaptive) system can be simply described as a system comprised of a large number of entities that display a high level of interactivity. The nature of this interactivity is mostly non-linear, containing manifest feedback loops.

Teaching-learning sites share many of the features of complex adaptive systems in that they are nonlinear, which means that simple cause-and-effect approaches to understanding interactions are unhelpful as they inevitably reduce and fail to acknowledge the importance of this complexity. As we explore below, this is particularly relevant when considering the use of observation as a mechanism for investigating teaching and learning. Despite what we think we know about the interrelationship between teaching and learning, classroom interactions are incredibly difficult to predict with any degree of reliability, particularly in relation to their impact on learning. Let us take, for example, an everyday scenario that occurs in lecture theatres and seminar rooms in any HEI, a group discussion between academic staff and students about subject matter covered during a course module. The teaching-learning interactions that ensue between staff and students are novel and, by definition, unpredictable. While the subject matter of the discussion may be known in advance by both parties, the focus and direction of the discussion invariably follows a fluid and spontaneous path, which makes it very difficult to be able to predict with any certainty things such as learning outcomes. Interactions occur both between participants and between them and the resources, media and spaces they choose to interact with and/or are exposed to, which cannot be controlled or measured reliably and/or predictably. As a consequence, learning outcomes or what each student gains from the discussion are likely to differ considerably across any given group of students. Similarly, in a typical question and answer session, what may seem like a straightforward response from a teacher to a student's question might have a far-reaching impact on the way that student makes sense of a particular topic and how they assimilate it to their wider subject knowledge. In contrast, a casual conversation over a coffee may prove instrumental in helping to develop a student's understanding of a concept or area of knowledge in a way that the formal learning encounter may not. In short, the interrelationship between teaching and learning is shaped by a range of complex variables that may not necessarily be directly related to the act of teaching yet can have a significant influence on how something is conceptualised by the student.

Another feature of complex adaptive systems that is shared by teaching-learning sites is the permeability of their boundaries. They cannot be drawn by the physical confines of the sites themselves, as a complex network of internal and external factors have an impact on, for example, students' ability and readiness to learn, as well as the many factors that can and frequently do impact upon what teachers do and their decision-making. In recent years, globalisation and the increasing digitalisation of HE have added a further layer of complexity to this network of factors which means that it becomes even more difficult to talk about 'boundaries' in the context of subjects or disciplines as traditional boundaries have become blurred (e.g. Giddens 2003).

At this point, you may be wondering how this discussion of the complexity of teaching and learning relates to the central focus of this book on the use of observation in HE. As commented in Chapter 1 and explored in greater depth in subsequent chapters, observation has traditionally been relied upon mainly as a method of assessment of teachers' practice in education. It is this overreliance on the use of observation as a method of assessment that has led to its dominance as a performance-management tool across colleges and schools and is increasingly becoming more commonplace in HE, with growing interest across HEIs in monitoring and measuring the quality of teaching (e.g. O'Leary, Cui and French 2019). What these assessment-based models have in common is that they typically rely on reductive criteria that oversimplify the complexity of teaching and learning, as the observation instruments used view the interrelationship as linear and correlational. These instruments are also designed to make an evaluative judgement in the most time-efficient way, largely for the purposes of categorising and ranking the so-called effectiveness of teaching and teachers, with the purported aim of driving improvement in the overall quality of teaching and learning. However, research evidence from colleges and schools not only exposes the failure of assessment-based models of observation in achieving this improvement, but also highlights the counterproductive consequences of relying on observation as an assessment tool. While there is limited research evidence of the impact of such uses of observation in HE, there is a significant body of research from colleges and schools that acts as a helpful point of reference for HE to learn valuable lessons from in terms of not making the same mistakes and maximising the value of observation. For example, one of the findings from the UK's largest research project on the use of observation in education to date (UCU 2013) repeatedly drew attention to the perceived inadequacies of observation as a means of attempting to capture the complexity of classrooms and teachers' work. In their qualitative comments, participants in the project highlighted the difficulty of observing classroom environments given the number of factors and issues which simultaneously occur at any given point in time. This was illuminated in their reflections on the complexity of the classroom and the inadequacy of observation as a tool to capture it:

> We work in a hyper-complex environment in terms of teaching and learning. I mean there are so many aspects to a teacher's job that you can't possibly get an insight into just by observing. Surely, it's got to be a more holistic thing, hasn't it?
>
> (Penny, Director of Quality)

Other participants involved in this research manifested an understanding of the permeability of classroom boundaries and the fact that learning in any one lesson was part of a trajectory over time as opposed to an episodic event that occurred during the observed lesson. As argued above, this reinforces all the more how important it is to acknowledge that the boundaries of the classroom extend beyond its spatial and temporal elements (Cilliers 1998). To see learning as a process that can be compartmentalised into discrete and neat units that correspond to lessons as self-contained events is indicative of a failure to understand the complexities involved, not to mention the process of learning itself. This is a particularly pertinent point in the context of the modularisation of HE courses, as discussed in the previous chapter.

In the UCU (2013) research project, there was a considerable mismatch between a complexity view of teaching, as understood by some teachers, and the reductive conceptualisations that underpinned institutional and managerialist approaches that were intent on compartmentalising learning as it appeared at a given moment whilst also ranking teacher performance:

> There are many variables in the numerous complex relationships between teacher and students. I've been graded low when an observer selected a couple of learners to interrogate who were struggling with a concept. The learning for those students was achieved over a number of weeks and it was not a problem for me that they hadn't grasped it in that particular lesson. However, it was perceived as a problem by the observer.
>
> (Richard, engineering lecturer)

Richard's comments reflect an intuitive understanding of the classroom as an open, complex system, which is constantly being shaped and affected by external influences. Admittedly, observers may not be aware of these influences and their impact on teaching and learning. Nevertheless, what Richard's comments also do is to highlight the inadequacies of conceptualising teaching and learning as a form of instrumentalist technology where the means can be controlled and manipulated to bring about the desired ends. Such reductive interpretations simply serve to expose the inadequacies of observation as an evaluative instrument when it is relied on as either the sole or predominant method for analysing the complex interactions of classrooms and teachers' work. Despite attempts to standardise and control it, teaching is not a mechanical process involving the application of a prescribed set of approaches or techniques in order to achieve predetermined outcomes; it is a complex art that is constantly evolving.

Assessment-based models of observation not only fail to capture that complexity but exacerbate the focus on a 'what works' agenda that prioritises issues of technical validity. As Biesta (2017, p. 316) has argued, discussions about 'effective teaching' concern not only matters of technical validity but also what he refers to as 'normative validity', by which he means whether what is being measured represents what we value in education. Such questions of normative validity are often dismissed by politicians and policy makers as either being too ideological or being ignored because they are too complicated and difficult to resolve, choosing instead to focus on 'scientific knowledge about "what works"' espoused by the evidence-based practice movement (Biesta 2017, p. 322). As Biesta goes on to argue, 'scientific evidence can neither replace judgements about how to act, nor can it replace judgements about the aims and ends of professional action' (p. 323). Yet evidence-based practice has increasingly begun to displace and even replace the professional judgement of educators, resulting in their disempowerment and the loss of democracy from their professional roles:

> The call for an evidence-based approach is not a deepening of the knowledge and judgement of professionals, but rather an attempt to overrule such knowledge and judgement. In precisely this sense, the evidence-based approach is another erosion of the democratic dimension of professionalism.
>
> (Biesta 2017, p. 323)

What is particularly significant about Biesta's analysis is that the reliance on reductive instruments like assessment-based models of observation and sector-wide policy developments such as the TEF may actually hinder rather than help efforts to further our understanding of the complex interrelationship between teaching and learning in HE.

Richardson et al. (2007) suggest that if complexity thinking is used as an epistemology (i.e. as the basis for knowledge claims, in this case understanding teaching-learning sites and/or spaces), then any analysis of complex adaptive systems requires consideration from a number of perspectives. Viewed separately, each perspective inevitably remains incomplete, making it difficult to understand the system in its entirety. However, by using a range of data collection methods, different elements of the system can be captured and will allow for the generation of multiple-perspective understandings. In doing this, observation becomes merely one of these perspectives, requiring us to look for other forms of evidence, such as the work produced by students, the videoing of lessons, and discussions with peers, which allow us to deconstruct and understand the system in different ways, and the use of interview techniques to uncover the cognitive elements of student learning. Understandably, using several approaches to explore the teaching–learning interrelationship requires a considerable time commitment and this may not be feasible on a regular basis for institutions and individuals. Nonetheless, as we argue throughout this book, it is important that we begin to think outside of the assessment box when it comes to the use of observation and approach the process of data collection more creatively and more authentically to enable us to gain multiple perspectives on the teaching-learning interactions that occur. Observation undoubtedly has an important role to play as part of a multi-method approach, but it is clearly not enough on its own. To move beyond these limitations and to ensure meaningful and sustainable improvement requires us to think differently. This is one of the underlying aims of this book.

In summary, a complexity view of teaching and learning reveals how problematic it is to rely on reductionist frameworks of observation as a method of data collection for forming judgements about the quality of teaching and learning. What this then implies is that the use of observation as an assessment tool on which to base judgements about teachers' professional capabilities and the impact of their teaching on their students' learning, whether it be for internal or external performative purposes, has minimal value in terms of its impact on improving either teaching or learning. In contrast, the collegial, collaborative and exploratory approach that we advocate throughout this book is what our research has revealed as an effective means of maximising the value of observation, along with embodying the core principles of a sustainable and authentic Scholarship of Teaching and Learning (SoTL), which the final section of this chapter now discusses.

Scholarship of teaching and learning

Over the last three decades, there has been an increase in sector-wide and institutional teaching and learning initiatives and programmes for academic staff, from the introduction of formal courses leading to recognised teaching qualifications, to informal training and support. While these initiatives and programmes provide opportunities for staff to invest in their professional development and the scholarship of teaching and learning (SoTL), they are often driven by the needs of quality assurance systems and the priorities of policy makers, which, unwittingly or not, can end up perpetuating managerialist cultures and practices, rather than furthering academics' knowledge and understanding of the complex interrelationship between teaching and learning and how this can enhance students' learning experiences.

Professional development programmes such as the *Postgraduate Certificate in HE Teaching and Learning* offer an opportunity to engage with generalised scholarly knowledge on teaching and learning and provide staff with a platform to develop understanding outside their disciplinary domain.

However, much of the academic and/or theoretical content used in these programmes arguably lacks actionable quality when practitioners are confronted with education issues that are of a social or cultural nature. Besides, institutional support and training is often short and episodic, which makes it difficult for staff to pursue a sustained learning opportunity of inquiry into situated teaching and learning issues they encounter. Furthermore, despite the increasing importance of student voice in HE teaching and learning, there is often very limited direct involvement of students in institutional level teaching and development programmes.

As argued in the previous section, teaching and learning are part of a complex, dynamic and interdependent relationship that comprises multiple elements (students, teachers, resources, environment etc.). They are also socially situated, intellectual activities (Lave 1993). How we understand teaching and learning in HE requires the creation of knowledge and meaning situated in such complex contexts. As Lave's work (1993, 1988) demonstrates, meaning has a relational character, generated in the interaction between teachers and students in the teaching and learning environments and spaces they cohabit. HE teachers' experiences and understandings of teaching and learning are often shaped by their disciplinary culture and practice (Neumann 2001). Although disciplinary knowledge is created through collective intellectual work, many academics' pedagogic knowledge and practices originate from their personal educational experiences.

In their research into how teachers make sense of and develop their teaching, Cajkler and Wood (2016) identified a set of indicative characteristics that they refer to as 'pedagogic literacy', drawing on the work of Shulman (1986, 1987) and his concept of 'pedagogic content knowledge'. They argue that it is by focusing on their pedagogic development that teachers can move from a trial-and-error approach to teaching, to one in which they have an informed awareness and understanding of the 'why' and 'how' of effective pedagogy and its impact on their students. Cajkler and Wood (2016) claim that it is by developing an appreciation and assimilation of the wide range of knowledge, skills, values and contexts inherent in what they refer to as the 'pedagogic environment', which leads to the growth of teachers' effective practice and their subsequent development of pedagogic literacy. They emphasise the importance of values as the foundation for shaping teachers' perceptions of the HE environment and the wider surroundings. They argue that values act as a central frame of reference for guiding teachers' pedagogic decision-making and provide a rationale for their actions and interactions with students. Skelton (2012, p. 267) identifies pedagogic development and academics' engagement with it as creating 'important spaces' in which they have the opportunity to develop their values and understand them against the constraints they may encounter within and outside of the workplace:

> Initial and continuing professional development ... about teaching and learning represent[s] important spaces where people can explore and develop their educational values and learn from the examination of value conflicts. To be authentic, such spaces need to acknowledge the micro, meso and macro level constraints that may make it difficult to realise particular educational values and to support people in developing personal responses to such circumstances.

Kreber (2013, p. 6) argues that to engage meaningfully in SoTL requires a commitment on the part of academics to 'adopting a critically reflective approach not only towards the content we teach but also towards the technical and, most importantly, the moral aspects of teaching, including reflection on the wider goals, social purposes and present policies of higher education'. This commitment is something that should apply to all academics, regardless of whether they view their role primarily as one that is teaching or research focused. A key concept running through Kreber's work is *authenticity*, which, she argues, is a cornerstone of an academic's meaningful engagement with the process of SoTL and is 'inextricably linked to doing what is in the most important interests of students and this involves helping students grow into their own authenticity' (p. 13). For Kreber, the concept of authenticity is not confined to the practice of teaching but embodies a much broader, far-reaching idea of both being and becoming a caring and conscientious citizen:

> Authenticity *in* and *through* (the scholarship of) university teaching is a striving for meaning, purpose and connectedness, aimed at creating a better world in which to *teach* and *learn* and, ultimately, a better, that is a fairer, more compassionate and sustainable, *world*. When we engage in (the scholarship of) teaching authentically we seek to enrich not only the students' academic learning, our repertoire of teaching practices and the knowledge base of teaching. We also have an interest in who we and our students are *becoming* and how, through our work, we can contribute to the common good. Thus, through authentic engagement in (the scholarship of) teaching we demonstrate that the world *matters* to us.
>
> (p. 13)

Kreber's conception of authenticity and the central role it plays in SoTL therefore clearly extends beyond the practice of teaching in a procedural sense, as she sees it as having a bigger role to play in addressing issues around social justice, equality and civic responsibility. For Kreber, authenticity has an inherently reciprocal quality. She emphasises this by saying that 'our own striving for authenticity is inextricably linked to us promoting the authenticity of others' (p. 48). What this means for HE teaching and learning is that in creating the conditions for students to develop their own authenticity, it is anticipated that they will subsequently become committed to promoting the authenticity of others. As Kreber says, 'it is in this sense that authentic engagement in (the scholarship of) university teaching seeks to promote social justice and equality *through* higher education' (p. 49). In a similar vein, Boyer (1987) argued that helping students to develop the ethical and moral judgement needed for purposeful civic engagement was an important element of the mission of HEIs and their contribution to society:

> ... the college should encourage each student to develop the capacity to judge wisely in matters of life and conduct ... The goal is to set them free in the world of ideas and provide a climate in which ethical and moral choices can be thoroughly examined, and convictions formed.
>
> (p. 284)

How the nurturing of authenticity and personal development occurs in the context of a HE teaching and learning environment depends largely on the formation and growth of meaningful, reciprocal relationships between academic staff and students, which, regardless of subject specialism, are fundamentally built on dialogic interaction. For such relationships to work, both parties need to openly commit to investing in and nurturing this dialogic relationship. As we discuss in Chapter 8 when sharing our experiences of the creation and implementation of a cycle of collaborative observation between staff and students, improving student learning requires teachers and students to develop a reciprocal, contextualised awareness and understanding of their learning and teaching experiences and what it means to learn collaboratively in the context of their course. At the same time, it would be naïve not to recognise the fact that the teacher–student relationship is inherently a hierarchical one in which the former wields more power and authority than the latter, not least because of their subject expertise. Similar challenges exist in respect of academic staff collaborating with each other on teaching and learning enhancement work. To avoid superficial, piecemeal-like engagement, they need to be afforded sufficient time and space in their workload allocations to build productive working relationships in which they can focus on developing the pedagogic literacy referred to earlier by Cajkler and Wood (2016). Chapter 6 explores a cycle of peer observation between staff that can be used to achieve this.

Kreber (2013) argues that authentic teachers actively seek ways to redress the power imbalance between them and their students by sharing their subject expertise with them and inviting them to become directly involved in the co-construction of knowledge by situating the subject in the students' experience. In the case studies we discuss in Chapter 8, we see examples of this co-construction of knowledge between students and staff in contextualised settings. Power can also be shared by academic staff disclosing their own vulnerabilities and the challenges they have experienced in trying to make sense of their subject and engaging in academic study. This personalisation and empathy building on the part of staff can be an important means of shifting power over to students as Kreber (2013, p. 51) argues:

> When teachers show personal investment in both the subject and the students, they share not only 'expertise power' but also reveal part of their own humanity. Students in turn are encouraged to explore whether the subject holds personal meaning also for them. Moreover, students are 'empowered' in a sense that their difficulties in connecting with the subject are honoured and their own sense of initial sense-making is encouraged and validated.

The implications for those academic staff looking to develop authenticity in their teaching is that they should actively seek to create opportunities to minimise their control over their students by sharing their knowledge openly and inviting them to engage in knowledge construction collaboratively. In no way does this devalue the academic's subject knowledge and expertise; this remains a cornerstone of the relationship between the two. Instead, what is envisaged is a closer partnership between the two rather than the hierarchically delineated teacher–student relationship that is often associated with traditional conceptions of teaching–learning relationships. Although teaching–learning encounters between staff and students provide ongoing opportunities for the co-construction of knowledge to occur, another context in which the two can come together as collaborators is through researching the teaching and learning experience. A recent study by the British Academy (2022) suggests that the original Humboldtian ideal of research and teaching as interconnected elements of HE study may have lost its meaning in the twenty-first-century university. The report recommends the need for greater institutional support for academics to engage in researching their own teaching, in collaboration with their colleagues and students so as to 'encourage the development of a culture of greater reflective practice and of pedagogical practices which enhance the relationship between teaching and research' (p. 5). While it is not within the scope of this chapter to explore the teaching–research relationship, it is an important subject that will be returned to in Chapter 8 when we discuss a staff–student collaborative research project that focused on the teaching and learning experiences of both parties.

Conclusion

This chapter started by interrogating what teaching means in the HE context, exploring some of the features that are generally associated with teaching and learning in HE as well as identifying those that distinguish it from schools and colleges. At the core of the HE identity and commonly associated with its civic mission is the idea that HEIs have an important role to play in developing students' intellectual autonomy, preparing them to become critical thinkers who question and challenge beliefs and assumptions, not just in relation to academia and their chosen subjects but also in a wider social sense. Our discussion of the scholarship of teaching and learning continued the focus on the social purposes of HE and the policy contexts in which we teach and our students learn, examining the moral aspects of teaching as well as the procedural or technical. To help us to develop a holistic understanding of the complex, nuanced interrelationship between teaching and learning, this chapter has also drawn on aspects of complexity theory to make sense of the different constituents involved and how they interact with each other. The golden thread running through our philosophy of the scholarship of teaching and learning and how academic staff are best supported to develop their pedagogic expertise is the importance of authenticity. Having drawn on Kreber's work to examine the significance of authenticity to the teaching–learning interrelationship in the final section of this chapter, it is a topic to which we will return in Chapter 4, when we develop our theory of what it means for academics to engage in a scholarly approach to inquiring into teaching and learning.

References

Barnett, R., 1990. *The Idea of Higher Education*. Buckingham: Open University Press.
Biesta, G., 2010. *Good Education in an Age of Measurement: Ethics, Politics, Democracy*. Boulder, CO: Paradigm Publishers.

Biesta, G., 2017. Education, measurement and the professions: Reclaiming a space for democratic professionality in education. *Educational Philosophy and Theory* 49(4), 315–330.

Blackmore, P., Blackwell, R. and Edmondson, M., 2016. Tackling wicked issues: Prestige and employment outcomes in the teaching excellence framework. *HEPI Occasional Paper 14.* Available at: http://www.hepi.ac.uk/2016/09/08/tackling-wicked-issues-prestige-employment-outcomes-teaching-excellence-framework/#comments Accessed 21.6.2021.

Boyer, E. L., 1987. *College: The Undergraduate Experience in America.* New York: Harper & Row: The Carnegie Foundation for the Advancement of Teaching.

British Academy, 2022. *The Teaching-Research Nexus – Project Summary Report.* British Academy, June 2022.

Cajkler, W. and Wood, P., 2016. Lesson study and pedagogic literacy in initial teacher education: Challenging reductive models. *British Journal of Educational Studies* 64(4), 503–521.

Cilliers, P., 1998. *Complexity and Postmodernism: Understanding Complex Systems.* London: Routledge.

Davis, B. and Sumara, D., 2006. *Complexity and Education: Inquiries into Learning, Teaching, and Research.* Mahwah NJ: Routledge.

Department for Business, Innovation, and Skills, (DfBIS), 2009. *Higher Ambitions: The Future of Universities in a Knowledge Economy.* London: HMSO.

Department for Business, Innovation, and Skills, (DfBIS), 2015. *Fulfilling Our Potential: Teaching Excellence, Social Mobility and Student Choice.* London: HMSO.

Department for Business, Innovation, and Skills, (DfBIS), 2016. *Success as a Knowledge Economy: Teaching Excellence, Social Mobility and Student Choice.* London: HMSO.

Giddens, A., 2003. *Runaway World: How Globalization is Reshaping Our Lives.* London: Routledge.

Gill, J., 2015. David Willetts interview: "What I did was in the interests of young people". *Times Higher Education.* Article published online 18th June 2015. Available at: https://www.timeshighereducation.com/david-willetts-what-i-did-was-in-the-interests-of-young-people. Accessed 04.05.2020.

Hargreaves, A. and Fullan, M., 2012. *Professional Capital: Transforming Teaching in Every School.* New York: Teachers' College Press.

Higher Education and Research Act, 2017. London: HMSO.

Kreber, C., 2013. *Authenticity in and through Teaching in Higher Education.* London: Routledge.

Lave, J., 1988. *Cognition in Practice: Mind, Mathematics and Culture in Everyday Life.* Cambridge: Cambridge University Press.

Lave, J., 1993. The Practice of Learning. In Chaiklin, S. and J. Lave, (eds.) *Understanding Practice.* Cambridge: Cambridge University Press, 3–32.

Mason, M., 2008. *Complexity Theory and the Philosophy of Education*. Chichester: Wiley and Sons Ltd.

Morrison, K., 2002. *School Leadership and Complexity Theory*. London: Routledge.

Neumann, R., 2001. Disciplinary differences and university teaching. *Studies in Higher Education* 26, 135–146.

O'Leary, M., Cui, V. and French, A., 2019. *Understanding, Recognising and Rewarding Teaching Quality in Higher Education: An Exploration of the Impact and Implications of the Teaching Excellence Framework*. University and Colleges Union. Retrieved from: https://www.ucu.org.uk/media/10092/Impact-of-TEF-report-Feb-2019/pdf/ImpactofTEFreportFEb2019.

Richardson, K.A., Cilliers, P. and Lissack, M., 2007. Complexity Science: A 'Gray' Science for the 'Stuff in Between'. In P. Cilliers, (ed.) *Thinking Complexity: Complexity and Philosophy volume 1*. Mansfield MA: ISCE Publishing, 25–35. Retrieved from: http://citeseerx.ist.psu.edu/viewdoc/download?doi=10.1.1.94.7038&rep=rep1&type=pdf. Accessed 21.10.2020.

Shulman, L. S., 1986. Those who understand: Knowledge growth in teaching. *Educational Researcher* 15, 4–14.

Shulman, L. S., 1987. Knowledge and teaching: Foundations of the new reform. *Harvard Educational Review* 57, 1–22.

Shulman, L. S., 2004. *The Wisdom of Practice: Essays on Teaching, Learning, and Learning to Teach*. San Francisco, CA: Jossey-Bass.

Skelton, A., 2012. Value conflicts in higher education teaching. *Teaching in Higher Education* 17(3), 257–268.

Su, F. and Wood, M., 2012. What makes a good university lecturer? Students' perceptions of teaching excellence. *Journal of Applied Research in Higher Education* 4(2), 142–155.

University and College Union (UCU), 2013. *Developing a National Framework for the Effective Use of Lesson Observation in Further Education*. Project Report, November 2013. Available at: http://www.ucu.org.uk/7105.

Wong, B., Chiu, Y.-L. T., Copsey-Blake, M. and Nikolopoulou, M., 2021. A mapping of graduate attributes: What can we expect from UK university students? *Higher Education Research and Development* 41(4), 1340–1355.

4 Developing a scholarly approach to higher education teaching and learning

A scholarly approach to higher education teaching and learning

In previous chapters, we introduced and briefly discussed the concept of a scholarship of teaching and learning (SoTL). The original concept of SoTL is often attributed to Boyer's seminal work *Scholarship Reconsidered: Priorities of the Professoriate*. Prior to Boyer, a number of other scholars (e.g. Shulman 1987) talked about how the concept of SoTL should be extended to consider other aspects of HE teaching and learning such as the production of course content and learning resources. Boyer saw the concept of scholarship as fundamental to reimagining HE core activities such as research and teaching and learning. He categorised these into four types of scholarship: *a scholarship of discovery, a scholarship of integration, a scholarship of application* and *a scholarship of teaching*. As discussed in Chapter 2, Boyer's conceptualisation and definition was his attempt to address what he perceived as the imbalanced attention given to research compared to teaching in HE. Therefore, rather than considering aspects of teaching such as curriculum knowledge as scholarly or scholarship activities, Boyer's conceptualisation of scholarship in HE was inclusive of all academic endeavours.

Since Boyer first coined the term 'scholarship of teaching', there has been a wealth of publications that have sought to conceptualise and define what constitutes SoTL. A particular feature associated with SoTL is its interdisciplinary coverage, which typically involves drawing on a diverse range of research methods and disciplinary perspectives. Indicative of how SoTL is not, and arguably should not be, constrained to particular disciplines or methodologies, Felten (2013, 121) refers to it somewhat disparagingly as a 'methodological and theoretical mutt'. Though it has to be said that Felten was referring specifically to what he perceived as the 'amateur culture' in which SoTL was undertaken in the US HE sector. Some have argued that the diversity of SoTL has caused a lack of coherence and clarity to how it has been conceptualised (e.g. Miller-Young and Yeo 2015), but equally the international SoTL community believes that it is this all-encompassing nature that makes it a relevant and suitable concept to apply to HE teaching and learning. In the chapters that follow, we introduce and discuss our approaches to improving teaching and learning through observation, drawing on some of the key SoTL literature. But first, we feel it is important to share with readers how we developed the conceptual and theoretical framework underpinning our work by highlighting some of the literature that has influenced our thinking to date.

In its early days, inquiries into the scholarship of teaching focused on trying to identify what it was and what it involved. As Andresen (2000, 137) observed, 'if the notions of scholarship, scholar and scholarly are to avoid emptiness and become useable as descriptors of teaching, as Ernest Boyer hoped, the concept behind these terms needs clarifying'. For Kreber and Cranton (2000), the scholarship of teaching includes both ongoing learning about teaching and the demonstration of teaching knowledge. To date, it is widely acknowledged that SoTL involves three ways of being *scholarly* in the context of teaching and learning: 1) reflecting critically on practice, 2) using ideas from relevant literature in the field and 3) contributing to the relevant literature in the field (Baume and Popovic 2016).

Laurie Richlin (2001) made a clear and important distinction between scholarly teaching and the scholarship of teaching. She argued that although these two are closely related, they differ in both their intent and outcomes. As Richlin explains,

> The purpose of scholarly teaching is to impact the activity of teaching and the resulting learning, whereas the scholarship of teaching results in a formal, peer-reviewed communication in the appropriate media or venue, which then becomes part of the knowledge base of teaching and learning in higher education.
>
> (p. 58)

Building on Richlin's distinction between scholarly teaching and the scholarship of teaching, we would argue that scholarly teaching involves engaging in ongoing learning about teaching through critical reflection on practice as well as making use of ideas from the relevant literature. This critical reflection involves inquiring into our own practice but also that of our peers within our community, which inevitably evokes a communitarian element that we see as fundamental and which we discuss in more detail later in this chapter. In the case of the scholarship of teaching, it not only includes engaging in scholarly teaching but also the active contribution to the knowledge base and relevant literature in the field.

Richlin insisted that if academics were to engage in a scholarly approach to exploring their teaching, they needed to undertake systematic classroom observations of their teaching, which would enable them to identify a problem or situation they would like to improve or an opportunity for exploration and/or development that they would like to pursue. Here, the term *systematic observation* refers to a method of observation that was heavily influenced by the positivist tradition (e.g. Croll 1986), though Richlin seemed to advocate the adoption of the broader principles of a systematic approach rather than the strict application of the specific method of systematic observation. While Richlin's use of terminology and the particular approach she proposed were rooted in what is traditionally referred to as the 'scientific method', the idea of exploring teaching and learning systematically is one of the core features that unites scholarly teaching and SoTL. What is particularly appealing about such an approach is that it enables academics to learn about and improve their pedagogical practice without having to rely on trial and error. We believe this is crucial to the sustainability of quality enhancement work on HE teaching and learning. As knowledgeable scholars in their respective subject areas, it is academic teaching staff who bring with them insights into their students' learning, and knowledge of curriculum content and pedagogical experience, and thus are best placed to lead such systematic inquiries. As Prosser (2008, 4) argues,

> We need to systematically reflect upon evidence of our own students' learning within our own classes and disciplines. We need to draw upon the generic research, but carefully situate that within our disciplines. We then need to monitor the success or otherwise of our efforts to improve our students' learning, and then communicate the outcomes of those efforts to our colleagues. The scholarship of teaching and learning from this perspective is not research in the traditional sense. It is a practically oriented activity, conducted collegially, and increasingly being conducted alongside traditional research within the disciplines.

This kind of classroom-based scholarly inquiry can take a number of forms, including collaboration between academic teaching staff, between staff and students, and between academic teaching staff and professional support staff (e.g. academic developers). What both Richlin and Prosser proposed had much in common with Schön's (1995) notion of scholarly action research where teaching is seen as a form of scholarship and an inquiry-based approach is the norm for improving teaching and learning or solving particular teaching and learning problems. This is what we see as the underpinning principle to a scholarly approach to HE teaching and learning. Admittedly, not every teaching-learning inquiry results in a scholarship publication or what many SoTL writers refer to as *going public* (e.g. Felten 2013; Miller-Young and Yeo 2015). However, every inquiry that intends to develop a meaningful understanding or make a meaningful contribution to improving teaching and learning should be underpinned by the key principles of a scholarly approach. Drawing on the key findings from some of the SoTL literature discussed here, we would summarise these key principles as: 1) situating the inquiry in the teacher's own classroom context and practice; 2) adopting a systematic approach to the teaching-learning inquiry; 3) engaging with the focus of inquiry critically and reflectively; and 4) working in partnership with others.

As discussed in Chapter 3, HE learning can be subversive and unsettling, as it requires learners to question, challenge and change engrained thinking and practices. While such thinking is generally associated with student learning at a higher level, the same principles arguably apply to academics' professional learning when taking a scholarly approach to teaching and learning. At its very core, this subversive and unsettling mindset underpins all scholarly activities across research, learning and teaching. As Kreber (2013, 74) argues, 'all academics who teach have a professional responsibility to approach their teaching with the same level of curiosity, knowledge and care as they adopt in relation to other aspects of their academic work'. Furthermore, adopting a critically reflexive stance to a scholarly approach to teaching and learning and SoTL more widely is fundamental if academics are to develop an understanding of the ways in which teaching and learning interact with, and are influenced by, wider social agendas and policies. This is how Boyer (1990) conceptualised scholarship in all aspects of academic work. To commit to a scholarly approach to teaching and learning thus requires all those who are involved to maintain an open and critical mind to what kind of knowledge they engage with in teaching-learning encounters, how they engage with it and how they engage with others who are also involved in the same teaching-learning encounters.

Authentic teaching and learning in higher education

As we discussed in Chapter 2, one of the consequences of the neoliberal agenda that has dominated HE policy in recent years is that it has distorted the way in which teaching and learning, along with its key protagonists i.e. teachers and students, have been conceptualised and are engaged with as an area of policy development. Instead of creating a culture in which HEIs are encouraged to explore authentic and meaningful interventions that make a tangible improvement to teaching and learning experiences, the dominant performative policy focus has given rise to a culture of 'hyperrealism' (Canning 2019), with institutions executing strategies and policies that are largely directed at satisfying regulatory metrics. Ironically, as we found in our research into the impact of the TEF in the UK (O'Leary, Cui and French 2019), while academic teaching staff welcomed the renewed policy interest in teaching, opportunities for them to play an active role in shaping institutional policy and practice were limited as policy enactment was largely managerial and prescriptive rather than inclusive and dialogic. In contrast, we have found the thinking and research methodologies proposed in some of the literature on scholarly approaches to teaching and learning, and SoTL more widely, have provided much more fruitful and thoughtful stimulus for advancing our understanding about the quality of HE teaching and learning. At the heart of this difference is the notion of authenticity in teaching and learning. If our critical analysis of recent policies is that they have resulted in inauthentic insights and practices, then what exactly do we mean when we talk about developing authentic insights and practices into HE teaching and learning?

Authenticity is a multidimensional concept that has become increasingly prevalent in some of the literature on teaching and learning in HE in recent years. In general, there are two interconnected strands of academic literature that explore the concept of authenticity in teaching and learning in HE. The first focuses on students' learning experiences, particularly their perceptions of learning tasks and the forms of assessment they undertake. This particular strand explores the extent to which students' learning experiences can be considered authentic i.e. their learning experiences are situated within the 'real world', students perceive them as relevant and therefore are more likely to engage in their learning tasks. The second strand has a broader focus on the civic mission of HE, particularly in relation to what Barnett (2004) referred to as the 'ontological turn' of HE pedagogy and the roles and responsibilities of HEIs in equipping students not just with the necessary knowledge and skills for the workplace but also helping them to become fully rounded citizens. As Kreber (2013, 13) explains in her understanding of what authenticity means for academic staff and students,

> When we engage in (the scholarship of) teaching authentically we seek to enrich not only the students' academic learning, our repertoire of teaching practices and the knowledge base of teaching. We also have an interest in who we and our students are *becoming* and how, through our work, we can contribute to the common good.

It is this second strand of authentic teaching and learning that we explore more in this book.

As observed by Kreber and Klampfleitner (2013), the significance of authenticity needs to be situated in the bigger picture of Western society's general interest in and concern for authenticity in both our personal and professional lives. Despite this recent interest, authenticity as a concept has a long history in Western philosophy, particularly during the nineteenth and twentieth centuries in the fields of existentialism and phenomenology, as explored by authors such as Nietzsche, Sartre and Heidegger. Kreber (2010, 2013) and Kreber and Klampfleitner (2013) provide a comprehensive analysis of the philosophical and theoretical understandings of authenticity in HE teaching from Western paradigms. According to Kreber and Klampfleitner (2013), the philosophical perspectives on authenticity in teaching can generally be categorised into three broad perspectives: 1) the existential perspective; 2) the critical perspective and 3) the communitarian perspective. Table 4.1 includes a summary of each of these perspectives based on Kreber and Klampfleitner's analysis.

In reality, authentic teaching often involves features of all three perspectives. However, it is interesting to note that Kreber and Klampfleitner's research identified the existential and critical perspectives as those which students and academic recognise and which they associate most commonly with authentic teaching in HE. While work by Kreber (2013) and Kreber and Klampfleitner (2013) has offered us a helpful philosophical lens through which to examine and reflect on our understanding and application of authenticity in HE teaching, we are mindful that their work focuses on authenticity in and through *teaching*. For us, teaching and learning are inextricably bound in a reciprocal relationship; they are two sides of the same coin and need to be explored together if we are to develop our understanding of teaching–learning interactions in physical and/or virtual spaces. From here on, we continue our discussion of the notion of authenticity by focusing on both teaching and learning.

Table 4.1 Existential, Critical and Communitarian Perspectives on Authenticity in Teaching

Perspective	Views on Authenticity	Implications for Teaching and Learning
Existential perspective	Authenticity as a process of becoming aware of our own unique purposes and possibilities in life and emphasises that we are authors of our own life, who take responsibility for our actions and stand by our inner commitments.	Academics who engage in teaching authentically have a genuine interest in their own development and regularly question the assumptions underlying their personal teaching practice as well as the larger context in which teaching takes place. They avoid complacency in their professional lives and are willing to challenge themselves. They also avoid compliance by openly contesting institutional practices or larger policy initiatives they do not agree with.
Critical perspective	Authenticity can happen only through reflective critique, whereby we realise how our ways of thinking and acting are influenced by assumptions, values and beliefs that we uncritically assimilated at an earlier time and now take for granted. Viewed from this perspective, authenticity involves recognising power relations that systematically distort our perceptions through critical reflection and critical self-reflection.	Normative ways of thinking about and enacting our teaching may not be conducive to our own well-being as academics, let alone the well-being, learning and development of students.
Communitarian perspective	Authenticity is not something to be achieved in isolation of the wider social context to which we belong. It is only by acknowledging our social interrelatedness that authenticity can become significant to the human condition.	Authenticity demands recognition of the fact that we are part of a professional community of teachers by whose socially constructed and historically evolved norms, values and ideals we are already bound and shaped. Authenticity in teaching involves placing teachers' individual reflective pursuits within a wider horizon of shared ideals in HE teaching. Specifically, authentic engagement in teaching is linked to the shared ideal of recognising the importance of doing what is in the important interests of students, and thus of supporting the students' authenticity or flourishing.

(Based on Kreber and Klampfleitner 2013, p. 466)

For us, authentic HE teaching and learning is underpinned by three interconnected elements. Firstly, it embraces the complexity of the teaching-learning phenomenon and recognises the importance of understanding teaching and learning in HE as a complex adaptive system. In Chapter 3, we discussed how teaching and learning can be understood through the lens of complexity theory and why this is an important perspective to consider when it comes to understanding the interrelationship between the two. In essence, authentic pedagogic practices need to allow learning and teaching to unfold organically without excessive instructional control by academic staff. As discussed previously, teaching and learning at HE level involves students and teachers working together and co-constructing knowledge in their shared teaching-learning sites/spaces and through teaching-learning events. While the teacher clearly has a specific role to facilitate and/or even lead this process of knowledge co-construction, there needs to be an affordance of autonomy and spontaneity if teaching is going to be able respond to learning reciprocally and authentically.

This leads us to the second aspect of authentic teaching and learning that is its transformative potential. As Boyer (1990) and Barnett (1990) identified, HE should always have an emphasis on students' *becoming*. In a similar vein, Kreber (2013) argued that the scholarship of teaching is inextricably linked to doing what is in the important interests of students. For us, this transformative potential also applies to teachers and the process of teaching at HE level. Jarvis captures the essence of this aspect of authenticity when he says that '(authentic) action is to be found when individuals freely act in such a way that they try to foster the growth and development of each other's being' (Jarvis cited in Cranton 2001, 84). What this means is that students and academics who share teaching and learning sites/spaces and events can foster their own as well as each other's learning and development through their authentic actions. Kreber and Klampfleitner (2013) maintain that all three perspectives on authenticity listed in Table 4.1 are consistent with this particular feature of HE teaching and learning, though they particularly emphasise importance of the communitarian perspective. In their work, Kreber and Klampfleitner have highlighted a notable gap in current work that explicitly addresses the link between authenticity in teaching and the fostering of authentic being in students. In Chapter 8, we share our approach to how we developed a collaboration between students and academic staff through a longitudinal project that used a specially designed cycle of collaborative observation as a lens for exploring their teaching-learning encounters on their university courses. In that chapter, we also discuss the reciprocal nature of authenticity in learning and teaching by using a range of illustrative examples from our case study courses.

Our third and final aspect of authenticity relates to how teaching and learning problematises and challenges some of the policy demands on HE. This centres on how and what academic staff and students perceive as the mission of HE, its underlying purposes, contribution to and impact on society. As discussed in Chapter 2, the HE sector globally has increasingly been subjected to policy interventions that have largely focused on the economic benefits of HE to national economies and the employability of students. Many scholars (e.g. Collini 2012) and students (Tomlinson 2017) consider this a very narrow conception of the place and purpose of HE. Authentic teaching and learning, therefore, has to interrogate and challenge the ideology underpinning such policy control over HE provision if it is to promote the genuine interests of students and academics. This connects with another core characteristic of HE that we discussed in the previous chapter, namely that of autonomy.

In Western education thinking, autonomy has a long-standing association with learner-centred traditions of education, particularly associated with thinkers such as John Dewey and Carl Rogers. Such conceptions of education regard autonomy as integral to the process as well as the end product of meaningful educational experiences. In other words, the development of intellectual autonomy and the nurturing of students as autonomous thinkers are considered core criteria for evaluating the success of the educational experience. While autonomy and authenticity in the learner-centred and humanist traditions of education tend to focus on the individual, we believe that autonomy and authenticity should also be prioritised and practised at a collective level in HE. What this means for us is that in addition to focusing on an individual student's and/or academic's learning and development, teaching and learning in HE should also be concerned with encouraging both students and academics to work collaboratively towards authenticity and autonomy. This is particularly significant when situated against the backdrop of the massification of HE where institutions are now made up of such diverse bodies of students and staff. Striving for authentic teaching and learning collectively is a way for such diverse bodies of students and staff to share and learn about each other's views, aspirations, experiences and practices. Throughout this book, we maintain that teaching and learning is a socially situated practice. As such, we align our views with the communitarian perspective of authenticity which argues that authenticity can only be achieved once we acknowledge our social interrelatedness. This is one of the reasons why we are critical of HE initiatives that individualise teaching and learning by focusing predominantly on the quality of an individual's knowledge and/or practice (e.g. the HEA/Advance HE fellowship scheme), regardless of whether or not they promote authentic pedagogical practices by individuals. This is a point that we now develop in more detail in relation to the intersubjective nature of teaching and learning and the usefulness of intersubjectivity as a theoretical tool for understanding the value of collaborative partnerships in making sense of the teaching-learning interrelationship.

Intersubjectivity in HE teaching and learning

Towards the end of Chapter 3, we discussed the importance of developing partnerships in promoting authenticity in teaching and learning. This is something that equally applies to both partnerships between academic staff and between staff and students. In the case of the latter, this may require the breaking down of hierarchically delineated barriers that often characterise traditional teaching-learning relationships between staff and students in HE before being able to develop authentic partnerships between the two. Here we suggest that the concept of intersubjectivity might be a useful theoretical tool to draw on.

Intersubjectivity is essentially the sharing of one person's experience or perception of reality with another, with a view to bringing about a shared understanding as a result of dialogic interaction between the two. As part of this interaction, each person recognises and respects that they are social beings who exist as a being with others. Thus, empathy is a fundamental element for intersubjectivity to occur. Dewey (1938, 39) argued that teachers need to 'have that sympathetic understanding of individuals as individuals which gives [them] an idea of what is actually going on in the minds of those who are learning'. One of the ways in which academic teaching staff can cultivate this 'sympathetic understanding' is by engaging in authentic dialogue with their colleagues and students about teaching and learning. In the case of the latter, as we argued in the previous chapter, this requires both the recognition of their hierarchical position of power and a conscious commitment to breaking down this hierarchy with the aim to empowering their students by building intersubjectivity and sharing control of teaching-learning spaces and encounters. Nonetheless, developing meaningful relationships and effective communication for intersubjective understanding is dependent on the provision of sufficient space and time over a sustained period if reciprocal trust between those involved is going to occur. This is a principle that applies to all relationships, whether it involves staff working with their students or their colleagues.

Biesta (1995) emphasises the importance of understanding intersubjectivity as a collaborative and dialogic process in which meaning is created *through* interaction. De Jaegher et al. (2016, p. 492) capture this succinctly when they state that, 'intersubjectivity is characterised as participatory sensemaking: the embodied, interactive coordination of sensemaking'. This has important implications for the professional learning of academic teaching staff in the context of observation approaches, especially in terms of how such work is conceptualised and operationalised to create the optimum conditions for meaningful learning to occur. It is a topic which we explore in greater depth in Chapter 9 when discussing the radical model of *unseen observation*.

Critical engagement in learning about teaching and learning

Being critical is arguably a defining concept of HE. Literature on criticality directed at HE is wide-ranging, covering philosophical debates about the concept itself, the praxis of critical thinking, critical reflection and how criticality can be incorporated into learning, teaching and assessment. In our work on learning about teaching and learning through the lens of observation, critical reflection, critical action and critical perspectives on pedagogy are essential elements of the approaches we developed, which we discuss in more detail in Chapters 6, 8 and 9. As it is in this chapter that we outline the theoretical and conceptual thinking that underpins our work, the final aspect that we wish to focus on is our understanding of criticality in the context of its relevance and application to HE pedagogical practices. For us, criticality involves critical engagement with four domains: 1) pedagogical knowledge; 2) the socio-political environment; 3) one's self; and 4) each other. The first two cover the epistemology of pedagogical practices, i.e. the knowledge that underpins how students and teachers go about learning and teaching. The latter two cover the ontology of pedagogical practices, i.e. students' and teachers' state of *being* in HE and their relationship with each other. These four domains are interconnected and reflexive as the ontologies impact on the kind of epistemologies that students and teachers subscribe to and the epistemologies that shape students' and teachers' perspectives on their own identity and their relationship with each other. We deliberately use the term *critical engagement* here as we intend to capture critical thinking, critical reflection and critical action in pedagogical practices by students and academic teaching staff.

Critical engagement with pedagogical knowledge

Returning to Boyer's *Scholarship Reconsidered* (1990), he emphasised that academic teaching staff must be able to build bridges between their own understanding of the subject and that of their students and must 'continuously examine' their pedagogic practices (p. 24). This is certainly essential for authentic teaching and learning to take place in the context of mass participation in HE. This context means that students come from a diverse range of socio-economic, cultural and educational backgrounds, with a wide-ranging set of needs, thus resulting in highly complex teaching and learning environments. Students also bring with them their lifetime experiences of learning in different contexts, along with their understanding of the interrelationship between the two. This makes traditional apprenticeship approaches to developing staff's teaching knowledge and practices insufficient (e.g. Knight and Trowler 2000). In their research, Becher and Trowler (2001) and Knight and Trowler (2000) have illustrated how powerful disciplinary and departmental-level cultures can be in shaping the teaching philosophies and practices of academic staff. Research by Trowler, Saunders and Bamber (2012) has also highlighted how even within the same discipline and department, individual academics draw on different sets of discursive and value-laden resources and their philosophies of teaching and learning may differ. Besides, the disciplinary, acculturated perspectives and approaches academics embody provide them with a frame of reference that can often differ from many of their undergraduate students, who are yet to be part of these same academic disciplinary communities.

The kind of pedagogical knowledge Boyer refers to is what Shulman (1987) called *pedagogical content knowledge*. Pedagogical content knowledge is the knowledge that links content and pedagogical knowledge, which Shulman (1987, p. 9) defined as knowing 'the ways of representing and formulating the subject that make it comprehensible to others'. As we discussed previously, HE classroom teaching and learning is complex, the knowledge learners and teachers are dealing with is often considered cutting edge, and the pedagogical aims are to create and nurture criticality, authenticity and transformative learning. This certainly requires teachers to take a critical approach to examining their own knowledge formation and how they go about assimilating that knowledge into their pedagogical practices. This kind of pedagogical knowledge reflects a teacher's capacity to teach and enables a teacher to be creative, to take risks, and to adopt different methods to suit the local context. Kreber (2013, p. 61) refers to this form of engagement with teaching as 'academic professionalism', which is 'characterised by informed, focused and critical reflections on the policies, practices and processes of university teaching and learning'. Brookfield's (1995) work is helpful in drawing a distinction between 'reflection' and 'critical reflection', with the latter extending the process of academics reflecting on their teaching beyond the self and the confines of teaching-learning spaces, and locating it in the wider social and political structures and environments in which teaching operates and their work is governed. This is also important in terms of acknowledging how academic teaching staff are responsible for making moral and professional judgements in their work.

Critical engagement with the socio-political environment

Teaching and learning in HE as a form of knowledge production and dissemination has never existed in a vacuum. As we mentioned above, work by scholars such as Becher and Trowler (2001) provided convincing evidence for how the social, political and cultural environment at a departmental and institutional level shape staff's teaching and learning practices. In a similar vein, we highlighted in Chapter 2 the impact of policy interventions at an institutional level on teaching and learning. In the following chapter, we also go on to discuss how teaching observations have become a performative tool for management to monitor and assess the teaching performance of academic staff. These examples serve to illustrate our rationale for why we emphasise the importance for both students and staff to engage critically with the wider socio-political environment when collectively reflecting and collaborating on their learning and teaching.

Drawing on the work of Shulman (1987, 1999) and Elton (1992), Kreber (2013) puts forward the case for why HE teaching should always be underpinned by a scholarly disposition. This involves academics engaging with the latest research findings in their discipline (their content knowledge) through a critically reflective and informed stance in relation to the policies, practices, processes and purposes of university teaching. This means all core activities by academics are underpinned by 'being curious, being reflective, and a desire to continue deepening their knowledge base' (p. 72). Looking at HE teaching and learning through the lens of authenticity, regardless of the philosophical perspective one takes (see Table 4.1), there is always a dimension of critical engagement with the socio-political environment that shapes and impacts on knowledge production and dissemination at the individual and collective level. Beyond critiquing the wider social, political and cultural agendas, HE pedagogical practices also need to action the genuine interests of students and academics as we discussed above.

Critical engagement with the socio-political environment by students and academic teaching has two layers. What we have discussed above focuses largely on the institutional impact and influence of the socio-political environment on HE. However, as we highlighted in the previous chapter, HE also has a civic mission that goes beyond what takes place inside individual HEIs. Historically, this kind of critical engagement in teaching and learning has been framed as a type of activism. As Barnett (1997) argues, this has always been a domain of HE's core business whether that involves serving the interests of the local communities where the HEI is located, advocating and sustaining the importance of democratic ideologies and practices in the wider world, or enabling students to act critically and authentically. Thus, in contemporary HE pedagogical practices, there must always be a space afforded to the nurturing of this kind of critical engagement by students and staff and opportunities for them to action such critical engagement.

Critical engagement with one's self

In Chapter 3, we touched upon the subject of higher-level learning and what this means. One of the aspects we discussed was the idea that HE learning is subversive and unsettling as it requires learners and academics to question, challenge and even change engrained and unanalysed thinking and practices. Related to this is the idea that the HE learning experience holds a transformative potential which requires students and academics to take a critical position on the 'ontological turn' of HE's impact on the student learning experience (Barnett 2004). We propose that the notion of authenticity can bring about meaningful insights into and engagement with HE teaching and learning, as it allows for teaching and learning to occur organically, enabling the transformative potential of HE and promoting students' and academics' genuine interests.

Returning to the three perspectives on authenticity explored earlier in Table 4.1, one common characteristic is the need to critically engage with one's self. This means becoming aware of our own existence, ways of thinking and acting in relation to the external environment, along with taking responsibility for our actions. It is only by doing so that we can engage authentically with learning about teaching and learning, as it is through this process of critical awareness where we begin to create meaning to our identities, our values and our pedagogical practices. As we touched on earlier, intersubjectivity has the potential to support academics' understanding of the importance of sharing their thinking, beliefs and assumptions about teaching and learning with their colleagues and their students. One of the ways in which academic teaching staff can stimulate this initial dialogue is through the production of a self-reflective account in the form of a teaching philosophy statement.

Schönwetter et al. (2002, p. 84) define a statement of teaching philosophy as 'a systematic and critical rationale that focuses on the important components defining effective teaching and learning in a particular discipline and/or institutional context'. While the issue of what constitutes 'effective teaching' is highly contested and is beyond the scope of this chapter to explore, this concise definition provides a clear starting point for discussion. The underlying aim of the teaching philosophy statement is to provide a space for academic staff to engage in a process of critical introspection, reflecting on some of the core issues relating to teaching and learning. So, for example, some of the areas covered in the statement that staff would be expected to reflect on include: the purpose of teaching and learning, the role of the teacher and student in teaching-learning encounters, pedagogic methods used, evaluation and assessment of teaching and learning, along with the contextual factors that influence the decision-making of staff in the planning, delivery and evaluation of their teaching. Schönwetter et al. (2002, p. 85) argue that as 'a broad philosophical statement of teaching practice, it translates the conceptualization of teaching into action by providing a set of principles'. The statement can thus be used as an ongoing point of reference for discussion.

Recognising that the production of a comprehensive teaching philosophy statement akin to that proposed by Schönwetter et al. (2002) may be an overwhelming and unwieldy exercise for academic teaching staff to undertake, we decided to produce a much shorter, more practically oriented version when developing our cycle of peer observation (CoPO). In the first stage of CoPO (discussed in more detail in Chapter 6), academic staff are required to produce a written self-reflection. This provides an opportunity for them to think holistically about their role, their practice, their approach to teaching, those aspects of their practice that they feel confident with as well as those areas of their practice they wish to explore and/or develop further. Among the questions that they are encouraged to reflect on are:

- How would you describe your approach(es) to teaching? What are the key factors that shape/have shaped your approach(es)?
- Which aspects of your teaching do you feel relatively confident with, and why?
- How do you understand your students' needs and adapt your practice to meet them?

- How do you plan for your sessions?
- How do you determine the key aims/outcomes of your sessions? How do you know when they have been met?

To a certain extent, the precise form that a teaching philosophy statement should take is unimportant as it is ultimately a means to an end rather than an end in itself. It is the process that matters more than the end product. What lies at the heart of this process is the creation of a space in which academic staff can critically reflect on their teaching, their professional identity and their students' learning experiences.

Barnett (1997) reminded us that self-reflection as a form of self-monitoring can be read essentially in two ways. It can either indicate an internalisation of others' agendas (i.e. self-censorship) or it can stand for powers of self-agency. Considering how powerful disciplinary and institutional cultures and traditions can be on learning and teaching, self-censorship certainly is a concern for pedagogical practices in HE. This is why we advocate for scholarly work on teaching and learning to take place between the key protagonists i.e. between staff and between staff and students. Later in Chapter 7, we discuss how using coaching skills can help to support meaningful critical self-reflection. In addition, to enable the transformative potential of critical self-reflection to be realised, scholarly inquiry into teaching and learning needs to be driven by the learning and development interests and goals of the key protagonists rather than a top-down agenda determined by others.

Critical engagement with each other

There are two dimensions to our use of the term 'each other' in this final section. The first relates to collaboration between academic teaching staff i.e. peers and/or colleagues working together. The second refers to collaboration between academic teaching staff and students.

Much of the literature and research in HE that explores critical engagement between academic staff in the context of teaching and learning tends to focus on peer observation. This is hardly surprising given how peer-based models have largely accounted for the engagement of HE academic staff with observation to date, as we discuss in the following chapter when reviewing the use of observation as a method in different educational contexts. While peer observation is not a term, or indeed a practice, that is unanimously understood and applied in HE, we use it consistently in Chapters 6–9 when referring to the applied models of observation that we have created. Thus, we define peer observation as a 'collaborative, reciprocal, model of observation where peers get together to observe each other's practice' and where 'the observation is not regarded as an end in itself but as a springboard for sharing ideas and stimulating reflective dialogue' (O'Leary and Price 2016, pp. 114–115).

In Chapters 6 and 9, we discuss two distinct collaborative models of peer observation between staff. In both cases, observations of teaching were identified as a common touchpoint and catalyst for dialogue for all academic teaching staff. Each model is designed to prioritise collaborative inquiry, critical reflection, professional dialogue and collegial development. A structured cycle was developed for each model to facilitate effective dialogic interaction between peers. Furthermore, another common bond between our different models of observation is the way in which we reconceptualise and reconfigure the use of observation. We do so by removing it from an assessment context and transforming it into a method of educational inquiry, from which new possibilities emerge for harnessing observation as a tool for developing collegial understanding about the reciprocal relationship between teaching and learning. Building on this work, we adapted the cycle of peer observation (CoPO) that we created for academic staff (see Chapter 6) to create a new cycle of collaborative observation (CoCO) to include students as co-researchers and co-observers. We drew on the work of Bowden and Marton's (2004) *collective consciousness* as the conceptual inspiration and theoretical underpinning for this co-constructed partnership, using CoCO as the vehicle for developing a partnership between students and staff that would help to generate this collective consciousness of learning and teaching (see Chapter 8).

The scholarship of teaching and learning encourages and values the co-construction of knowledge between teachers and students, assuming a learning partnership, instead of a traditional didactic relationship (Trigwell et al. 2000). A key argument put forward by Boyer is the idea that scholars (i.e. students and academics) are co-learners:

> (…) faculty, as scholars, are also learners (…) While well prepared lectures surely have a place, teaching, at its best, means not only transmitting knowledge, but transforming and extending it as well. Through reading, through classroom discussion, and surely through comments and questions posed by students, professors themselves will be pushed in creative new directions.
>
> (1990, p. 24)

SoTL calls for a collective approach to create and sustain a scholarly culture and mindset towards teaching and learning. This means that rather than seeing improving teaching and learning as the responsibility of individual students and academics, it is viewed as the responsibility of the wider department, faculty, institution and academic community. The emphasis is on the 'we' rather than the 'I', with collaboration central.

Conceptualising students and academics as co-learners who belong to the same academic community enables us to reimagine the type of pedagogical engagement that members of such an academic community can have with each other. Crucially, it opens up the ethical and affective dimensions of pedagogical practices when members of an academic community come together to make sense of what happens in their teaching-learning spaces and how the activities and experiences impact on both students and academic teaching staff. As we reveal when we share some of the key findings from our research in later chapters attest, the difference in the quality and value of the learning and teaching experiences of students and staff when they are engaged in an authentic academic community is palpable.

Concluding thoughts

The first part of this chapter discussed the notions of a scholarship of teaching and a scholarly approach to teaching. While we identified the production of peer-reviewed publications or outputs that are shared with the wider academic community as one of the aspects that distinguishes the former from the latter, there are certainly more similarities than differences between the two. In summary, some of the core characteristics that we associate with a scholarly approach to teaching and learning in HE include: 1) academic teaching staff inquiring into their own teaching, that of their peers and their students' learning within their respective communities; 2) adopting a systematic approach to the exploration of their chosen teaching-learning inquiries; 3) engaging with the focus of their inquiries critically and reflectively; and 4) working in partnership with others within their communities i.e. colleagues, peers and students. Following on from this, we have explored the notion of authenticity in teaching and learning in HE and how this has influenced the conceptual and theoretical foundations of our work and its relevance to developing a scholarly approach. We identified three discernible elements of this authenticity which we summarise as: 1) the recognition of the transformative potential of HE and its role in the *becoming* of both students and academic staff; 2) the importance of understanding teaching and learning in HE as a complex adaptive system; and 3) the centrality of criticality in interrogating and challenging the internal and external environment in which HEIs operate. The last part of this chapter has focused on critical engagement in learning about teaching and learning and what this entails. For academic teaching staff, we established that being critically reflective means a lot more than just thinking about our own teaching. For critical reflection to be authentic and have a meaningful impact, it must involve developing a clear understanding of the beliefs, thinking and decision-making of academic teaching staff. It also needs to be underpinned by a sense of critical self-awareness and social, political and ethical awareness. In the chapters that follow, we turn our attention to focusing on the practice of observation and its role in relation to understanding and improving teaching and learning.

References

Andresen, L. W., 2000. A useable, trans-disciplinary conception of scholarship. *Higher Education Research and Development* 19(2), 137–143.

Barnett, R., 1990. *The Idea of Higher Education*. Buckingham: Open University Press.

Barnett, R., 1997. *Higher Education: A Critical Business*. Buckingham: Open University Press.

Barnett, R. 2004. Learning for an unknown future. *Higher Education Research and Development* 23(3), 247–260.

Baume, D. and Popovic, C., 2016. *Advancing Practice in Academic Development*. London: Routledge.

Becher, T., and Trowler, P., 2001. *Academic Tribes and Territories: Intellectual Enquiry and the Culture of Disciplines*. London: McGraw-Hill Education.

Biesta, G. J. J., 1995. Pragmatism as a Pedagogy of Communicative Action. In J. Garrison, (ed.) *The New Scholarship on John Dewey*. Dordrecht: Kluwer Academic Publishers, 105–127.

Bowden, J. and Marton, F., 2004. *The University of Learning: Beyond Quality and Competence*. London: Routledge.

Boyer, E., 1990. *Scholarship Reconsidered: Priorities of the Professoriate*. San Francisco CA: Jossey-Bass.

Brookfield, S. D., 1995. *Becoming a Critically Reflective Teacher*. San Francisco CA: Jossey-Bass.

Canning, J., 2019. The UK Teaching Excellence Framework (TEF) as an illustration of Baudrillard's hyperreality. *Discourse: Studies in the Cultural Politics of Education* 40(3), 319–330.

Collini, S. 2012. *What are Universities For?* London: Penguin.

Cranton, P. A., 2001. *Becoming an Authentic Teacher in Higher Education*. Malabar FL: Krieger.

Croll, P., 1986. *Systematic Classroom Observation*. London: Falmer.

De Jaegher, H., Pieper, B., Clénin, D. and Fuchs, T., 2017. Grasping intersubjectivity: An invitation to embody social interaction research. *Phenomenology and the Cognitive Sciences* 16(3), 491–523.

Dewey, J., 1938. *Experience and Education*. New York NY: Macmillan.

Elton, L., 1992. Research, teaching and scholarship in an expanding higher education system. *Higher Education Quarterly* 46(3), 252–267.

Felten, P., 2013. Principles of good practice in SoTL. *Teaching and Learning Inquiry* 1(1), 121–125.

Knight, P. and Trowler, P., 2000. Department level cultures and the improvement of learning and teaching. *Studies in Higher Education* 25(1), 69–83.

Kreber, C., 2013. *Authenticity In and Through Teaching. The Transformative Potential of the Scholarship of Teaching*. London: Routledge.

Kreber, C. and Cranton, P., 2000. Exploring the scholarship of teaching. *The Journal of Higher Education* 71, 476–495.

Kreber, C. and Klampfleitner, M., 2013. Lecturers' and students' conceptions of authenticity in teaching and actual teacher actions and attributes students perceive as helpful. *High Education* 66, 463–487.

Miller-Young, J. and Yeo, M., 2015. Conceptualizing and communicating SoTL: A framework for the field. *Teaching & Learning Inquiry* 3(2), 37–53.

O'Leary, M. and Price, D., 2016. Peer Observation as a Springboard for Teacher Learning. In M. O'Leary, (ed.) *Reclaiming Lesson Observation: Supporting Excellence in Teacher Learning*. Abingdon: Routledge, 114–123.

O'Leary, M., Cui, V. and French, A., 2019. *Understanding, Recognising and Rewarding Teaching Quality in Higher Education: An Exploration of the Impact and Implications of the Teaching Excellence Framework*. London: University and Colleges Union. https://www.ucu.org.uk/media/10092/Impact-of-TEF-report-Feb-2019/pdf/ImpactofTEFreportFEb2019.

Prosser, M., 2008. The scholarship of teaching and learning: What is it? A personal view. *International Journal for the Scholarship of Teaching and Learning* 2(2), ISSN 1931–4744. https://doi.org/10.20429/ijsotl.2008.020202

Richlin, L., 2001. Scholarly Teaching and the Scholarship of Teaching. In C. Kreber, (ed.) *New Directions for Teaching and Learning: No. 86*. San Francisco CA: Jossey-Bass, 57–67.

Schön, D. A., 1995. The new scholarship requires a new epistemology. *Change* 27(6), 27–34.

Schönwetter, D.J., Sokal, L., Friesen, M. and Taylor, K. L., 2002. Teaching philosophies reconsidered: A conceptual model for the development and evaluation of teaching philosophy statements. *The International Journal for Academic Development* 7, 83–97.

Shulman, L. S., 1987. Knowledge and teaching: Foundations of the new reform. *Harvard Educational Review* 36(1), 1–22.

Shulman, L. S., 1999. Taking learning seriously. *Change* 31(4), 11–17.
Tomlinson, M., 2017. Student perceptions of themselves as "consumers" of higher education. *British Journal of Sociology of Education* 38(4), 450–567.
Trigwell, K., Martin, E., Benjamin, J. and Prosser, M., 2000. Scholarship of teaching: A model. *Higher Education Research and Development* 19, 155–168.
Trowler, P., Saunders, M. and Bamber, V., (eds). 2012. *Tribes and Territories in the 21st Century: Rethinking the Significance of Disciplines in Higher Education*. London: Routledge.

A review of the role of observation in teaching and learning

5

Contexts, models and purposes of the observation of teaching and learning

An overview

Observation is a multi-purpose mechanism that is used for a multitude of reasons and in different contexts in education. In the contexts of teacher training and teacher development, for example, it has a well-established role as a formative tool in the education, training and ongoing professional learning of teachers globally. While its use in higher education (HE) is less commonplace compared to schools and colleges, there has certainly been an increase in the number of higher education institutions (HEIs) adopting observation as a form of institutional practice for staff in recent years (O'Leary, Cui and French 2019a). The reasons for this are related largely to the increasing interest and policy focus on the quality of teaching and learning over the last two decades, which cannot be decontextualised from a neoliberal policy agenda that has resulted in the 'transformation of social relations into calculabilities and exchanges' (Ball 2012, p. 29), with the continuing international commodification and marketisation of HE.

Historically, observation has predominantly served as a dual-purpose mechanism across educational sectors. Its principal use has been as both a formative and a summative method of assessment for monitoring and measuring the competence and effectiveness of teaching and teachers' classroom performance. However, it has also played a developmental role in nurturing the pedagogic skills and knowledge base of teachers at all stages of their career. That said, this duality has become dichotomised in recent years, mainly due to global education policies that have prioritised an agenda of performance management and quality assurance over teachers' professional growth, which has meant that the use of observation has been restricted to a particular purpose, as discussed further below.

The use of observation in schools

The use of observation has a much longer and more varied history in primary and secondary schools than it does in tertiary colleges and HE (Grubb 2000). It should therefore come as no surprise to hear that much of the literature and educational research undertaken into observation as a method has taken place in the schools' sector. This is something that not only applies to the UK context but also internationally (e.g. Martinez, Taut and Schaaf 2016). In terms of the focus of studies to date on observation in schools, it can be broadly divided into two key areas of interest that reflect the differing lenses adopted for using observation, along with the underlying purpose and agenda behind each lens. The focus of the first lens is the use of observation as an assessment method for evaluating teacher performance and/or the effectiveness of teaching. In contrast, the focus of the second lens is on the use of observation to study children's behaviour, particularly in relation to how they learn as well as their interactions with their peers and their teachers; this has particularly been the case in early years and primary settings. In the case of secondary schools, the focus has largely been on the former i.e. its application as a method of assessing teaching and teacher performance.

In terms of publications on observation in the schools' sector, these can be separated into two broad areas. Firstly, there are those textbooks that focus on the practical application of observation and typically adopt a task-based approach for teachers to use observation in classrooms, to observe either their students or other teachers (e.g. Fawcett and Watson 2016; Wajnryb 1993). Secondly, there are research-based texts (e.g. journal articles, research reports, theses) that explore different aspects and applications of observation. For example, there are those that focus on the design, implementation and evaluation of standardised observation instruments. From an ontological and epistemological perspective, such instruments are invariably the product of researchers who align themselves to a positivist paradigm and are based on the premise that teaching and learning are phenomena that can be systematically observed and recorded (e.g. Bell et al. 2012; Pianta, La Paro and Hamre 2007). Methodologically, these instruments typically adopt a quantitative approach where the observer is required to count and/ or rank what they observe.

One of the most widely cited textbooks on observation to date in England is Wragg's *An Introduction to Classroom Observation* (1999). The book is situated in the context of English primary schools and covers a wide range of themes related to the practical application of observation as a pedagogic tool. From the start of the book, Wragg raises one of the most commonly debated issues regarding the use of observation as a method of assessment i.e. the issue of reliability. In stating that 'we often "observe" what we want to see' (1999, p. vii), Wragg draws attention to the subjectivity of observation and how events are 'inevitably filtered through the interpretive lens of the observer' (Foster 1996, p. 14) with traditional assessment-based models of observation. The subjectivity of observers' interpretations is a common theme in the schools-based observation literature, particularly when discussing notions of *good* or *effective* practice (e.g. Tilstone 1998). Added to this, even evidence from large-scale projects like the Measures of Effective Teaching (MET) project in the USA highlights how problematic the issue of observer or 'interrater' reliability is when it comes to making judgements on the observation of teaching.

The MET project (2011–2013), sponsored by the Gates Foundation, was a large-scale, longitudinal study involving 3,000 volunteer teachers from a range of school districts in the USA. It was designed to identify the skills and qualities characterising the 'effective teacher', along with testing which methods of evaluation were the fairest and most reliable in capturing this information. Although the project's findings were inconclusive as to what makes an effective teacher and offer little in the way of guidance about developing valid and reliable teacher evaluation systems, it has played a key role in raising the profile of teacher evaluation research. Classroom observation featured as a specific strand of the project and was one of the main instruments used to assess teacher effectiveness. In relation to the use of observation as a method of evaluation, one of the key findings from the project emphasised how a 'single observation by a single observer is a fairly unreliable estimate of a teacher's practice' (Ho and Kane 2013, p. 13), echoing other related research discussed below in this chapter. MET project researchers concluded that at least two different observers, each observing four different lessons (thus totalling eight discrete observation evaluations) may be needed to overcome issues of observer subjectivity over a sustained period of time. However, in their research into teacher effectiveness, Campbell et al. (2004, p. 133) claimed that 'even successive observations of a teacher will only ever supply a collection of snapshots rather than a full picture of teacher behaviour over the year'. While they acknowledged the importance of observation as a source of evidence for systems for evaluating teacher performance, they also remarked that as a method of data collection 'it is often used with little regard for, or knowledge of, its characteristics' (Campbell et al. 2004). What they meant by this comment was that despite its widespread use as a means of gathering data, there is a lack of rigour in its application and insufficient awareness on the part of those carrying out observation of its limitations as a method. This is a matter that we will discuss in more detail in Chapter 7 when exploring the practice of observation preparation and training.

In an international study that examined a sample of sixteen classroom observation systems in schools across six different countries (Australia, Chile, Germany, Japan, Singapore and the USA), Martinez, Taut and Schaaf (2016, p. 27) concluded that:

> There is little empirical evidence to suggest that large-scale standardized observation, and high-stakes teacher evaluation in general, constitutes a good vehicle for countries to exert improvements and achieve educational success (Feuer, 2012), while at the same time there is little dispute that high quality teaching is the main factor modifiable by educational policy that predicts students' educational outcomes.
> (Nye, Konstantopoulos and Hedges 2004)

Wragg (1999, p. 60) maintains that 'mostly when we talk about a "good" teacher, an "effective" strategy or a "bad" lesson, we are referring to our own subjective perception'. To reinforce his argument, he recalls a session in which thirty-five highly experienced teacher educators were shown a videotape of a student teacher's lesson and were asked to grade it on a scale of A–E (A at the top end of the scale and E at the bottom). Their grades varied from a D at the lowest end to a B+ at the top end of the scale. Such differing judgements highlight the reality of how problematic observer subjectivity can be when using observation as a method for assessing teaching and reinforce the limitations of observation as a sole method of assessment, especially when ranking scales are used to measure and evaluate performance.

The use of hierarchical ranking or classification systems of so-called 'excellence' or 'quality' when assessing teaching through observation is another common theme in the schools' literature. Wragg (1999) is critical of hierarchical ranking systems, as he claims that 'the nature of the levels can still be vague and diffuse, using words like "adequate" or "considerable" that are open to widely differing interpretations' (Wragg 1999, p. 103). The idea that there is a shared understanding among those involved in the observation process as to the precise meaning and interpretation of value-laden terms such as 'poor', 'good', 'excellent' or 'outstanding' is a matter of considerable dispute among researchers and the teaching profession. Although there are those researchers in the field who claim to have developed observation frameworks that purport to increase consistency by linking teaching standards, observation criteria and rubrics (e.g. Danielson 2011), the reality is that such qualitative terms are inherently relative and not imbued with an unambiguous and universal understanding. Wragg (1999) argues that such terms, together with the assessment criteria that underpin them, need to be carefully defined when used and attempts made to establish a collective understanding. However, we would argue that even when such attempts are made, there is no compelling evidence to suggest that they make a significant difference in minimising the threats to the reliability of the observer's assessment. For example, despite observers undertaking standardisation training for the use of observation instruments and their accompanying assessment criteria, the extent to which such training leads to a standardisation in their understanding and application of them is difficult to control or know with any degree of certainty, not least because there is rarely any systematic analysis of their subsequent judgements. In other words, whilst such practice might be useful in raising collective awareness among observers, it is unrealistic to expect the assessment criteria to be uniformly and consistently applied. Besides, related research suggests that experienced assessors are likely to judge intuitively, even ignoring published criteria. Though it has to be said that this is not a phenomenon specific to observation as a method of assessment but reinforces more widely held beliefs among key researchers in the field that 'assessment is not an exact science and we must stop presenting it as such' (Gipps 1994, p. 167).

Historically, the grading of performance management observations has been a contentious issue in schools in England. The largest unions representing schoolteachers, the National Education Union (NEU) and the National Association of Schoolmasters/Union of Women Teachers (NASUWT), have both produced guidance for their members on observation, which was updated following Ofsted's shift in policy on the grading of lesson observations in inspections. Both unions believe that grading encourages school management to view observation as a surveillance mechanism with which to monitor the quality of teachers' work, instead of seeing it as a valuable means of stimulating professional dialogue. Marriott (2001) maintains that the grade can take on such importance that it threatens to undermine the value of the dialogue and feedback between the observer and the observee. Both parties can 'become hung up on what the grade means rather than how to improve the teaching' (2001, p. 46). Such is the anxiety surrounding grading that the 'teacher may become over-concerned about whether he or she has "passed"' (Marriott 2001).

In their two-year monitoring study of teacher appraisal in English primary and secondary schools, Wragg et al. (1996) highlighted what they described as a 'snapshot' approach to classroom observation (i.e. one-off observations) as one of the main obstacles to identifying incompetent teachers. The reason for this was because such teachers could deliver the 'rehearsed' lesson as a one-off performance, hence avoiding detection. Marriott (2001, p. 8) has also highlighted the limitations of a snapshot approach as 'the impact of teaching on learning, and therefore progress, is harder to evaluate in the context of one lesson'. O'Leary's research (2020) has also highlighted the prevalence of the 'showcase lesson' in performance management observations. In addition to concerns surrounding the validity and reliability of episodic observations, there is also the issue of what such practice reveals about institutional approaches to monitoring the quality of teaching. In other words, that an institution should choose to rely on isolated observations of staff as a tool for monitoring teacher performance arguably says more about the inadequacy of an institution's policy than it does about the quality of teaching.

Wragg (1999, p. 3) succinctly summarises some of the paradoxes involved with observation when comparing the ways in which teachers respond to the different contexts in which it occurs and its application as a multi-purpose tool in the following comment:

> Skilfully handled, classroom observation can benefit both the observer and the person being observed, serving to inform and enhance the professional skills of both people. Badly handled, however, it becomes counter-productive, at its worst arousing hostility, resistance and suspicion.

The nature of the relationship between the observer and the observed teacher and how they interact differs according to who is observing whom, in what context and for what purpose. Underpinning Wragg's comment above, and the relationship between the observer and the observed teacher, are the notions of power and authority. As Wragg comments, 'the actual or perceived power relationship between observer and observed is not just a sociological concept, but rather a reality that needs to be recognised' (Wragg 1999, p. 62). For example, if a senior leader undertakes an assessment-based observation of a probationary teacher for their probation, there is a clear delineation of power and authority between the two, which would result in the senior leader driving the interaction between the two. In this instance, it would be normal to expect the observed teacher to adopt a more passive role, with less likelihood of them challenging or contesting their observer's views. This is because the context and purpose of such an observation are high stakes, with the observer making a summative judgement of the teacher's performance, which could have far-reaching consequences for the observed teacher. In contrast, if two teachers observe each other as part of a peer-based model of observation designed to support a collegial approach to professional development, the nature of the relationship is very different and the stakes are naturally much lower in comparison to the previous scenario. Although these two contrasting scenarios reflect some of the differing contexts, models and purposes of observation, what separates and unites them are notions of control, ownership and professional autonomy and the extent to which these are embodied in these different approaches.

The success of many observation programmes in schools seems to depend on the extent to which teachers are able to own the process as opposed to it being something that is 'done to them'. Tilstone (1998, p. 59) uses the term 'partnership observation' to capture what she sees as a more collaborative, equal relationship between observer and observee. She argues that 'such partnerships will only work if the [observer] is not regarded as an authoritarian figure and is able to take on the role of facilitator with the teacher in control of direction of the observation and consequent actions' (Tilstone 1998, p. 60). This echoes studies across different education sectors and seems to be a common denominator in those models of observation that teachers value most in terms of helping to develop their pedagogic thinking and practice. Two such examples in the schools sector are 'unseen observation' and 'lesson study'.

'Unseen observation' is an innovative approach, developed by O'Leary (2020), that is increasingly being embraced by schools and colleges in England, with practitioners acknowledging its positive impact on attitudes to observation and reporting significant improvements in their teaching and their students' learning. The term 'unseen observation' might seem odd or even a contradiction given that it is a model of observation that does not involve observing a taught lesson. It is a teacher-centred model where the fundamental work takes place in the pre- and post-session conversations that form the foundation of the unseen observation cycle (see Figure 5.1).

The teacher's recounting and reflection on the taught lesson is what provides the stimulus for the professional dialogue between them and their coach/peer, as well as a pre-session meeting (Stage 2) between the two in which they discuss the proposed session plan. What is particularly distinctive about unseen observation is the shift in the locus of control from the

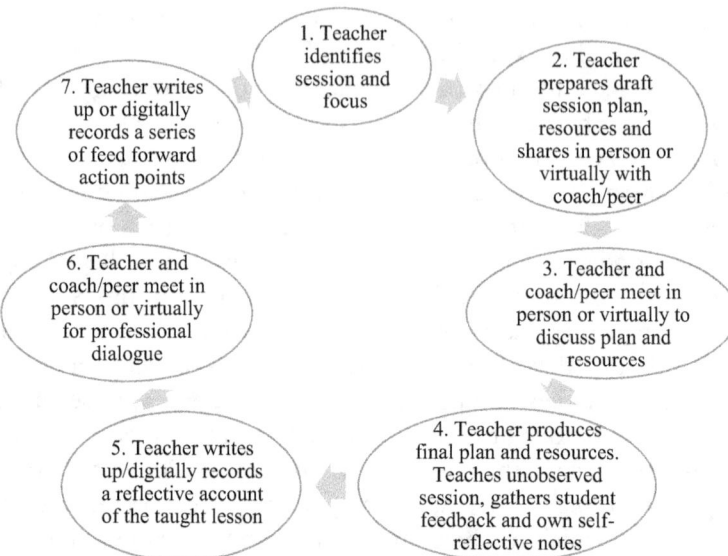

Figure 5.1 An overview of the 7 stages of the unseen observation cycle

'observer' to the 'observed', reducing some of the counterproductive effects of traditional observations and in turn creating a more equitable working relationship. As individual teachers are empowered to decide the focus of their unseen observation, this provides them with increased autonomy to take ownership of their practice, along with the freedom to reflect more meaningfully and deeply on their practice and its impact on their students. It is built on the premise that teachers are the best people to decide their own professional needs and those of their students. This rethinking and reconfiguring of observation and the roles of observer and the observed may help to explain the increasing popularity of unseen observation and why it has been embraced so enthusiastically by teachers. This particular approach to observation is discussed in depth in Chapter 9.

Another model of observation that has gained traction in schools internationally over the last two decades is 'lesson study'. Lesson study (*jugyokenkyu*) originated in Japan, where it has a long and well-documented history that dates back to the late nineteenth century and where it has been used traditionally as the most common form of teacher professional development in the improvement of mathematics and science education in particular. As Wood and Rawlings-Smith (2017, p. 91) explain, lesson study is 'a collaborative development process that focuses on improving teacher practice through deep, collaborative reflection and investigation of student learning'. Unlike conventional models of observation that tend to be based on an atomistic approach to separating out aspects of teaching and learning into discrete units (planning, resources, teaching strategies etc.), lesson study adopts a more holistic approach. Conventional models of observation typically rely on the information gathered during a single, isolated observation of an individual teacher's classroom practice on which to base judgements and formulate follow-up improvement action plans. Lesson study 'challenges the status quo of teachers and their classrooms as islands – relatively unaware of events on other islands – with students floating in between' (Wang-Iverson 2002, p. 1).

Far from being seen as a corrective mechanism to improve the practice of individual teachers, the planned impact of lesson study is meant to be collaborative and fully inclusive of all teachers. Hence teachers usually work together in small groups of 3–5 on an agreed 'learning challenge their students face' (Wood and Rawlings-Smith 2017, p. 91), which is typically something that may be difficult or problematic for them to understand. The primary focus is to develop educators' understanding of their students' learning, with a view to this then informing and feeding into their own practice and, ultimately, into improving students' understanding of the targeted learning challenge.

Reflecting a shift in the lens of observation away from individual teacher performance and onto students' learning and engagement with the subject area, lesson study places the emphasis on the observation of a curriculum unit rather than an isolated lesson. Its ultimate aim is thus to examine in depth how those who teach that unit can enhance greater student understanding and achievement. In short, lesson study is based broadly on an action-research approach to studying what goes on in classrooms where teachers work collaboratively as active researchers. Furthermore, one of its unique characteristics is how it seeks to involve the learners in the discussion and analysis of the observed lessons. According to Lieberman (2009), lesson study puts student and teacher learning at the centre of the observation process rather than teacher evaluation.

There is evidence of a growth in the use of lesson study as a form of intervention in teacher development, particularly in schools. Lieberman (2009), for example, has reported on the popularity of lesson study increasing in the USA. Its use has also increased in schools in England (e.g. Wood 2017; Wood and Cajkler 2016). In her research, Lieberman (2009) found that lesson study encouraged greater openness among staff, which helped to expose vulnerability as an issue that affects both experienced and novice teachers. Lieberman argues that lesson study has helped to foster a collegial approach to teacher development through peer observation and thus prompted teachers to take more risks in their teaching.

'Instructional rounds' or 'learning rounds' is another recent development in the field of observation and the professional development of teachers in schools. Instructional rounds is a practice that was first developed in the USA (City et al. 2009; Roberts 2012) and has since been adopted by various education systems internationally. Instructional rounds are essentially a collaborative, team-based approach to observation where educators come together to observe teaching across different classes within a school, with a view to bringing about school-wide improvement rather than focusing on the practice of individual teachers as is often the case with conventional models of observation. Philpott and Oates (2015, p. 23) provide a concise explanation:

> Instructional rounds is a method for collaborative professional development in which educators come together to observe teaching and learning across a number of classrooms in a single school. In a post observation debrief they use notes and other forms of recording, such as diagrams, taken during the observations to build up a detailed picture of teaching and learning in the school. The intention is to use this to develop understanding of the teaching and learning practice in the school and make plans for what needs to be done next to develop that practice.

There are four steps to the process of instructional rounds: 1) identifying a 'problem' of practice, 2) observing, 3) debriefing and 4) focusing on the follow-up actions for development. While the originators of instructional rounds acknowledge that variations of their design can emerge, they are adamant that the four steps to the process cannot be compromised if it is to be considered as an authentic representation and to be done properly (City et al. 2009). Underpinning the first step in the process (i.e. identifying a problem of practice) is a focus on what City et al. refer to as the 'instructional core', which they define as 'the teacher and the student in the presence of content' (2009, p. 22). In other words, in order for instructional rounds to be effective, they need to prioritise their focus on the iterative relationships between the teacher, the student and the subject matter, as well as how changes to any one of them requires or creates changes in the other two. Besides, the specific focus of the round needs to be something that is observable and actionable. What is clear is that the identification of a problem of practice is not a straightforward, procedural task but one that requires an in-depth, complex understanding of the way in which these three elements interact and impact on each other.

The second step in the process (i.e. observing) appears to reflect some of the characteristics of the non-judgemental model of observation discussed in the next chapter. The process of observation in instructional rounds is linked closely to the debriefing stage in the third step insomuch as there are four stages to the debriefing that shape the way in which observers are expected to record what they see. These four stages are: 1) description, 2) analysis, 3) prediction and 4) evaluation. There is particular emphasis on the importance of the first stage of description, which mirrors the approach taken to the Cycle of Peer Observation (CoPO) discussed in the following chapter where observers undergo training in recording non-judgemental notes of the observation. The fundamental principle is that observers are asked to record what they see in a descriptive, factual way, without imposing their interpretation of what they think about what they see. As City et al. (2009, p. 84) acknowledge, this is not an instinctive, natural skill but one that 'must be learned, and some other habits – like using general or judgmental language or jargon – must be unlearned'. This raises fundamental questions about the act of observing, which are explored in depth in Chapter 7. In addition, the more detailed the descriptions recorded, the better.

Cultural change is a linchpin for the effectiveness of instructional rounds. As others have argued about maximising the potential of observation as a tool for enhancing the quality of teacher development and students' learning experience (e.g. O'Leary 2020), wider cultural change at an organisational level is crucial for such reforms to have a meaningful and sustainable impact on institutional policy and practice. Developing a shared culture in schools where teachers and leaders collaborate is therefore essential to the success of instructional rounds. Instructional rounds are simply a means to an end. The development of cultural change within an institution drives improvement rather than the practice of models like instructional rounds per se. Besides, such practice needs to link closely to an institution's overarching improvement strategy.

A variation of instructional rounds known as 'learning rounds' gained official support from the Scottish government for use in Scotland's schools in the noughties. Philpott and Oates's research (2015, p. 22) found that 'what teachers in Scotland do when they say they are doing learning rounds varies widely from school to school and deviates significantly from the practice of instructional rounds'. Their research reveals that the practice of learning rounds in Scotland tends to focus mainly on observation and debrief at the expense of other equally important parts of the process. Instead of developing a problem of practice from the evidence gathered during instructional rounds, the model of learning rounds used in the schools included in Philpott and Oates' research identified a pre-determined observation focus from the outset. In short, while there were aspects of the process of instructional rounds present in these schools' adaptation, there were important elements that appeared to be absent such as the 'theory of action' and a deeper understanding of the importance of developing a 'rich problem of practice'.

In summary, Philpott and Oates (2015, p. 24) list the defining features of instructional rounds as:

- A rich problem of practice based on shared evidence focused on the 'instructional core'
- Fine-grained descriptive data about what is happening (not what isn't happening) in classrooms that can be used for later analysis and prediction and, finally, evaluation
- A wider strategy for improvement that is linked to the problem of practice and the observations
- A developing theory of action about how different actions affect outcomes
- A changed culture for schools and districts

In a subsequent paper, Philpott and Oates (2017) discuss the use and impact of learning rounds in terms of their role in fostering teacher agency in professional learning communities. Their findings revealed that although the learning rounds in their research were largely organised by the teachers themselves, 'the nature and purpose of the process can be seen as defined by policy and by local authority and school management' (2017, p. 329). Despite the teachers participating voluntarily, Philpott and Oates questioned the extent to which they had genuine ownership of the practice as a whole given that they were not involved in the decision-making about how the process was defined and its purposes. The issue of teacher ownership is one we will return to in the final section of this chapter.

The use of observation in tertiary colleges and further education providers

Compared to schools, observation has historically been an under-researched area in the further education (FE) sector, though the last decade has seen a marked interest in observation-related studies (e.g. Edgington 2013; O'Leary et al. 2019b; Page 2014; UCU 2013). In terms of the use and/or role of observation, the reasons for its emergence in FE are consistent with those discussed above for schools, i.e. the implementation of performance management systems and the wider audit and accountability culture.

Hardman's research (2007) adopted a case study approach in which observation was explored in three FE colleges and three HEIs. In seeking to identify differences between the two sectors, she reported that OTL was much more heavily associated with quality assurance (QA) and performance management systems in FE colleges where there was an emphasis on grading staff. This contrasted with HE where there was a tendency for it to occur in developmental contexts, reflected in the prevalence of informal peer-based models of observation as the most common model of practice, as discussed further in the following section. The three FE colleges in Hardman's study all had observation policies and procedures that sought to combine the purposes of QA requirements for Ofsted and other external regulators, together with their own quality improvement (QI) agendas. Hardman (2007, p. 41) remarks that:

> As observation schemes are resource intensive and most QA systems entail considerable investment in staff time, FE managers aim to combine the achievement of both QA and QI objectives using one scheme. One consequence is that the effectiveness of the QI process is diminished in proportion to the predominance of the schemes' evaluative or judgemental features.

Observation schemes are undoubtedly time-intensive and expensive for colleges. With limited budgets, it is hardly surprising that colleges should attempt to dovetail two different purposes into one scheme. However, as Hardman suggests, the effectiveness of such a strategy is questionable. QA requirements appear to take precedence over the Continuing Professional Development (CPD) needs of tutors. Furthermore, the use of observation for QA purposes is not without its controversies.

Recent research carried out in FE has uncovered how the use of lesson observation has been predominantly shaped by a performance management agenda (e.g. Boocock 2013; Edgington 2013; O'Leary 2013; Page 2014; UCU 2013). This has been reflected in the contexts and purposes for which observation has been used for assessing the performance of experienced, in-service teachers but also in the training and assessment of novice, pre-service teachers. This performance-driven focus has culminated in a prescribed and codified model of what it means to be an effective teaching professional in some circles, with limited opportunities for the use of observation to stimulate collaborative discussion about the process of teaching and learning.

A key finding from O'Leary's doctoral research (2011) carried out across ten FE colleges was how graded observation (i.e. observations ranked according to the Ofsted 4-point scale of: 1. Outstanding; 2. Good; 3. Requires

Improvement and 4. Inadequate) had become normalised as a performative tool of managerialist systems fixated with measuring teacher performance rather than actually improving it. The vast majority of colleges involved in O'Leary's research adopted what he refers to as a 'restrictive approach' (O'Leary 2013) to the use of observation, typified by their reliance on the use of the Ofsted 4-point graded scale to measure performance, prioritising the needs of performance management systems over the individual development needs of their staff. Yet, in contrast, in those colleges where there was evidence of an 'expansive approach' (O'Leary 2013), grading was seen as less important, as the professional development needs of staff underpinned the way in which observation was used.

O'Leary's doctoral research revealed repeated examples of teachers being encouraged to demonstrate normalised models of so-called effective practice based on prescribed notions of 'excellent' or 'good' teaching, often cascaded from senior management, who were understandably keen to promote 'best practice' given the high-stakes nature of such observations, particularly during external inspections. This encouraged teachers to perform inauthentically and led to the emergence of the 'rehearsed' or 'showcase lesson', where the teacher concerned 'played the game' in order to succeed.

In a qualitative case study involving sixteen teachers working in a single FE college in England, Page's (2014) doctoral research explored her participants' perceptions, experiences and engagement with being observed teaching over a six-year period. Through a series of face-to-face narrative interviews, Page's research also used these teachers' experiences of observation as a means of exploring their sense of professionalism, their attitudes to being held accountable through observation and how being observed influenced their perceptions and practices of 'good teaching'. Her findings revealed 'the multi-layered, deep-rooted emotions teachers associate with being observed and how these impact on their perception of a professional teacher and their understanding of what "good teaching" is' (2014, p. 3). She argued that teachers have become 'docile servants of the micro and macro-level control levers placed on them' (ibid.) through observation, resulting in cultures of fear and mistrust. She concludes by calling for an urgent review of observation practices with the needs of teachers placed at the heart of reform.

Edgington's (2013) qualitative research also included in-depth interviews with fourteen FE staff. Drawing on her personal reflections as an FE teacher, along with her creative writing skills, Edgington's research created fictionalised accounts as a means of anonymising the voices and experiences of her participants' narratives. As part of her theoretical framework, she drew on concepts from social constructionist and psychoanalytical perspectives. Through a series of detailed case studies, Edgington examined the real impact of performance management approaches to observation on the emotional selves of the observers and observees who participated in her doctoral research. Adopting a poststructuralist and psychoanalytical approach to exploring and explaining her participants' perceptions of observation allowed her to unearth their emotional experiences. In doing this, her research has helped to shed new light on a common area of practice that has been largely under-theorised and under-researched for many years, as it provides a valuable insight into how observation experiences impact on educators as emotional beings and, ultimately, how it affects them and their professional practice.

In 2012/13, the largest union representing further and higher education staff in the world, the University and College Union (UCU), funded a national research project to investigate the use and impact of lesson observation on the professional lives of staff working in FE (UCU 2013). The project remains the largest and most extensive study in the English education system to date on observation. The research adopted a mixed-methods approach involving quantitative and qualitative methods of inquiry. The sample for the first phase of the data collection (online survey) comprised UCU members, ranging from part-time tutors to senior managers. Approximately 4,000 respondents completed the survey (n=3976). The second phase involved staff from a range of colleges across England, including UCU members and non-members, who participated in a series of focus groups and interviews.

A key finding from the UCU research was the widespread discontent felt amongst participants towards the use of lesson observation as a form of performative teacher assessment. This use of observation was repeatedly criticised by a significant majority of participants for being a 'box-ticking' exercise and, in some instances, a 'disciplinary stick' with which 'to beat staff'. Such observations were also identified by many respondents as being a major cause of increased levels of stress and anxiety amongst teaching staff.

Another compelling finding to emerge from the study's data was the increasing appetite for change to how observation was used in many institutions across the sector. While only a small minority of participants expressed a desire to see an end to the use of lesson observation per se as a form of teacher evaluation, the majority acknowledged that it had an important role to play in teacher assessment and development. They did so, however, on the proviso that certain models/approaches to observation were deemed to be more beneficial than others, particularly peer-based models with a focus on enhancing professional learning and development. Furthermore, many participants expressed the need to explore alternative approaches and to move away from dominant normalised models of observations driven by performance management agendas.

In summary, the UCU project report raised serious questions about the fitness for purpose of prevailing observation assessment systems in FE and the extent to which these systems were able to achieve their purported goals (UCU 2013). The overwhelming message from participants was that normalised models of graded observations had minimal, if any, positive impact on raising the quality of teaching and learning across the sector. In many instances, they appeared to have become a perfunctory mechanism with observers, as well as observees questioning their effectiveness as a method of assessment. The views of practitioners working at different levels within the sector all pointed to one pressing outcome and that was the need for a change to sector-wide policy and practice. The findings from this report were subsequently to play a major part in influencing the inspectorate's (Ofsted) decision to discontinue the practice of grading individual lesson observations during college inspections and in turn had a cascading effect on policy and practice institutionally across the FE sector.

One of the most recent observation approaches to emerge in FE is 'teaching triangles'. In a research project exploring the links between leadership and the improvement of teaching and learning in FE (see O'Leary et al. 2019b), teaching triangles emerged in one of the case study colleges as an innovative model of observation that had been a key driver in transforming the improvement of teaching and learning across the organisation.

Teaching triangles share many of the qualities of peer-based models of observation and lesson study, with some distinctive features. The ethos underpinning teaching triangles links to Hargreaves and Fullan's (2012) notion of social capital in terms of the value attached to reciprocal learning when observing and collectively reflecting with peers. It also connects with social theories of learning such as *Communities of Practice* (CoP). At the heart of the concept of the CoP is the idea that we learn by engaging in social practice with other members of the CoP (Wenger 1998). In the case of teaching triangles, this works on the premise that by providing teachers with opportunities to come together to discuss, compare, share ideas and experiences about teaching collaboratively with their peers, this is a fundamental component of improving the professional expertise of teachers.

Compared to previous assessed performance-management models of observation, the introduction of teaching triangles was seen as 'a breath of fresh air' by teaching staff at the college involved in the research. The contrast between the two regimes and the impact on staff perceptions and their experiences was significant, with the overwhelming majority of staff enthusiastically embracing teaching triangles and considering them a success. The overriding narrative to emerge was one that accentuated the collaborative, supportive and developmental focus of the teaching triangles, with staff no longer afraid to 'take risks' but positively encouraged to do so, as the focus had shifted from a judgement of performance on to collegial support. Teaching triangles proved effective in creating a virtuous cycle of trust amongst colleagues, who felt supported and encouraged to experiment with and diversify their teaching. Conceptualising improvement as an ongoing process that requires drive and a commitment to continuously wanting to do better was a philosophy that the teaching triangles certainly seemed to play a key role in bringing about. The teaching triangles had clearly had a significant impact on helping to promote longer-term thinking and collaboration about teachers' professional practice and how they could continue to improve themselves.

The use of observation in higher education

In recent decades, there has been an increase in the prevalence of QA systems in HE. As discussed in Chapter 2, the massification, commodification and marketisation of the HE sector have all given rise to such systems, which have since become embedded firmly in the organisational cultures and structures of HEIs globally. Given that teaching is at the heart of what HEIs do and that the quality of teaching is one of the most important factors influencing students' learning outcomes (e.g. Seidel and Shavelson 2007), it is to be expected that HEIs should seek to measure and evaluate the effectiveness and quality of teaching, as well as identify areas for improvement. As an OECD (2009) report acknowledged, it is important to understand teachers' strengths and those aspects of their practice that could benefit from further development. However, the evaluation of the effectiveness and quality of teaching is relatively new territory for HEIs as the focus has traditionally been on research and the outcomes from research-related activity. While accountability systems for evaluating the effectiveness of teaching and learning in HEIs vary internationally, the educational experience and learning outcomes of students figure prominently in most systems. For example, in the UK, data relating to the recruitment, retention, progression and attainment of students, along with module evaluations and data from an annual survey (National Student Survey) targeted at all final-year degree students in England, Wales and Northern Ireland all feature prominently in HEIs' accountability systems and have a big influence on policy and practice. In the case of the latter, students are required to evaluate the quality of the teaching on their courses as well as their experiences of the assessment and feedback of their work among other things. Nevertheless, as many studies have identified, 'the literature does not provide compelling evidence that student evaluations of teaching allow for reliable and accurate appraisals of teaching effectiveness' (Jarrell 2018, p. 8). But what role does observation play in the context of evaluating and improving the quality of teaching in HEIs?

It is only in recent years that observation has begun to emerge as a prominent area of practice in HEIs. This has been partly fuelled by demands for greater accountability but, more increasingly, as a result of its potential for supporting the professional development of academic staff (e.g. McMahon, Barrett and O'Neill 2007; Shortland 2004). Unlike FE and the schools' sector, its use has traditionally been much less commonplace or prescribed. For example, there is less evidence of links to formal, centralised QA systems and it has tended to operate mostly on an informal, voluntary and departmental basis. Having said this, with teaching excellence now firmly on the policy agenda of governments worldwide, the use of observation is increasing in HE. In the UK, for example, following the introduction of the Teaching Excellence Framework (TEF) in 2016, observation has become more commonly used as a QA tool to gather information on teaching standards and to evidence staff performance (e.g. O'Leary, Cui and French 2019a). It has also become a feature of formal programmes of professional study for staff new to teaching in HE. An example of this is the Postgraduate Certificate in Learning and Teaching in the English HE sector, a compulsory qualification that new staff are expected to complete in order to satisfy their probationary requirements. In general, there is limited evidence of links between observation and the summative assessment of the teaching performance of academic staff in HE. The most common models of observation in use in HEIs have been peer-directed, allowing academic staff greater autonomy and control over its use and the opportunity to explore its potential as a means of stimulating critical reflection and professional dialogue about practice among peers.

The use of observation in HE can broadly be divided into two recognisable contexts and domains. In the first instance, it has been used as a long-standing method for supporting and assessing student teachers undertaking teacher training/education courses at both undergraduate level (e.g. Bachelor of Arts in Primary Education, Bachelor of Science in Mathematics with secondary education) and postgraduate level (e.g. Postgraduate Certificate in Education). In the second instance, peer-based models of observation have been used as a form of collaborative professional development by academic staff to stimulate reflection and provide a catalyst for thinking about and discussing teaching.

Various studies into the use of peer observation of teaching (POT) in HE have highlighted the value of observing others' teaching as opposed to being observed and receiving feedback (e.g. Bell and Mladenovic 2008; Hendry, Bell and Thomson 2014). In a recent case study of POT in a Canadian university, Kanuka and Sadowski (2020) found that peer observation feedback was of value for both the observed and the observer. In relation to the latter, their research identified the fostering of collegial relationships and the opportunity to observe a peer whose teaching practices were unfamiliar as two concrete benefits. The main aim of Kanuka and Sadowski's study was 'how to facilitate collegial engagement in the form of critical dialogue about teaching as well as self and mutual reflection' (p. 2). As they acknowledge from the outset of their study, trust and collegiality are fundamental tenets if such approaches to POT are to be effective. Related to this, they also recognise the importance of creating the conditions in which critical dialogue among colleagues can occur without fear of punitive consequences or reprisal. This is a recurring challenge discussed by others in previous studies of POT (e.g. Adshead, White and Stephenson 2006; Peel 2005). The biggest obstacle to creating the optimum conditions for a collegial culture in which academic staff can engage openly and productively in critical dialogue about teaching is when observation is used as an evaluative tool to assess teaching performance. As we discuss in depth in the following chapter, breaking the links between observation and assessment in POT is a crucial step in helping staff to embrace it as a supportive rather than a judgemental process. It can make a big difference to the way in which academic staff engage with observation as a mechanism, along with the value they derive from it.

Previous studies into the use of POT in HE have revealed common, recurring issues that acknowledge the opportunities that POT can offer yet equally the threats associated with its use. For example, Peel (2005) warned of its potential danger as a surveillance tool on an institutional level. Research carried out among GP teachers revealed opposition to schemes that used peer observation to address the twin aims of teacher development and QA. Such schemes were considered 'unlikely to succeed if seen to be conveying quality assurance in the guise of tutor support' (Adshead, White and Stephenson 2006, p. 72). The transparency of the aims and objectives of any peer observation scheme in HE is thus regarded as fundamental to avoid it being viewed with suspicion by lecturers.

Gosling (2002, p. 2) talked about the need for staff to be seen as 'genuine peers in which there is real mutuality and respect for each of the participants as equal'. He suggests that the process can be undermined if the observer is senior in hierarchy to the observee, although his claim is unsubstantiated. His concerns seem to be based on the premise that such a relationship is likely to result in more senior members of staff taking charge, hence threatening the equality of the interaction. Similarly, the 'identification of individual needs' is an aspect discussed by Carroll and O'Loughlin (2014) in their research exploring the particular challenges facing new entrants to HE teaching who have no or little experience of peer observation. The nature of relationships within peer observation is thus a particular factor highlighted in much of the cognate literature as integral to the success and sustainability of any approach and is paramount to encouraging authentic engagement and commitment to developing thinking and practice.

One of the most commonly cited benefits of POT is as a stimulus for HE teachers to reflect on and discuss their practice with colleagues. It can help teachers to develop a shared understanding of some of common issues and challenges relating to the teaching and learning experiences of their peers and their students, as well as their own. Working collaboratively with colleagues can also help to counteract the issue of pedagogical solitude (Shulman 1993).

In their review of the literature including POT, but which they refer to as 'collegial faculty development', Esterhazy et al. (2021) identified a number of common contextual factors that shape the way in which HEIs engage with and implement POT. At an institutional level, these include things such as leadership models, organisational policies and workload allocation models. In turn, these tend to be closely connected to national-level factors such as QA requirements and national policies that influence the way in which HEIs mediate, interact with and operationalise their institutional responses to such policies. These interrelated contextual factors subsequently shape how practices like POT are applied, experienced and, ultimately, the extent to which they are valued by academic staff. Among some of the other 'relational factors' identified by Esterhazy et al. (2021) in their review were faculty communities, trust, credibility and mutual respect, and power dynamics. Based on their synthesis of the empirical findings from the literature they reviewed, they produced an overview of recommendations for conducting collegial faculty development in practice. Coincidentally, many of the recommendations they include are reflected in the collegial peer observation scheme discussed in the following chapter.

In a recent small-scale study, Compton's (2019) doctoral research focused on the use of three different developmental approaches to observation as part of PG Cert-type programmes at three different universities. The three approaches were: 1) peer-supported reviews, 2) extended microteaching and 3) student reviewers. One of the findings to emerge that echoes previous studies is that the value of engaging in observation is as beneficial to the observer as it is to the observee, and sometimes even greater for the former. Compton therefore recommends greater emphasis should be placed on the value of observer learning in all observation approaches. Another finding to emerge from Compton's research that overlapped each of the three approaches in his study was how observation provided academic staff with opportunities to see things through the eyes of others (i.e. peers, students, different disciplines).

In a recent two-year project funded by the Higher Education Funding Council for England, O'Leary and Cui (2020) developed an innovative cycle of collaborative observation (CoCO) involving both academic staff and students at Birmingham City University. It was a faculty-wide project that comprised five case studies from a range of undergraduate education and health programmes, with each case study including two members of academic staff and two student participants. The five case studies included: (1) Early Childhood Studies; (2) Primary Education; (3) Radiotherapy; (4) Child Nursing and (5) Adult Nursing. The underpinning ethos of the project was that any initiative designed to improve student learning must be inclusive and therefore be based on students and academics working together to develop an awareness and understanding of learning collaboratively in the context of their respective programmes of study. The project used the shared classroom experience through the lens of observation as a central reference point, with students and teachers coming together to identify and discuss the critical aspects and reciprocally reflect on their understanding of these experiences.

CoCO was underpinned by Brookfield's (1995) idea of the 'critically reflective practitioner', with student learning one of four key lenses through which teachers are encouraged to evaluate the effectiveness of their teaching according. In CoCO, students and staff all take an active role in critically reflecting on their practices, viewing the 'same' classroom experience from their perspective and exchanging their observations and reflections with each other. The project methodology drew individual perspectives together to observe teaching and learning at a programme-specific level rather than focusing attention on an individual's practice or a one-off session. Central to the project's philosophy of improving teaching and learning was the need for students and teaching staff to take shared responsibility for developing mutual understanding, by using a shared frame of reference from which to generate new understandings of situated teaching and learning experiences. Chapter 8 provides an in-depth exploration of CoCO and the case studies involved in the project.

Summary of the key themes and issues relating to observation from current research

There are clearly recurring themes surrounding the use of observation in all three sectors. For example, its value as a means of stimulating reflection on practice by engaging in critical dialogue with colleagues and students seems to be a shared interpretation among researchers and practitioners in all three sectors, albeit with the caveat that specific ground rules need to be in place for this to work successfully i.e. notions of mutual trust, respect, ownership etc. At the same time, there are divergences between the three that partly reflect their historical status and the history of policy in each sector. In FE and schools, observation has been used mainly to satisfy policy-driven agendas of performance management systems. In HE, its role is less prescribed, thus allowing lecturers more autonomy and control over its use, though arguably the climate is beginning to change with the increased marketisation of the sector and the introduction of the TEF in HE, which promotes overt competition with universities and their students compelled to compete with one another.

Some of the existing research in the field has highlighted how the performative nature of high-stakes observations has resulted in a decline in the creativity and innovation of teachers' work in the classroom. There is a reluctance to want to 'take risks' for fear of being given a low grade or being ranked unfavourably. Teachers are aware of the need to 'play the game', which can result in them following a collective template of 'good practice' during observation. Even in the context of ITE, trainees are often discouraged from taking risks during assessed observations as the outcomes can have significant consequences. Yet recent research into the use of lesson study and other more collaborative approaches to observation among qualified teachers seems to suggest a counterbalance to this.

With regard to the use of observation as a formative tool for professional learning, there would appear to be a commonality across much of the literature in terms of some of the key concepts discussed i.e. collaboration, equality, autonomy, ownership, trust etc. Much of this work has focused on the use of peer-based models of observation, which are explored further in subsequent chapters of this book. Ownership of observation needs to be devolved down as much as possible to the participants in the teaching process. The closer the ownership of the process is located to the actual participants, the more likely it is that the aims will be achieved, and the outcomes accepted by all concerned. In short, whatever model of observation an organisation adopts, teacher ownership needs to run right through it like a golden thread if you want to bring about meaningful and sustainable improvement in teaching and learning. Furthermore, this needs to happen at every stage of the process i.e. from the initial conceptualisation and creation of the model to the implementation and evaluation of it. Teacher ownership is a core ingredient that ultimately makes or breaks the effectiveness of models of observation.

Wragg (1999, p. 17) argued that 'good classroom observation can lie at the heart of both understanding professional practice and improving its quality'. When it is used insightfully observation can have a profound impact, which 'can lead to a more open climate, greater trust between colleagues, and the development of strong professional relationships' (Marriott 2001, p. 3). Similarly, in relation to the use of POT in HE, Sachs and Parsell (2014, p. 2) argue that when it is done well, it 'opens the classroom to review in a safe and supporting way with a focus on improvement and professional learning. However, they warn that 'at its worst, it becomes a management tool to monitor and control the practices of teachers'. (p. 2). One of the biggest obstacles to the creation of a supportive and developmental climate would appear to be performance management-driven models of observation that assess and categorise teachers' classroom performance against grading or ranking scales.

The purpose of observation is ultimately what should determine how it is used and the roles of those involved. This chapter's review of existing research across education sectors has highlighted how the boundaries between different contexts, models and purposes have become blurred and contested. At the heart of these contestations lies a conflict between 'structure' and 'teacher agency', and related notions of power and control that often manifests itself in the paradoxical agendas of policy makers, the institution and its teaching staff. This conflict is epitomised by the way in which the developmental needs of staff and the requirements of performance management systems are forced to compete as they are often conflated into a 'one-size-fits-all' model of observation in schools and colleges, with the latter overshadowing the former.

To conclude, across all three sectors previous studies have revealed that observation is regarded as an important means of evaluating, reflecting on and improving the quality of teaching and learning as well as contributing to a greater understanding of these processes. Whether this occurs as part of QA systems or professional development programmes, the central role that observation has to play in the professional practice of teachers seems incontestable. Where the contestations start to emerge, however, is in relation to the stated aims behind its use, the extent to which the outcomes match these aims and the way in which the process of observation is operationalised.

References

Adshead, L., White, P. T. and Stephenson, A., 2006. Introducing peer observation of teaching to GP teachers: A questionnaire study. *Medical Teacher* 28, 68–73.

Ball, S. J., 2012. *Global Education Inc. New Policy Networks and the Neoliberal Imaginary*. Abigndon, Oxon: Routledge.

Bell, A. and Mladenovic, R., 2008. The benefits of peer observation of teaching for tutor development. *Higher Education* 55(6), 735–752.

Bell, C. A., Gitomer, D. H., McCaffrey, D. F., Hamre, B. K., Pianta, R. C. and Qi, Y., 2012. An argument approach to observation protocol validity, *Educational Assessment* 17(2–3), 62–87.

Boocock, A., 2013. Observation of teaching and learning: Teacher development or micropolitics and neo-Fordism. *Journal of Further and Higher Education* 37(4), 482–503.

Brookfield, S. D., 1995. *Becoming a Critically Reflective Teacher*. San Francisco CA: Jossey-Bass.

Campbell, J., Kyriakides, L., Muijs, D. and Robinson, W., 2004. *Assessing Teacher Effectiveness – Developing a Differentiated Model*. London: Routledge Falmer.

Carroll, C. and O'Loughlin, D., 2014. Peer observation of teaching: Enhancing academic engagement for new participants. *Innovations in Education and Teaching International* 51(4), 446–456.

City, E. A., Elmore, R. F., Fiarman, S. E. and Teitel, L., 2009. *Instructional Rounds in Education; A Network Approach to Improving Teaching and Learning*. Cambridge MA: Harvard Education Press.

Compton, M., 2019. *Rethinking professional development observations of HE lecturers: Cases of the unorthodox*. unpublished EdD Thesis, UCL, Institute of Education: UK.

Danielson, C., 2011. *Enhancing Professional Practice: A Framework for Teaching* (3rd Edition). Alexandria, Virginia: Association for Supervision and Curriculum Development (ASCD).

Edgington, U., 2013. Performativity and affectivity: Lesson observations in England's Further Education colleges. *Management in Education* 27(4), 138–145.

Esterhazy, R., de Lange, T., Bastiansen, S. and Wittek, L., 2021. Moving Beyond Peer Review of Teaching: A Conceptual Framework for Collegial Faculty Development. *Review of Educational Research* 91(2), 237–271.

Fawcett, M. and Watson, D. L., 2016. *Learning Through Child Observation* (3rd Edition). London: Jessica Kingsley Publishers.

Foster, P., 1996. *Observing Schools – A Methodological Guide*. London: Paul Chapman Publishing.

Gipps, C., 1994. *Beyond Testing: Towards a Theory of Educational Assessment*. London: Falmer Press.

Gosling, D., 2002. *Models of Peer Observation of Teaching.* London: LTSN Generic Centre.

Grubb, W. N., 2000. Opening classrooms and improving teaching: Lessons from school inspections in England. *Teachers College Record* 102(4), 696–723.

Hardman, J., 2007. *The Use of Teaching Observation in Higher Education: An Exploration of the Relationship between Teacher Observation for Quality Assurance and Quality Improvement in Teaching in Higher Education, in the Light of Further Education Sector Experience.* Report produced for Escalate, August 2007. Available at: https://dera.ioe.ac.uk//13058/. Accessed 07.07.2021.

Hargreaves, A. and Fullan, M., 2012. *Professional Capital: Transforming Teaching in every School.* New York: Teachers' College Press.

Hendry, G. D., Bell, A. and Thomson, K., 2014. Learning by observing a peer's teaching situation. *International Journal for Academic Development* 19(4), 318–329.

Ho, A. D. and Kane, T. J., 2013. *The Reliability of Classroom Observations by School Personnel.* Seattle WA: The Bill & Melinda Gates Foundation.

Jarrell, A., 2018. *Assessing Teaching in Higher Education: Current Issues, Trends and Recommendations.* Report submitted to the 13th Session of the Joint ILO–UNESCO Committee of Experts on the Application of the Recommendations concerning Teaching Personnel (CEART). Available at: https://www.ilo.org/sector/activities/sectoral-meetings/WCMS_675253/lang--en/index.htm. Accessed 28.6.2021.

Kanuka, H. and Sadowski, C., 2020. Reflective peer observations of university teaching: A Canadian case study. *Journal of University Teaching & Learning Practice* 17(5). Available at: https://ro.uow.edu.au/jutlp/vol17/iss5/11. Accessed 28.06.2021.

Lieberman, J. 2009. Reinventing teacher professional norms and identities: The role of lesson study and learning communities. *Professional Development in Education* 35(1), 83–99.

Marriott, G., 2001. *Observing Teachers at Work.* Oxford: Heinemann.

Martinez, F., Taut, S. and Schaaf, K., 2016. Classroom observation for evaluating and improving: An international perspective. *Studies in Educational Evaluation* 49, 15–29.

McMahon, T., Barrett, T. and O'Neill, G., 2007. Using observation of teaching to improve quality: Finding your way through the muddle of competing conceptions, confusion of practice and mutually exclusive intentions. *Teaching in Higher Education* 12(4), 499–511.

O'Leary, M., 2011. *The role of lesson observation in shaping professional identity, learning and development in further education colleges in the west midlands.* unpublished PhD Thesis, University of Warwick: UK.

O'Leary, M., 2013. Expansive and restrictive approaches to professionalism in FE colleges: The observation of teaching and learning as a case in point. *Research in Post-Compulsory Education* 8(4), 348–364.

O'Leary, M., 2020. *Classroom Observation: A Guide to the Effective Observation of Teaching and Learning* (Second Edition). London: Routledge.

O'Leary, M. and Cui, V., 2020. Reconceptualising teaching and learning in higher education: Challenging neoliberal narratives of teaching excellence through collaborative observation. *Teaching in Higher Education* 25(2), 141–156.

O'Leary, M., Cui, V. and French, A., 2019a. *Understanding, Recognising and Rewarding Teaching Quality in Higher Education: An Exploration of the Impact and Implications of the Teaching Excellence and Student Outcomes Framework.* UCU Project Report. DOI: 10.13140/RG.2.2.22769.94566.

O'Leary, M., Smith, R., Cui, V. and Dakka, F., 2019b. *The Role of Leadership in Prioritising and Improving the Quality of Teaching and Learning in Further Education.* Final Project Report for the Further Education Trust for Leadership. Available at: https://fetl.org.uk/publications/the-role-of-leadership-in-prioritising-and-improving-the-quality-of-teaching-and-learning-in-further-education/. Accessed 02.07.2021.

Organisation for Economic Co-operation and Development (OECD), 2009. *Teacher Evaluation: A Conceptual Framework and Examples of Country Practices.* Paris: OECD.

Page, L., 2014. *Further Education Teachers' Perceptions of Being Observed Teaching: A Single Institution Case-study.* unpublished PhD Thesis, University of Lincoln, Lincoln: UK.

Peel, D., 2005. Peer Observation as a transformatory tool? *Teaching in Higher Education* 10(4), 489–504.

Philpott, C. and Oates, C., 2015. What do teachers do when they say they are doing learning rounds? Scotland's experience of instructional rounds. *European Journal of Educational Research* 4(1), 22–37.

Philpott, C. and Oates, C., 2017. Teacher agency and professional learning communities; what can learning rounds in Scotland teach us? *Professional Development in Education* 43(3), 318–333.

Roberts, J. E., 2012. *Instructional Rounds in Action.* Cambridge MA: Harvard Education Press.

Sachs, J. and Parsell, M., 2014. *Peer Review of Learning and Teaching in Higher Education – International Perspectives.* London & New York: Springer Dordrecht Heidelberg.

Seidel, T. and Shavelson, R. J., 2007. Teaching effectiveness research in the past decade: The role of theory and research design in disentangling meta-analysis results. *Review of Educational Research* 77(4), 454–499.

Shortland, S., 2004. Peer Observation: A tool for staff development or compliance? *Journal of Further and Higher Education* 28(2), 219–228.

Shulman, L. S., 1993. Teaching as community property. *Change* 25(6), 6–7.

Tilstone, C. 1998. *Observing Teaching and Learning – Principles and Practice*. London: David Fulton.

University and College Union (UCU), 2013. *Developing a National Framework for the Effective Use of Lesson Observation in Further Education.* Project report, November 2013. Available at: http://www.ucu.org.uk/7105.

Wajnryb, R., 1993. *Classroom Observation Tasks*. Cambridge: Cambridge University Press.

Wang-Iverson, P., 2002. 'What is lesson study?' Research for better schools. *Currents* V(2), 1–2. Available at: http://www.rbs.org/SiteData/doc/currents_0502/320e53d8a9347dcbe2243a74532a6a41/currents_0502.pdf. Accessed 20.06.2020.

Wenger, E., 1998. *Communities of Practice Learning, Meaning, and Identity*. Cambridge: Cambridge University Press.

Wood, P., 2017. Lesson Study. An Opportunity for Considering the Role of Observation in Practice Development, in M. O'Leary, (ed.) *Reclaiming Lesson Observation: Supporting Excellence in Teacher Learning*. Abingdon: Routledge, 163–171.

Wood, P. and Cajkler, W., 2016. A participatory approach to lesson study in higher education. *International Journal for Lesson and Learning Studies* 5(1), 4–18.

Wood, P. and Rawlings-Smith, E., 2017. Spotlight on: Lesson study: A collaborative approach to teacher growth. *Geography* 102(2), 91–94.

Wragg, E.C., 1999. *An Introduction to Classroom Observation* (2nd Edition). London: Routledge.

Wragg, E. C., Wikeley, F. J., Wragg, C. M. and Haynes, G. S., 1996. *Teacher Appraisal Observed*. London: Routledge.

Designing and implementing a collegial peer observation scheme*

Introduction

Classroom observation has long occupied a prominent place in the formal assessment and development of teachers in primary, secondary and further/tertiary education globally. In recent decades, it has become predominantly associated with the performance management of teachers in these education sectors, with a reliance on its use as a performative tool of summative assessment with which to monitor and measure teacher effectiveness (e.g. O'Leary 2012, 2013), as discussed in the previous chapter. In contrast, its use in higher education (HE) has traditionally been less commonplace, with practice less developed across the sector. Peer-based models of observation have largely accounted for engagement among HE staff to date, though this has varied markedly within and across institutions and countries (e.g. Hendry and Oliver 2012). However, with teaching excellence now firmly on the policy agenda of governments worldwide, the use of observation is increasing in HE. In the United Kingdom (UK), for example, following the introduction of the Teaching Excellence Framework (TEF), observation has increasingly become employed as a quality assurance tool to gather information on teaching standards and to evidence staff performance (e.g. O'Leary, Cui and French 2019). It is in the context of these policy developments and

---

* This chapter is based on an article that originally appeared in the journal *Professional Development in Education*; O'Leary, M. and Savage, S., 2020. Breathing new life into the observation of teaching and learning in higher education: moving from the performative to the informative. *Professional Development in Education* 46(1), 145–159. Included with permission.

DOI: 10.4324/9780429341908-6

the wider global interest in understanding and improving teaching and learning in HE that this chapter is situated. Drawing on a recent faculty professional development project involving academic staff from a modern English university, the chapter discusses the conceptualisation, implementation and evaluation of an innovative, research-informed approach to the use of the observation of teaching and learning.

The first part of this chapter explores some of the literature on the peer review or observation of HE teaching as well as that of coaching, with these two fields framing the conceptual underpinnings of the project's approach and operationalisation. The second part of the chapter moves on to discuss the methodology of the project. From its conceptualisation to subsequent implementation and evaluation, we provide an outline of the origins and development of our approach, its rationale and its application. The final part discusses some of the project's findings relating to staff attitudes, perceptions and experiences of this innovation.

Peer review of higher education teaching

The use of peer review in HE teaching can differ markedly within and across institutions and countries. In comparison to the peer review of research, arguably a more well-established and familiar process to academics internationally, the peer review of teaching is generally less developed or systematic. For example, Wingrove et al.'s (2018) study highlights how academics are used to their performance in research being measured but less so when it comes to teaching. The differences between these two processes is unsurprising given the historic importance attached to research and the priority it has traditionally held over that of teaching in the HE sector (see, for example, Parker 2008; Vardi and Quin 2011).

Peer review of HE teaching and peer observation are terms that are often used interchangeably by researchers (see, for example, Sachs and Parsell 2014); both are commonly used for formative and summative purposes (Bell and Mladenovic 2008; Sachs and Parsell 2014). Traditionally, peer observation has operated largely on an informal, voluntary basis, but more recently it has become part of formal programmes of professional study for staff new to teaching in HE. An example of this is the Postgraduate Certificate in Learning and Teaching in the English HE sector, a compulsory qualification that new staff are expected to complete in order to satisfy their probationary requirements. In addition, observation is now increasingly being used as a tool of accountability for evaluating teaching quality and standards across programmes (See, for example, O'Leary, Cui and French 2019).

Despite the widespread use of peer observation, it is not a term or practice that is universally or consistently interpreted and applied in HE, differing significantly from one setting to another as a result of variables such as context, ethos, purpose, method, participants and their roles etc. (e.g. Fullerton 2003; McMahon, Barrett and O'Neill 2007). In the case of the project discussed in this chapter, our conceptualisation and application of the term 'peer observation' is best described as 'a collaborative, reciprocal, model of observation where peers get together to observe each other's practice' and where 'the observation is not regarded as an end in itself but as a springboard for sharing ideas and stimulating reflective dialogue' (O'Leary and Price 2016, pp. 114–115). We also found Tilstone's (2012, p. 59) term 'partnership observation' useful in encapsulating the notions of equality, collaboration and collegiality that underpin the approach adopted in the project.

For Tilstone (2012, p. 60), the fundamental elements of any successful partnership are 'trust, commitment, common understanding and the identification of individual needs'. Other studies in the field of peer observation have identified the importance of trust between participants as being central to the success of peer relationships and the process as a whole (e.g. Gosling 2002; Hammersley-Fletcher and Orsmond 2005; Shortland 2004). Similarly, the 'identification of individual needs' is an aspect discussed by Carroll and O'Loughlin (2014) in their research exploring the particular challenges facing new entrants to HE teaching who have no or little experience of peer observation. The nature of relationships within peer observation is thus a particular factor highlighted in much of the cognate literature as integral to the success and sustainability of any approach and is paramount to encouraging authentic engagement and commitment to developing thinking and practice. We worked hard to achieve and to protect these elements when creating our faculty scheme and the preparation and training of staff involved, as discussed further in the project methodology below.

There is some contention about the value of peer observation and the degree of formality associated with its use and underpinning purpose (Lomas and Kinchin 2006). Arguably, the more informal the approach, the more prone it can leave itself open to accusations of a lack of criticality and rigour, with questionable value for those involved. Yet equally high levels of formality can be considered to endorse performance management rather than performance enhancement agendas and thus may not necessarily increase the meaningfulness and/or value of the activity (see, for example, Thomson, Amani and Hendry 2015). One might also argue that the greater the degree of formal processes introduced, the more onerous involvement can become for all parties, thus threatening to reduce its overall effectiveness and impact. That said, it is important to differentiate between a systematic and a procedurally formal approach to peer observation, as the application of the former can conceivably enhance its success and sustainability. As Buskist, Emad and Groccia (2014, p. 50) maintain, 'successful peer review is the product of planned and intentional discussion of pedagogy with the teacher and detailed analysis of the teacher's pedagogical practices and how those practices impact student learning'. Thus, there is clearly a balance to establish in adopting a systematic approach, whilst allowing room for flexibility and spontaneity.

In a small-scale study of a peer observation scheme in a university in Ireland, McMahon, Barrett and O'Neill's (2007, p. 505) research participants were in no doubt that having control over the five key dimensions of: 1) choice of observer, 2) focus of observation, 3) form and method of feedback, 4) resultant data flow and 5) the next steps encouraged them to focus on the improvement of practice rather than the demonstration of existing good practice. Similarly, in our project, being able to exercise professional agency over these five dimensions proved crucial to ensuring staff engagement with our approach from the outset but equally for it to remain sustainable as an ongoing practice. Wingrove et al. (2018), amongst others, have also highlighted the importance of an ethos of collegiality and respect for peer observation to be successful and sustainable when comparing the experiences of HE academics in Australia and England.

The role of coaching in peer observation

To develop our non-evaluative approach to observation and our conceptualisation of the role of the observer, we drew upon the theory and practice of coaching relationships as a model for observer–observee interaction. There is considerable variance in the literature regarding a definition of coaching (e.g. Lofthouse 2019) and even less agreement on the difference between *coaching* and *mentoring* (e.g. Garvey, Stokes and Megginson 2018; Hargreaves 2010). Broadly speaking, mentoring is often linked with 'knowledge transfer' from a more experienced to a less experienced staff member (Pleschová and McAlpine 2015), whereas coaching is more often associated with the role of a non-judgemental observer, who, rather than providing direct advice, facilitates the coachee's own exploration of the challenges they experience (Costa and Garmston 2016). For the purposes of this project we therefore adopted the term 'coaching' with a focus on learning relationships underpinned by an ethos of inquiry and a willingness to explore 'unasked questions' (Bokeno 2009; Fletcher 2012). The model embodied in our approach is closest to 'peer coaching' where staff with relatively equal levels of experience and status work collaboratively to provide a formative experience for coachees (Ladyshewsky 2014; Parker, Kram and Hall 2013).

Throughout the literature, inquiry is identified as a central tenet of a coaching approach. Whitmore (2002) advises that coaches' primary verbal interaction should be interrogative in the form of questions rather than declarative statements; this was an ethos we sought to instil in our observers from the outset in the training programme we developed (discussed further below). Similarly, Bokeno (2009) underscores the need to ask open questions that suspend beliefs and assumptions about the correct way to do things. The use of questions encourages coachees' deeper reflection and problem-solving abilities, promoting self-reflection to explore one's thinking, beliefs and assumptions (Costa and Garmston 2016; Parsloe and Leedham 2009). 'Questions can enable teachers to cast a new lens over their landscape, to make the familiar strange' (Charteris and Smardon 2014, p. 16). While providing direct advice can arguably create dependence and undermine original thinking, coaching questions encourage the coachee to take responsibility for their professional learning and become self-empowered and self-directed to discover their own solutions (Costa and Garmston 2016). Whitmore (2002, p. 42) emphasises that a coach does not need to be a subject expert; their function should be more of a 'detached awareness raiser' than a provider of solutions. The role of the coach is to develop dialogic interaction (e.g. Bokeno and Gantt 2000; Charteris and Smardon 2014) and to invite a colleague to see themselves in a new light (Costa and Garmston 2016). Coaching questions are thus a means to achieve transformative, as opposed to transmissive, professional development for educators (Kennedy 2014).

A non-evaluative approach to observation highlights the value of observers as coaches and/or facilitators of an inquiry-based approach to using observation to explore teaching and learning. Having severed the link between observation as an assessment of individual performance, coachees are able to develop their own reflective skills and increase their self-efficacy (Ladyshewsky 2014). Nonetheless, many workplaces are increasingly dominated by cultures of performativity, where observers can find it challenging to refrain from making judgements about what they see. As Costa and Garmston (2016, p. 4) argue, 'coaches must undergo a paradigm shift from teaching others to helping others learn from situations; from holding power to empowering others; from telling to inquiring'. This last point was a crucial focus in the observer training programme we developed which we discuss below.

As highlighted in the discussion on peer observation above, there is also broad agreement in the coaching literature that good rapport and a relationship of trust are necessary for the ethos of inquiry to develop and succeed. Coachees are only likely to feel safe to explore their own practice and to experiment once the fear of reprisal is removed (e.g. Costa and Garmston 2016; Cox 2012). In her study of peer coaching in a university faculty, Cox (2012) found that the success of the coaching relationship was predicated on the development of trust. The notion of trust was not restricted to an individual level between colleagues, but extended to an organisational level, incorporating employees' trust in the organisation's motives. Thus efforts need to be made to minimise the elements of distrust such as fear, scepticism, cynicism, wariness, watchfulness and vigilance (Lewicki, Tomlinson, and Gillespie 2006).

Where an organisation monitors a coaching scheme for performance management purposes, there is the danger that these characteristics may creep in (Cox 2012). Lofthouse and Leat (2013) argue that the development of peer coaching in organisations dominated by cultures of performativity is highly problematic because the systems, policies and practices of such organisational cultures tend to militate against the development of trust and reflection, both of which are considered core ingredients for successful coaching relationships to thrive.

Jewett and MacPhee (2012) also raise concerns about performative associations with the term 'observation' and instead prefer 'event'. But Western (2012) suggests coaches should reclaim 'observation' in the spirit of Žižek (1992), who encourages observers to 'look awry' in order to reframe and question normative practices. According to Žižek, it is only by looking awry that we are able to really see what is going on, which reinforces one of the fundamental principles of our approach that using a different lens through which to view observation enables us to gain a fresh perspective. When used in this way, observation can act as a catalyst for dialogue and reflection (Lofthouse and Hall 2014). We too acknowledge the difficulty associated with the term 'observation', which can trigger associations with judgements of the quality of teaching and/or teacher performance. While we decided to retain the term 'observation' in our project, we chose to reconceptualise and reconfigure it from an assessment tool to a method of educational inquiry for gathering situated evidence of professional practice, as discussed in more detail below.

Some writers argue that the use of non-judgemental language within coaching conversations can foster independent thought; this can help to maintain the agency of coachees, often generating personalised and innovative thought by preserving the coachee's words and the coach asking questions that contain fewer presuppositions (e.g. Arnold 2009). This resonates with the view that the observer aspires to provide an objective view of the session, reflecting with the observee as a mirror to inform thinking about future practice (Hammersley-Fletcher and Orsmond 2005). It can also help to reduce any tendency towards evaluative or judgemental feedback, thus fostering a reciprocity of equality within professional partnerships based on mutual respect and trust (O'Leary 2020).

Project context and methodology

Project conceptualisation and implementation

This project was undertaken in a large faculty of a modern English university that specialised in health- and education-related programmes. The conceptualisation and implementation of observation in the project was underpinned by an exploratory rather than an explanatory approach (Robson 2002). This is a crucial distinction in the epistemological and methodological positioning of the project. Both researchers had extensive experience of working with observation in a range of contexts and education sectors from supporting and assessing new entrants to teaching, to coaching and mentoring experienced practitioners.

The project's bespoke observation approach was designed to prioritise collaborative inquiry, critical reflection, professional dialogue and collegial development. Shaped and informed by contemporary research, thinking and practice in the field (e.g. O'Leary and Wood 2017; UCU 2013), a key starting point for the project was to sever the link between observation and its use as a method of assessing teaching performance in order to overcome what we perceived as some of the limitations of conventional approaches to observation. Instead, we embarked on a process of reconceptualising observation as a data collection tool of exploratory inquiry into teaching practices among staff in the faculty, providing a platform for collaborative development. This was one of the unique and innovative characteristics of the project's epistemological and methodological positionality, distinguishing it from existing approaches to the peer observation of teaching that invariably involve some form of evaluation or judgement of the teaching performance of peers. Our previous research in the field helped to crystallise our belief that disassociating observation from the realm of assessment was a crucial step to take to engender a safe, nurturing and trusting environment for reflection and dialogue between staff.

Observations of teaching were conceptualised and applied as a common touchpoint and catalyst for dialogue between observer and observee. The Cycle of Peer Observation (CoPO, see Figure 6.1) was developed as a framework to facilitate effective dialogic interaction between observer and observee. Pairings were organised between peers within departments or similar subject areas. One of the recommendations to emerge from the pilot study (discussed below) was that schools and departments within the faculty should have the freedom to manage their own allocations at a local level. Together with empowering observees with the choice of their observation focus, these were two aspects of the framework considered fundamental to promoting a culture of trust and agency.

Observers are instructed to compile a descriptive log/field notes of what they observe along with associated questions and/or reflective comments to discuss during the professional dialogue stage rather than make evaluative judgements. It is made clear to all staff that observers are not there to provide answers or solutions to all their questions but to support them as peers to reflect on their practice. Furthermore, all staff are instructed to anonymise the documentation generated during CoPO in order to protect their identities. Having received ethical approval, this documentation was stored securely and other than the participants themselves, access was limited to the two researchers.

All observers undertake an intensive one-day observation training programme and are required to organise a reciprocal observation with a fellow observer as a means of practising their skills before formally undertaking their roles. The training programme has since been extended to all faculty staff and not just those undertaking the role of observer. The first part of the training focuses on staff discussing and critically reflecting on their understandings, perceptions and prior experiences of observation. We have since come to articulate this stage of the training as a process of *conceptual catharsis*, having learnt that unless academic staff are allowed to divest themselves of prior experiences and associations with observation in an assessment context, then expecting them to engage with a reconceptualised approach is likely to be more problematic and ultimately less successful. In short, encouraging teaching staff to detach observation from assessment and embrace it as an exploratory tool requires a significant shift individually and collectively, and it is important to integrate time for this in the training.

The second part of the training provides staff with opportunities to develop an understanding of the epistemological and methodological underpinnings of CoPO, to discuss the processes of the cycle, as well as practise some basic coaching and observation skills through a series of interactive tasks. For example, they practise carrying out non-judgemental observations via a selection of video clips of HE teaching and compare their observation notes and reflections with their peers. This is to help to develop an awareness of what different observers notice when they observe, and then reflect on their values of learning and teaching and how these values inform their observations and reflections. They also practise conducting conversations using coaching questions, which are divided into three sections: 1) pre-observation; 2) post-observation and 3) future planning. Example questions from the first two sections included: *Which areas of your teaching would you most like to develop? What did you feel was the most successful part of the session? Why? Can you apply any learning from how you designed this successful approach to how you teach other sessions?* Chapter 7 discusses the development of coaching and observation skills in more detail.

A pilot study was conducted in 2015/16, comprising a sample of a team of 10 observers and 23 observees. Participants' experiences of the effectiveness and value of the approach, along with the procedural elements of the cycle, were captured via an online survey and a pilot project review day. After analysing these data, amendments were made to elements of CoPO, which was subsequently implemented in full across the faculty in 2016/17. One such change was a request from observers to do their own post-observation reflective write-up as well as observees (see Stage 6 in Figure 6.1 below). There was a consensus among observers that their own practice and professional learning was informed by observing others, reinforcing previous research in this area (e.g. Tenenberg 2016). In 2017/18, two accompanying guides for observers and observees were created to outline the rationale for each stage and provide anonymised examples of documentation from staff who had completed the cycle in its first iteration. Thinking prompts for self-reflection were also developed based on feedback; these are an optional stimulus for those who find them a useful point of reference. The original observer and observee guides have since been updated and a single, combined guide is included in Appendix 6.1 at the end of this chapter for the reader to use. Stage 7 was also introduced more recently and is discussed further below.

How the Cycle of Peer Observation (CoPO) works

As Figure 6.1 shows, there are seven stages to CoPO. Stage 1 provides the observee with an opportunity to think holistically about their teaching through a self-reflective writing account, encouraging them to reflect on their strengths and identify areas for further professional learning. This self-reflection is shared with the observer and forms a catalyst for professional dialogue and in the pre-observation meeting (Stage 2), where they have the opportunity to establish a professional rapport and explore themes

Designing and implementing a collegial peer observation scheme 109

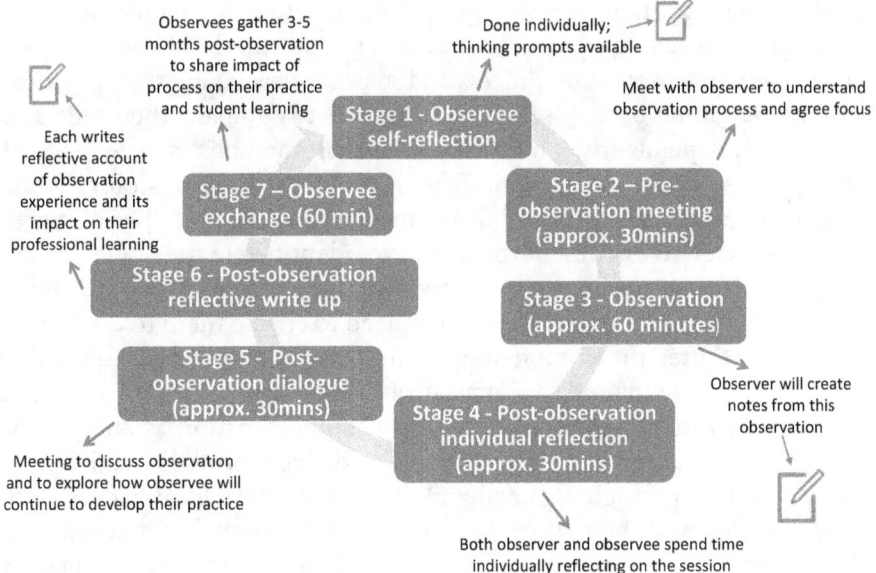

Figure 6.1 Cycle of Peer Observation (CoPO)

articulated by the observee in their self-reflection. Where appropriate, the observer uses coaching questions to establish an ethos of inquiry as the observee articulates their chosen observation focus, and both agree the logistical details of the observation.

Stage 3 is the observation, which typically lasts about an hour. In contrast to assessment-based models of observation, observers are not required to use a pro forma when taking notes as there is no checklist of behaviours or assessment criteria. They are asked simply to record what they see, with the understanding that they should avoid judgement and evaluation. Their goal is to act as 'detached awareness raisers' (Whitmore 2002, p. 42), a lens through which the observee can gain an additional view of the events of the observation and to use the observer's notes as a springboard for collegial dialogue.

Following the observation, individual reflections (Stage 4) are carried out by both observer and observee. The observer further develops their observation notes to add questions and comments in preparation for the post-observation meeting (Stage 5). Both bring their observation notes and Stage 4 reflections to the Stage 5 discussion and relate these back to what was discussed in Stage 2 in terms of the agreed focus of the session. The observer draws on non-judgmental coaching skills as they discuss the learning and teaching they experienced and observed, culminating in the observee's formulation of teaching objectives that encapsulate the learning they have taken from the observation process and steps for developing their practice.

Stage 6 requires both observer and observee to complete their reflective write-ups independently. The aim is to capture the holistic experience of both parties of the cycle, making connections between this observation experience and their past learning and teaching experiences. The observee is also expected to document the objectives identified in the Stage 5 meeting and reflect on how they intend to move their teaching forward, along with the resources/support they might need to enable them to do so. Several months after the completion of their observations, both observers and observees are invited to a focus group with their peers (Stage 7). The purpose is to move the focus away from the observation as an episodic event by creating further opportunities for dialogic professional learning as they share the insights gained and the impact these have had on both their teaching and their students' learning. The rationale for scheduling this meeting several months after the completion of the other stages of the cycle was twofold. Firstly, we wanted to allow time for the insights gained during their observation experiences to permeate their thinking/ practice and to discuss the impact on their teaching and their students' learning. Secondly, we wanted to ensure that CoPO did not become a closed, box-ticking exercise, with no influence on academics' practice; rather, we wanted to ensure that the process remained dynamic and relevant to all involved.

Data collection and analysis

To evaluate staff perceptions and experiences of the conceptualisation and operationalisation of CoPO, our project drew on multiple sets of qualitative data. As a means of canvassing a breadth of participants' perspectives across the faculty, an online survey provided the starting point for data collection. This was complemented by a range of other qualitative methods, including interviews, focus groups and documentation generated in the different stages of CoPO. As this was a 'live' project, it is important to stress that pre-determined codes for analysis were not drawn up, but themes were allowed to emerge from the data in a 'grounded' approach though not grounded theory. These themes were complemented and informed by relevant literature and theory associated with the field of observing learning and teaching. Thus, the process of data analysis was iterative.

Designing and implementing a collegial peer observation scheme

Findings and discussion

Three key themes to emerge from the data regarding staff attitudes, perceptions and experiences of CoPO are discussed in this section:

- Confronting the challenges of change
- The double-edged sword of time
- Restoring professional agency through CoPO

These themes recurred across various data sets and participant groups, thus strengthening their validity and reliability as themes that resonated with staff from different subject areas across the faculty.

Confronting the challenges of change

Our experience resonates with the views of Costa and Garmston (2014) that paradigm shifts take time. For some staff the *conceptual catharsis* we referred to above extended beyond the training and into their engagement with CoPO. For example, the data revealed isolated cases of initial guardedness among a small group of observees. Despite assurances to the contrary, some expressed scepticism about the purpose of CoPO and felt that it would still be used to monitor the quality of their teaching. Billet's (2004) research on participation in workplace learning offers a useful lens through which to make sense of this initial scepticism and reluctance on the part of a minority of staff. As Billet (2004, p. 321) maintains, 'participation may be actively supported, welcomed, resented or actively opposed ... despite efforts to regulate participation, there can be no guarantee that these intents will be fully realised. Individuals will decide how they will participate in and what they learn from what they experience.' This interpretation was partly consistent with how during the first iteration of CoPO, most departments welcomed its introduction and wholeheartedly engaged with it without any coercion or regulation. Although there were small numbers of staff whose participation was prompted by requests from their line managers to do so, their initial reluctance was a reflection of concerns for adding to already heavy workloads rather than any opposition to engaging with CoPO per se.

One observer 'sensed a nervousness in some colleagues about what to choose as their focus' and as a result 'a lot [of observees] still choose something they're good at'. This was reinforced in the qualitative data from several observees, whose first reactions to hearing about the introduction of a new observation scheme in the faculty was to plan an 'all singing, all dancing lesson' on the premise that they 'had to prove [their] worth'. However, in the following extract from a focus group, an observer from a teacher education programme shares how his colleague's initial scepticism to CoPO dissipated once they began the cycle:

> I had an initial exchange with a colleague about the observation cycle and their immediate response was, 'Oh God, how can we jump through this hoop as quickly and as painlessly as possible?' ... But then what was really interesting is that once they identified something that was really challenging to them in their teaching, the meetings we had both before and after the observation were really productive, focused and forward looking. And they ended up admitting that it had been a worthwhile exercise after all!

Some observers worked with observees who had been conditioned to view the main purpose of observation as summative assessments of their teaching (O'Leary 2013). Observers reported several examples where observees explicitly requested advice on improving their teaching, but rather than offer opinions and advice, they were able to maintain an ethos of inquiry, which created the space for the observee to generate their own solutions. One midwifery lecturer still found this challenging, as commented in her online survey response: 'I understood the process to be non-judgemental and this was achieved, but to the extent where I actually craved some judgement and validation for what I was doing.' This was certainly a recurring theme across different data sets where both observers and observees identified a desire from some staff to receive comments about the effectiveness of their teaching, driven by what largely seemed a need for validation that they were 'doing a good job'. This raises interesting questions about the need for judgement and validation in HE professional practice. What opportunities are available for academic staff to receive positive affirmations of their teaching? Or, indeed, as we explore in the following section below, what opportunities are there for them to discuss learning and teaching in general? In this sense, CoPO seemed to provide a valuable shared forum to facilitate collegial dialogue.

It was clear that disassociating observation from its application as an assessment tool to monitor and measure the effectiveness of their teaching represented a significant challenge for some staff more than for others, particularly for those working in disciplines such as education where there is a long-standing association between observation and performance management/appraisal (e.g. Edgington 2016). Having an awareness of these prior experiences helped to contextualise comments such as 'I have often been paralysed by fear about observations' or that their experience of observations in colleges and schools was that they were 'box-ticking' exercises, which were associations that were addressed in staff briefings and training.

While some observees may have craved judgement, some observers also found it difficult to withhold. One of the main challenges for observers was thus the adoption of a non-evaluative approach to observing. A senior nursing academic commented in a focus group that 'the biggest challenge for me is not judging what I see and wanting to share over 15 years of experience'. A review of the faculty-wide data from the observers' notes (Stage 3) and their reflections on the post-observation discussion (Stage 6) revealed instances of a judgemental focus in their reporting style. This was perhaps unsurprising given how normalised and engrained the conceptualisation and application of observation as an evaluative tool has become in education, as discussed previously.

In a reflective account of their experience of CoPO, another observer from nursing commented on the difficulties involved in observing a session they felt required improvement:

> I started the post-session briefing with only asking questions, not giving any criticism or suggestions ... I found myself in a difficult situation, because my perception of the session and the student engagement was miles apart from that of the observee and it was difficult to communicate that there were improvements necessary.

The observer concluded their written reflection by listing nine suggestions for improvement that they subsequently shared with the observee. Whilst this practice was clearly at odds with the project's methodological and axiological approach, it raises some important questions relating to judgemental observation approaches. On what basis is such judgement warranted? As a result of hierarchical standing? Expertise and/or experience in the field? By invitation from the observee? How observers should respond when witnessing 'poor' or 'weak' teaching in sessions emerged as a key discussion point in the evaluation of the pilot. There was agreement that such instances, however rare they may be, should not be ignored on the grounds of professional responsibility and a duty of care to students. Nevertheless, participants felt that CoPO was not the forum in which to deal with issues of competence and capability, as it could jeopardise the underpinning ethos of the scheme. Observers were advised to follow established organisational systems and procedures that were more suited to this.

Some observers also found it difficult to pose questions that seemed open and did not imply judgement. The main reason for this was twofold, both of which have repercussions for the further development of our approach.

Firstly, with hindsight, the training and time devoted to practising coaching conversations and asking questions during the observer training programme was insufficient. Secondly, we realise now that it was unrealistic to expect observers to acquire this skill from the outset but requires sustained practice to develop proficiency.

While the adoption of a non-judgemental approach was clearly a challenge to some observers, others appeared to manage this more successfully and their observees acknowledged this, as the following excerpt from an interview with an early years lecturer illustrates:

> It was very useful as the discussion, after the observation, was almost like I was watching a video recording of my lesson. We were able to take sections of the lesson where I had made a pedagogical decision – intuitively or deliberately – and then unpick it to discuss the impact of my decision on the students' learning experience as well as allowing me the opportunity to reflect on my decisions which may impact on my future planning and delivery ... This was about "observing" – not telling me where I went wrong and how I could make it better. My observer's message was definitely more about us being equal professionals and not about one of us being better than the other.

In summary, incorporating a non-judgemental approach to observing and recording notes and questions about the observation was clearly an ongoing challenge for observers that would require further training and support. We have already responded to this challenge by creating additional development sessions for staff focusing on areas such as developing their coaching skills, making use of Socratic questioning and recording observation notes in a non-judgemental style.

The episodic nature of observing a single session dominated the focus of both observer and observee. In the first year, observee initial self-reflections focused almost exclusively on the observed session rather than a more holistic review of their practice. Although practice-based thinking prompts were distributed to observees as an optional tool, these did not seem to stimulate thinking beyond the scope of what they were planning to show the observer. Across schools and departments, most of the focus was on the observed session with less thought towards the implications for wider practice. This revealed the need for a more explicit focus on the relationship between the two in staff briefings and training. One of the key learning points from this has been the need for a consistency in lines of communication at all levels and ongoing dissemination, yet equally a flexibility in accommodating localised contexts and circumstances.

The double-edged sword of time

Time emerged as a double-edged sword for many staff when it came to their engagement with CoPO. While both observees and observers across the faculty acknowledged its value (discussed further below), the logistical obstacles involved in arranging mutually convenient times to meet for each stage of CoPO and to complete the cycle in a timely manner reflected wider systemic difficulties facing many staff. With many part-time staff in a practice-based faculty where students are often out on placement for large periods, both observers and observees reported difficulties fitting in CoPO meetings around scheduled teaching and other commitments. Despite good intentions from staff, the post-observation discussion (Stage 5) would sometimes take place several weeks after the observation itself (Stage 3), which, in some instances, participants acknowledged was not their preference but often the first available opportunity for them to be able to block out sufficient time to meet. Increased work demands are, of course, not new to HE staff. We recognise that time and dedication are needed to create meaningful professional dialogues. Equally, when done properly, CoPO can be a time-intensive process but we would argue that the return on the investment of staff time makes it a worthwhile investment. Furthermore, the adoption of a new workload allocation model by the faculty may allow the time commitment of observers and observees to be formally planned and recognised, thus valorising it even more.

The time of year an observation is scheduled emerged as an obstacle for some; there can be a rush to complete the observations at the tail end of the academic year when there can be little timetabled teaching to observe. Both observers and observees suggested that the scheduling of observations earlier in the academic cycle would have a greater impact on their practice. Nevertheless, this was not always possible and later observations prompted resourceful responses by some to move away from 'traditional' observations, typically involving large groups of students, to focusing on wider areas of teaching practice, such as one-to-one supervisions, academic support tutorials and the use of e-learning.

As HE teaching typically involves a multitude of differing scenarios, sites and interactions, staff have been encouraged to embrace a broad understanding of their teaching practice throughout the project when choosing 'teaching events' for their observations. Some have eagerly embraced the opportunity to experiment by choosing to focus on one-to-one interactions with students rather than whole-group teaching. For example, two senior education researchers chose to focus on a doctoral supervision session with a student. They shared meaningful reflections with each other about empathy while exploring the difficult balance a supervisor needs to maintain between providing pastoral care and offering academic challenge to move the student's thinking and writing forward, as the following excerpts from both supervisors written reflections illustrate:

> As a result of our discussions and reflections on the supervision, I realise that in some cases, empathy and a pastoral role is needed to support students. I come from an artistic background where critique is part of the process of creation. With some students, I've come to realise now that this has to be learned and therefore careful balance is needed with support and critique.
>
> (Supervisor 1)

> This supervision experience led onto other discussions linked to the pastoral nature of the role. We both agreed that there needs to be a fine balance of listening, guiding but also helping the student to explore new avenues. Questioning played an important role in this discussion, as the student revealed more concerns, it was important to ask questions to help them understand how they need to navigate and resolve the issues.
>
> (Supervisor 2)

The other side of this double-edged sword of time was that some welcomed the introduction of CoPO because in their eyes it had created 'protected time' for collaborative reflection and discussion, as a lecturer from life sciences explains in the following extract:

> One of the reasons why I like this scheme is that it protects time to allow you to observe your peers and spend time thinking about practice and talking about teaching and learning, which you wouldn't normally get as we're all so busy.

It seems somewhat ironic that opportunities for academic staff to come together to discuss and share ideas about the core business of the institution i.e. learning and teaching are heavily circumscribed. Yet as one senior academic from radiotherapy commented: 'it's the only time I've had to reflect and focus on my teaching in the 6 years I've been here'. In reference to a specific stage of CoPO, a lecturer from social work highlighted the value of the pre-observation (Stage 2) in their post-observation reflection. He commented that:

> ... the time taken to engage in the pre observation meeting and understand a little of my background was, I feel, an important part of the whole process and I think it made me value it much more than I might otherwise have done.

The enthusiasm for CoPO manifested to date would suggest that there is clearly a demand and appetite for allowing academics more space and time to devote to discussing practice and thinking about their practice. In the words of an early years lecturer, '[CoPO] has given us the oxygen to breathe ... when you're given the oxygen, it helps to breathe new life into your thinking and your teaching.'

Restoring professional agency through CoPO

As articulated in the discussion on coaching in the literature review, for an ethos of inquiry to develop and succeed between coach and coachee, the relationship needs to be underpinned by trust (Costa and Garmston 2016; Cox 2012). During the course of the observation training, the importance of establishing rapport and a sense of collegiality between observer and observee was emphasised as fundamental to create an atmosphere of trust and confidence that would encourage both to discuss and reflect on practice openly, particularly for colleagues who may not have known each other well. Observees overwhelmingly felt that the observers achieved this; repeatedly using words such as 'supportive', 'friendly' and 'professional' to describe their approach.

Echoing Buskist, Emad and Groccia's (2014, p. 50) emphasis on the importance of structure and planning for 'intentional discussion of pedagogy', both observers and observees remarked on how CoPO provided a useful framework for focused discussion. In particular, they underlined the 'vital role' of the pre-observation meeting (Stage 2) in the process. It allows the observer to clarify the purpose of the observation and to dispel any myths that may exist about the performative nature of the process. An observer from radiotherapy commented:

> The pre-observation meeting has been so important in agreeing and clarifying the focus and unpicking the observee's thinking and rationale for their focus. It's been interesting how deep some of those discussions about teaching have been too.

Equally, from the observees' perspective, the pre-observation meeting 'set the tone' by encouraging them to take the lead in the discussion and its focus, while also helping to establish the roles, responsibilities and expectations of each party in the process.

Observees valued the professional trust given to them. As one teacher education lecturer commented, 'the fact that we have the opportunity to choose our focus and not have to pander to others' agendas is very empowering to me'. Comments like this were common among observees across different data sets, reinforcing the importance of professional agency in the process and how this is valued by academics (e.g. McMahon, Barrett and O'Neill 2007).

The following astute remark by a nursing lecturer encapsulates the underpinning ethos of the project and helps to illuminate why staff have successfully embraced it:

> I specifically chose a session I wasn't comfortable with and I found this process to be much more supportive than previous experiences … my observer wasn't imposing their view of what they consider to be effective teaching on me and I really appreciated that because I think I'm probably the best person to know how to change [my teaching] … I just needed somebody to help me find the best way to do it.

She went on to describe how she used the observation as an opportunity to focus on an area of her teaching that she felt was 'too didactic', which had previously emerged as a problem based on student feedback and a lack of student engagement during sessions. As a result of her observation discussion, she trialled more interactive teaching approaches, which were well received by students. She is now in the process of changing all her teaching sessions to promote more interaction as a result of her observation experience.

Another senior lecturer from early childhood studies spoke of being in a small team who all observed each other and that 'the observations generated many conversations outside of this process. … The whole ethos of the course has since changed and the observation process was the catalyst for that.'

Like the staff in Tenenberg's study (2016), observers found the process of observation, reflection and professional dialogue was also beneficial to their own practice: 'It was really quite rewarding as an observer; I learnt more from the observee than they ever would have learned from me if I were forced into the role of trying to advise.' Another said 'being an observee made me reflect upon my own practice with greater breadth and question some things I do that have become unquestioned habits'. Such comments from observers were indicative of how through the process of observing their peers, not only did they have the opportunity to witness their colleague's practice but, at the same time, they were able to compare and reflect on their own through the lens of another's practice.

To conclude, CoPO completed its third full iteration at the end of the academic year 2018/19, with over 350 academic staff across the faculty having undertaken at least one full cycle. Survey results indicate high levels of engagement and satisfaction with the new approach, with 93 per cent of observee respondents (strongly) agreeing with the statement, 'The observation cycle helped me reflect on my teaching and student learning'. When asked to use a slider scale to answer the question, 'Was the observation process more informative/developmental or performative/judgemental?', the average rating was 92/100 in favour of informative/developmental. This was echoed in the qualitative comments of staff, with one lecturer describing it as a 'genuinely democratic process that values individuals for the strengths they have, rather than an attempt to identify and criticise perceived weaknesses' and another that it was an 'incredibly positive and supportive approach to observing and reflecting on our teaching and students' learning'.

Concluding comments

From its original conception, CoPO was designed with a clear ethos of encouraging collaborative inquiry, critical reflection and a commitment to using observation as a catalyst for professional dialogue between colleagues. The findings from the project discussed in this chapter add weight to the argument that removing observation from the context of high-stakes assessments of individuals' teaching performances can facilitate the creation of collegial cultures that encourage reflection and collaborative dialogue between academic staff (e.g. O'Leary and Wood 2017; UCU 2013). In reconceptualising and reconfiguring the use of observation by removing it from an assessment context and transforming it into a method of educational inquiry, new possibilities have thus emerged for harnessing observation as a tool for developing collegial understanding about the reciprocal relationship between teaching and learning.

There have clearly been some ongoing challenges throughout the project. For example, the issue of time remains a live challenge for all involved in terms of coordinating timetables to enable staff to complete all stages of CoPO in a timely manner. However, the introduction of a formal workload allocation model across the faculty has since helped to make more transparent to all what the time demands are, as well as establishing formal recognition of the importance of this activity by explicitly allocating time for staff participation in CoPO. As CoPO has developed and the overwhelming majority of staff have experienced it, there has been a noticeable increase in the recognition of its value, as manifested by its inclusion as a standing item on department meeting agendas.

The interrelated notions and skills of self- and peer reflection manifested themselves in differing degrees of depth and scope across participants. This emerged from analysis of the qualitative research data and the documentation generated across the different stages of CoPO. Given the breadth and diversity of subject areas and staff profiles across the faculty, this was perhaps unsurprising. However, it did highlight the need for the inclusion of additional theoretical input in the observation training on critical reflection. In addition, ensuring that observers are adopting a non-evaluative approach to observing represents another ongoing challenge and this is an aspect of CoPO that requires further development. That said, the project has been successful in developing a supportive and non-performative model that faculty colleagues are willing to engage with. While the transition from a performative, assessment-based model of observation to an informative, inquiry-based model has certainly been more of a marathon than a sprint, our experience would suggest that it is a journey worth embarking upon. Findings from the project to date have supported the rationale for its creation that by removing observation from the context of assessment, a safe, low-stakes environment for reflection and dialogue between academic staff can blossom. This in turn has facilitated staff to change and develop their practice. At the same time, it has also opened up new opportunities to engage with observation as a lens to inform and develop staff understanding of effective teaching and learning.

Appendix 6.1 – CoPO observee and observer guide

This guide will introduce you to the Cycle of Peer Observation (CoPO) discussed in this chapter and illustrated in Figure 6.1. It will provide a step-by-step explanation of what will happen at each stage of the cycle. The philosophy of CoPO is based on an ethos of non-judgemental collaborative inquiry, critical reflection and prioritising professional dialogue.

Designing and implementing a collegial peer observation scheme

Stage 1: Observee self-reflection on teaching and learning

Our Cycle of Peer Observation (CoPO) puts the observee at the heart of the process. It provides an opportunity for teaching staff to think holistically about their practice, to identify their strengths and build upon them, and to examine areas for further professional learning. Once observee–observer pairings/allocations have been confirmed, the first stage of the cycle begins by focusing on the observee's own self-reflection. Observees are asked to reflect holistically about their role, their approach to teaching, those aspects of their practice that they feel confident with as well as those areas of their practice they wish to explore and/or develop further (see Table 6.1 for exemplar prompt questions to support observee self-reflection). It is important that observees set aside sufficient time to engage fully with this self-reflection in Stage 1, as the quality and depth of this initial self-reflection can make a significant contribution to the overall success and value of the cycle.

Table 6.1 Some Thinking Prompts for Self-Reflection on Teaching and Learning

- How would you describe your approach(es) to teaching? What are the key factors that shape/have shaped your approach(es)?
- Which aspects of your teaching do you feel relatively confident with, and why?
- How do you ensure you build on the above strengths?
- Are there new things which you'd like to bring to your practice but haven't yet found the time/support/courage to do? Explore your interest in them and what is holding you back.
- Are there any areas of your practice where you lack confidence, or where you feel less effective than you'd like to be? Explore these and the feelings they bring up.
- How effective is your planning? Do you face any barriers to planning?
- How do you understand your students' needs and adapt your practice to meet them? Which approaches have been effective? Would you like to explore this more?
- If you lecture together with colleagues, how effectively do you work together?
- How do you plan for your sessions?
- How do you determine the key aims/outcomes of your sessions? How do you know when they have been met?
- How well do your sessions link to work students do outside university teaching?
- Are there any aspects of your practice where you feel the input of an observer would be useful, in order to reflect back what they have seen to aid your development? (You are encouraged to identify a particular area of focus for the observer – although you may also just ask for a more generalised observation if you choose.) This question is one to explore more in depth with your observer in Stage 2.

There are no tick boxes or checklists of expected behaviours, observees have the freedom to complete this self-reflection in the manner which works best for them, focusing on the areas *they* identify. Furthermore, observees are encouraged not to limit their reflections to their lecturing role but to include other teaching scenarios such as practice-based teaching, research supervision, 1-2-1 tutorials, skills demonstration sessions and studio-based activity, to name but a few typical teaching-learning scenarios. These self-reflections are also meant to provide an opportunity for observees to think about their practice holistically rather than focusing on individual teaching sessions.

At the suggestion of past observees that have participated in CoPO, we have developed some questions which can be used as a stimulus to support this self-reflection. Observees are not required to answer these questions in Table 6.1 but simply to use them as thinking prompts. The self-reflection must be a meaningful exercise for the observee so ultimately, they choose the focus and format of this reflective piece.

The observee needs to document their self-reflections either in a written document or audio file form and share this with their observer at least two days prior to the Stage 2 meeting (see more information on this Stage below). If there are any elements of the self-reflection that the observee would prefer not to share with their observer for any reason, then they need to produce an edited version to send to their observer. Table 6.2 provides illustrative examples of completed observee self-reflections.

Table 6.2 provides three anonymised examples of Stage 1 observee self-reflections.

Stage 2: Pre-observation meeting: establish rapport and choose focus

This initial meeting is an opportunity for the observee and observer to get to know each other better. There are several important areas to explore:

1. To ensure the observee understands CoPO and that they feel comfortable with the observation process. It is also important to emphasise the collegial and non-judgemental ethos of CoPO's approach. This is an opportunity to clarify any misunderstandings or misgivings there may be about the process and to emphasise the holistic nature of the observation process.

Table 6.2 Examples of Stage 1 Observee Self-Reflections

Observee A
Having reflected on some of my teaching strengths and weaknesses, I feel that I am strong at building a rapport with students, and I am a confident public speaker and presenter. However, as someone whose subject specialism is psychology, my teaching topics often compliment the themes of the module, as opposed to being the main theme. This sometimes makes it difficult for students to understand how the teaching and reading applies to their assessment.
Level 4 BSc Public Health students take a module called 'Perspectives in Health' in the first semester of their first year. The point of the module is to introduce them to a psychological approach to understanding health, as well as physiological and sociological approaches. The psychology portion of the module comes at the end. While students seem to enjoy the psychology sessions that I teach in their module, many of their assessments are particularly poor in this area compared to the sociology or physiology sections. I will be restructuring the sessions a bit this year and they have been somewhat re-focused and re-organised through the Transforming the Curriculum process. I would like to use new technology (Socrative) as a way to both engage the students and to recap material from the previous session to check their understanding before moving on to the next material. I am hoping that this will give me better insight into what the students are struggling to understand, as well as the opportunity to address it.

Observee B
*My **approaches to teaching** are varied but are informed by an emphasis on reflective practice (with preference for the DEADACRE approach to reflection developed by former staff within health promotion/public health at BCU). The DEADACRE approach to reflective practice focuses on the process of reflection and eight stages in this process: describing, expanding, accounting, denial/distortion, acceptance, consequences, resolve and expectation. I have also been moving to a stronger focus on blended learning. I have also found Meyer and Land's work (2006) on threshold concepts and barriers to learning very useful and have tried to apply this in my teaching. Finally, a key approach focuses on developing a growth mindset – helping students to recognise the extent to which their mindset limits or facilitates learning and supporting them to develop skills in increasing the amount of effort/application to their studies as well as the effectiveness of their learning strategies.*
***Key factors shaping my approaches** to teaching include the PG Cert at BCU which helped me to identify an over-reliance on a teacher-centred didacticism and a move to a more student-centred approach to learning. Other factors that constrain teaching are workload and the workload allocation system which limits the amount of time that can be allocated e.g. to developing blended learning approaches.*
***Aspects of my teaching** that I feel most confident with are my ability to support student processing of learning through small group work and activities.*

(Continued)

Table 6.2 (Continued)

Aspects of my teaching I would like to develop or improve on are finding an appropriate balance between the tensions of supporting students to achieve, progress and addressing retention issues (students who are often not "study-ready" on arrival at BCU and who have low confidence and limited life skills in managing time and workloads) whilst at the same time developing a student-centred approach that fosters deep learning and independent learners. The former tends to engender a more directive (didactic) approach, while the latter requires a huge investment of time. Currently, we are focusing on assessment within our programme including understanding of the assessment brief and skills and knowledge to meet learning outcomes. It is this that I would like the observation to provide feedback on. The session will be the final session in the module and will be consolidating/summarising learning on the module in relation to the learning outcomes.

The key aims/outcomes for the session are set for each session and are the information that should be understood by the end of the session. However, this is not formally assessed (and maybe it should be). Rather there is an opportunity – through small group work processing – to assess understanding throughout the session. There are a wide range of needs within the student group and a lot of emphasis is given to formative work and formative feedback as well as small group work which provides opportunities for more targeted support across the group.

Observee C

I am new to the university and teaching in an academic setting. I feel more confident teaching practical skills having been a teacher for XXX students previously. I am due to start my PG Cert this year which I hope will enable me to understand the theory behind the different approaches to teaching in HE. My lectures at the moment tend to be PowerPoint-based and I aim to involve the students in the discussion as much as possible. At present, I have little knowledge of meeting the differing needs of students within individual sessions, however, I try to make myself available through individual tutorials and ensure the students are aware of how to arrange this. To prepare for the sessions I update/edit the existing materials and discuss with experienced colleagues what techniques they have used successfully in the past. I am aware that my teaching style needs to develop particularly in relation to encouraging students to answer/participate in class discussions. The aims/outcomes for each session are based upon [regulatory] requirements and my own experience, I feel that it is important to tailor the sessions to these in order to ensure students are able to practice safely.

For this particular session, the measure of meeting the key outcomes is the production of two [outputs] from the students. I find it difficult to quantify the success of other sessions that do not involve a practical element, I hope to develop this skill as part of the PG Cert. I find student evaluation helpful and peer support has been invaluable in reviewing my skills. I also reflect upon the sessions informally and consider how to improve/change the session for the next delivery. The lectures I deliver are all part of... regulated courses, therefore the students will use the theory they have learned here at the university out in practice. Their practice is then assessed by a suitably qualified mentor within their [organisation]. I would like to be able to move around the classroom more whilst delivering a teaching session from PowerPoint. At the moment the slides need to be moved on from the keys/mouse at the podium, it would be nice to be able to do this from anywhere in the classroom. I feel that, as a teaching team, we have a good understanding of each other's strengths and tend to work instinctively within a session. I have been extremely well supported by experienced colleagues who continue to help me to develop.

2. Discussion of observee self-reflection, which should have been done in Stage 1 and shared with the observer with sufficient time for them to review it before the Stage 2 meeting. This discussion in Stage 2 is a chance to explore issues and themes which have arisen through the reflective process as well as an opportunity to expand on those reflections where appropriate. The observer needs to ensure that the observee uses this opportunity to reflect on their teaching as a whole and not simply focus on the specific session that will be observed. The observer may choose to use some of the thinking prompts in Stage 1 as coaching questions during this initial discussion.
3. Agreement of observation focus between the observee and observer. The observation process should encourage the observee to reflect on their practice overall. However, it is not possible to observe all aspects of your practice, observees therefore need to identify a specific focus and to choose a teaching session where they feel the input from a supportive observer would be useful. Observees may want to try something new or choose to focus on an area they would like to improve, or a specific skill where they lack confidence. It is important to remember that the observer is not there to judge the effectiveness of your teaching, but to provide you with another view of the event and to help stimulate your reflections on it. Once a specific focus has been agreed, both observer and observee should make a note of this.
4. Agreement of date and time for both the observation (Stage 3) as well as the post-observation dialogue (Stage 5) to take place.

Stage 3: The observation

Having agreed the time and date of the observation, the observee then decides if they wish to inform students of the observer's presence. In a large lecture theatre, the observer may not be noticeable, but in smaller teaching scenarios, it is important for the students to understand that they are not being observed. There is no prescribed template for the observer to record their notes on. The only expectation is that they record their notes and questions in some way. As CoPO adopts an exploratory approach to observation and is **NOT** an assessment, there is no accompanying assessment criteria for the observer. The observer therefore begins with a blank canvas. The decision not to have a template with pre-determined categories for observers is deliberate and informed by the most current research. The observer's role is to approach the observation with an inquisitive interest that is not contaminated by a set agenda. Observers are expected to remain as objective as possible and simply record what they see and hear during the observation, removing judgement and evaluation from their comments. Their goal is to be a 'detached awareness raiser, a lens through which the observee can gain an additional view of events during the session.

The observation should last up to a maximum of 60 minutes depending on the agreed focus and the duration of the key parts of the lesson. If, for example, the main focus of the session is a task that is scheduled to last 40 minutes, then the observer will observe for that period of time. What follows are examples of notes that have been completed by past observers. We have included two different extracts from longer observation notes in this section to provide a point of reference for the kinds of descriptive logs observers are expected to make. In both cases, the observers have noted questions they can bring to the Stage 5 discussion, but they have done so in very different ways. Observers are encouraged to experiment and find a way that works for them and to keep reminding themselves about the need to avoid judgement!

BOX 6.1   EXAMPLE A – EXTRACT OF OBSERVATION NOTES

Observer A

Handouts had been prepared and learners were provided with a plan for the day, which included the learning outcomes for the day and key texts. Tell me more about this. Question for post observation reflection.

The classroom was set out in a horse shoe: this enabled all learners to see each other and I could see learners took the opportunity this arrangement lent itself to for discussion and sharing ideas Question for post observation reflection.

Designing and implementing a collegial peer observation scheme

Learners were welcomed! and the context of the lesson was explained in detail. It was interesting to see that challenges learners might face were referred to. It seemed to send the message that this lesson was going to stretch them and push them out of their comfort zone. Was this intentional? Question for post observation reflection.

Twitter feeds on definitions of culture led to the overall topic of the lesson

Why twitter? Question for post observation reflection.

You kept offering learners opportunities to ask questions and check understanding. Learners answered peer's questions, as in 'what is epistemology?' instigated by 'who can tell her...' Is this normal practice? Question for post observation reflection.

Learners then worked in groups creating posters that explored [different themes]. Method for undertaking activity; modelling good practice? Question for post observation reflection.

Learners then presented; nominations for next presenters came from learners. Learners used iPads to share images to support and explain their ideas.

"Learn something new together – we're not experts, as these dance genres are embedded into tradition". What was your thinking behind this comment? Question for post observation reflection.

BOX 6.2 EXAMPLE B – EXTRACT OF OBSERVATION NOTES

Observer B

Observation	Question
The room is prepared in advance with note making materials. As the student arrive and settle, you move from table to table engaging the students in conversation, asking after their welfare and talking to them about first appointments.	
You start promptly at 1.15 pm You introduce the session and explain your expectations in terms of engagement and interaction. You outline your experiences on the topic of E-Safety and the potential 'unpleasant' aspects of the topic. Learning outcomes are listed in colour on the screen In talking through the learning outcomes you make the link between this session and generating evidence for the Part 2 Standard	What uncomfortable issues might arise in this session? Do they need identifying at the start so that students are aware? Is there any significance to the colours used on the screen?
A large group arrive a few minutes after the start of the first activity During the first discussion task, you move from group to group appointing a scribe, explaining that s/he will not be required to read aloud. You keep to the time limit strictly, bring the conversation to a close and the attraction back to you.	Are the students arriving within an acceptable time from the start of the session?
You talk through the statements on the screens	Might the students consider the implications of each statement?
You collect a chair for the two people who arrive later.	Are the students arriving within an acceptable time from the start of the session?
You ask [student] if everything is alright. There are some whispered conversations in the room.	Were you aware of this? What are your views about these conversations?

Observer B	
Observation	Question
As you talk you move from one side of the room to the other. As the students talk in a discussion task you move into the whole room as far as you able with the room so full. The second discussion task is also timed. The pairs near me have a varied approach to time restraints with one pair using their phone to time each other.	
You use a strategy to bring the group together, and link the feedback by referring to a conversation you have been part of. Feedback is collected from each table. You use humour to recognise the human behaviours common to all.	Were you aware of the impact of your comments and reactions to the contribution made by students?

Stage 4: Post-observation reflection by both observee and observer

Both observee and observer should take some time after the session to gather their thoughts and review their notes, particularly in light of the focus agreed in Stage 2. The reflective process may inspire both to notice aspects of the session that they had not previously thought about. The observee is encouraged to think about how this particular observed session relates to their teaching overall and what they might have learned so far. The reflections gathered during this stage can be used as stimulus for the post-observation between the two in Stage 5.

Stage 5: Post-observation dialogue: developing your practice

It is **NOT** the role of the observer to offer a judgement of the perceived effectiveness of the session. Instead, they will share with the observee their notes on what they observed along with exploring any questions they recorded based on the observed session. The observer's key role is as a supportive coach to encourage the observee to reflect, share and discuss their thinking about their practice. Rather than offer opinions, the observer will use coaching questions to stimulate your thinking. While the observer's notes will obviously provide an important point of reference for this post-observation dialogue, it is the observee who retains the locus of control of the focus and direction of the dialogue. They decide which aspect(s) of their practice they want the dialogue to focus on. There are two key objectives to the session:

1. The observer will share what they saw and use coaching questions to help stimulate the observee's reflections on the session and their wider practice.
2. The observer will help the observee to decide how they will use the insights gained in the observation cycle to identify objectives for developing their teaching in the future. By the end of Stage 5 the observee should have an idea how to take things forward. Have you identified some new skills you would like to introduce/develop? Have you decided to change the way you are doing something? Have you identified any support needs and available resources to meet those needs?

Stage 6: Post-observation reflective write-up

Both observee and observer will take individual time to reflect on the whole cycle and decide what learning each will take away from it. Each will then produce a reflective write-up of the cycle which they will share with each other (see Table 6.3 for anonymised examples). One of the things we learnt early on in the implementation of CoPO was that the benefits of participation in the cycle are reciprocal, with both observers and observees recognising the positive impact on their thinking and practice. In their write-up, the observee needs to document the objectives they identified in the Stage 5 meeting and agree an action plan as to how they intend to follow up on these. A key consideration here is not only how the observee wants to move their teaching forward but also the resources and support they might need to do so. Their action plan needs to explain how they intend to achieve this. There is no set template for the Stage 6 post-observation reflective write up for either observer or observee but below are some questions that the observer may wish to consider, followed by exemplar write-ups from past participants in CoPO.

- How did the cycle work for you and the observee? Was the observee able to positively engage with the process? Do you have any suggestions for improving/adapting CoPO?

Table 6.3 Examples of Stage 6 Self-Reflections by Observers and Observees

Observer C

The session raised an interesting question of the observer/observee dynamic. It was clear to me that [observe] was nervous when the topic turned to [X], which derived from the fact that I am [very experienced in this field]. This highlights an aspect of the observation process that can have unexpected consequences relating to power dynamics. Fortunately in this case I think the impact was minimal (and not noticed by students) as [observee] is an experienced lecturer, however, a more inexperienced lecturer might find this has a greater impact.

A recurring thread throughout the observation process has been the lack of time; from the lack of time to properly prepare through time to print registers, to the desire to develop technology-based skills. In order to ensure that students get the best possible learning experience and that staff are able to fully develop their teaching skills, there must be an adequate (and realistic) recognition of the time that this requires. I don't think this is appreciated by the wider university.

Observer D

I have found the opportunity to observe interesting but really really difficult to simply reflect and aim to aid your enquiry. I was really conscious of just how limited my observation was in capturing the detail of what was going on. The discussions before and after were really thought-provoking.

I really want to apply some of your thinking to my teaching. One aspect that aligns with my own action planning is being more specific about outcomes expected and sharing this explicitly with students. From your teaching I am keen to develop your highly structured use of supporting handouts or at least share this with my team as we write new modules.

Observee C

[Observer] was very supportive and felt the session met its key aims and was well planned with effective classroom management. [Observer] also pointed out that I had emphasised and given more detailed examples relevant to the topics, to make the content ... relevant to the students. We had concerns that some students had not acted on any of the instructions to make notes and supplement the slides given. We also discussed some of the wider issues and concerns about how we might tackle students' use of devises. One useful idea I felt from [observer] was to signposting for students at the beginning of the session when and where it will be acceptable for them to use them.

I felt the observation was a positive experience and even though I was more nervous than anticipated about being observed it went well. It gave me confidence to have a peer from a similar discipline think the learning and activity was fit for purpose. It also allowed me time to reflect on both the strengths and weaknesses of my session preparation, and space to think about what had happened and how I might change things at a later date. I hope the reflections throughout the process stages 1, 4–5 show some of this development process.

Some discussion was also had about producing student resources and the time and availability to do this. I also expressed concerns that sometime I had produced resources for Moodle such as videos or sophisticated links to files from images, that I didn't do regularly enough so felt deskilled. I know this is an ongoing personal development issue that I want to work on producing resources using new packages such as Wordwall and access faculty sessions to be aware of any new and upcoming learning resources.

(Continued)

Table 6.3 (Continued)

Observee D

At the start of the session I felt relaxed and confident and both [the lecturer with whom I was team teaching] and I chatted to students. I was aware that the tables were in groups. This is problematic for a lecture-style session as students have fed back that this is uncomfortable when looking at PowerPoints. I decided not to move the tables as the practical part of the session would be better facilitated with group tables. During the lecture [delivered by other lecturer] I found it difficult not to chip in at various points. I was anxious that all elements were covered. On reflection I realise that this is not a bad thing and that this can enhance the student experience. Although I do feel it is part of my difficulty in letting go of teaching due to my own personality. Reflecting back, I do feel that we should have identified clearly before the session how we were going to facilitate the group work. It worked well as we both naturally went to different groups, but it could have been chaotic.

Following the taught session I 'took over' the session and explained the group work and [the] quiz.

Were you on time as planned?

The timings had been vaguely discussed prior to the session and I feel we were about right. The lesson plan I had was a previous one and I had not shared it with [my colleague]. Reflecting back this would have been an appropriate time to have a break [between the lecture and group work]. During the practical element I noted students were becoming unsettled. I am aware that a student's attention span is about 15 to 20 minutes so should have factored in a break.

Did you have a strategy to ensure/encourage responses from all students?

I didn't have an identified strategy to ensure feedback from students. Reflecting back I can see that I do not always elicit responses from all students. It is easy to let the confident students answer whilst quieter students get 'missed'.

I felt and measured the success of the session in that each student had produced two [outputs]. I don't feel any part of the session didn't go as planned. The quiz questions were answered well and measured this by the responses the students gave. I would use this format again but would do a more structured way of answering to ensure that all students were able to engage. I do feel it encouraged better learning as it gave students the opportunity to practice navigating the [standards] a safe supportive environment. This is a skill that will be required in their future practice ... I also feel that this reflection has confirmed that this session is best delivered by joint teaching. It would have been interesting to see the student's perspective of the teaching session and whether their experience and feelings were the same as the three academics involved in this process. I feel that the opportunity to reflect upon my teaching has highlighted both good areas and also those area which I can develop.

My plan to move forward with my development is:
- Ensure I revisit learning aims and objectives prior to session
- Ensure teaching plans are current and identify clear time frames
- Look at the pedagogy for development/design of quiz and exam questions – how this can inform my current practice
- Ensure appropriate breaks are factored into sessions
- Look at using joint teaching where resources allow

Be more proactive in gaining student feedback on my teaching.

Observee E
Follow-Up Actions/issues to consider:

- Look into how consistent approaches regarding dyslexia-friendly strategies can be applied.
- Seek and support the development of fora within the School of [X] for sharing learning/CPD developed through [X] role to ensure that the team have an understanding of current issues and their implications.
- Seek a consistent approach to dealing with lateness.
- Be more explicit about how the strategies I use could be deployed in [practice].
- Continue to develop and embed manageable and efficient strategies to use formative assessment information to enhance the effectiveness of how sessions are tailored to meet the needs of individuals and maximise their progress.
- Consider how Moodle discussion forums and Twitter etc. could be used to enhance the engagement and motivation of trainees in relation to key issues.
- Be more proactive/aware in varying my position in the classroom when leading discussions

- How did it feel to step into the role of non-judgemental observer and coach? Are there any skills you need to develop in this context?
- Did engaging with another colleague's practice prompt you to reflect on your own teaching practice? If so, please elaborate.
- Did you and/or the observee identify any issues which could have a wider impact on your department/school/faculty? These could be anything, such as curriculum matters, room configuration, a wider developmental need across the team, etc. This is an opportunity to create a broader dialogue of areas for development beyond individual members of staff.

Stage 7: Observee exchange: collaborative inquiry

Several months after the completion of the observation cycle, observees are invited to a focus group. It is an opportunity for them share the insights gained and the plans made in Stage 6 and discuss how these have impacted their teaching and their students' learning. The purpose is to ensure that the observation process doesn't become a closed, administrative practice but opens up a community of collaborative inquiry where colleagues take ownership of their professional development and support each other through professional dialogue. It is an opportunity for them to have meaningful conversations about teaching and learning and ensure the peer observation process remains dynamic and relevant to their practice. By the end of Stage 7, observees will have reviewed the objectives set in Stage 6, considered the impact these have had and refined their plans for continuing to develop the practice.

References

Arnold, J., 2009. *Coaching Skills for Leaders in the Workplace*. Oxford: How to Books Ltd.

Bell, A. and Mladenovic, R., 2008. The benefits of peer observation of teaching for tutor development. *Higher Education* 55(6), 735–752.

Billet, S., 2004. Workplace participatory practices: Conceptualising workplaces as learning environments. *The Journal of Workplace Learning* 16(6), 312–324.

Bokeno, R. M., 2009. Genus of learning relationships: Mentoring and coaching as communicative interaction. *Development and Learning in Organizations* 23(1), 5–8.

Bokeno, R. M. and Gantt, V. W., 2000. Dialogic mentoring. *Management Communication Quarterly* 14(2), 237–269.

Buskist, W., Emad, A. I. and Groccia, J. E., 2014. A Practical Model For Conducting Helpful Peer Review Of Teaching. In Sachs, J. and Parsell, S. (eds.) *Peer Review of Learning and Teaching in Higher Education: International Perspectives*. Springer: Dordrecht, 33–52.

Carroll, C. and O'Loughlin, D., 2014. Peer observation of teaching: Enhancing academic engagement for new participants. *Innovations in Education and Teaching International* 51(4), 446–456.

Charteris, J. and Smardon, D., 2014. Dialogic peer coaching as teacher leadership for professional inquiry. *International Journal of Mentoring and Coaching in Education* 3(2), 108–124.

Costa, A. L. and Garmston, R. J., 2016. *Cognitive Coaching* (3rd Edition). London: Rowman and Littlefield.

Cox, E., 2012. Individual and organizational trust in a reciprocal peer coaching context. *Mentoring & Tutoring: Partnership in Learning* 20(3), 427–443.

Edgington, U. M., 2016. Performativity and the power of shame: Lesson observations, emotional labour and professional habitus. *Sociological Research Online* 21(1), 11. Available at: http://www.socresonline.org.uk/21/1/11.html. Accessed 28.11.2018.

Fletcher, S. J., 2012. Coaching: An Overview. In Fletcher, S. J. and Mullen, C. A. (eds.) *SAGE Handbook of Mentoring and Coaching*. London: SAGE, 24–40.

Fullerton, H., 2003. Observation of teaching. In Ketteridge, S. Fry H. and Marshall, S. (eds.) *A handbook for Teaching and Learning in Higher Education* (2nd Edition). London: Kogan Page, 226–241.

Garvey, B., Stokes, P. and Megginson, D., 2018. *Coaching and Mentoring: Theory and Practice* (3rd Edition). London: SAGE.

Gosling, D., 2002. *Models of Peer Observation of Teaching*. London: LTSN Generic Centre.

Hammersley-Fletcher, L. and Orsmond, P., 2005. Reflecting on reflective practices within peer observation. *Studies in Higher Education* 30(2), 213–224.

Hargreaves, E., 2010. Knowledge construction and personal relationship: Insights about a UK university mentoring and coaching service. *Mentoring & Tutoring: Partnership in Learning* 18(2), 107–120.

Hendry, G. and Oliver, G. R., 2012. Seeing is believing: The benefits of peer observation. *Journal of University Teaching and Learning Practice* 9(1), 1–9.

Jewett, P. and MacPhee, D., 2012. A dialogic conception of learning: Collaborative peer coaching. *International Journal of Mentoring and Coaching in Education* 1(1), 12–23.

Kennedy, A., 2014. Understanding continuing professional development: The need for theory to impact on policy and practice. *Professional Development in Education* 40(5), 688–697.

Ladyshewsky, R., 2014. Peer Coaching. In Bachkirova, T., Cox, E. and Clutterbuck, D. A. (eds.) *The Complete Handbook of Coaching* (2nd edition). London: SAGE. 285–297.

Lewicki, R. J., Tomlinson, E. and Gillespie, N., 2006. Models of interpersonal trust development: Theoretical approaches, empirical evidence, and future directions. *Journal of Management* 32(6), 991–1022.

Lofthouse, R., 2019. Coaching in education: A professional development process in formation, *Professional Development in Education* 45(1), 33–45.

Lofthouse, R. and Hall, E., 2014. Developing practices in teachers' professional dialogue in England: Using coaching dimensions as an epistemic tool. *Professional Development in Education* 40(5), 758–778.

Lofthouse, R. and Leat, D., 2013. An activity theory perspective on peer coaching. *International Journal of Mentoring and Coaching in Education* 2(1), 8–20.

Lomas, L. and Kinchin, I., 2006. Developing a peer observation program with university teachers. *International Journal of Teaching and Learning in Higher Education* 18(3), 204–214.

McMahon, T., Barrett, T. and O'Neill, G., 2007. Using observation of teaching to improve quality: Finding your way through the muddle of competing conceptions, confusion of practice and mutually exclusive intentions. *Teaching in Higher Education* 12(4), 499–511.

O'Leary, M., 2012. Exploring the role of lesson observation in the English education system: A review of methods, models and meanings. *Professional Development in Education* 38(5), 791–810.

O'Leary, M., 2013. Surveillance, performativity and normalised practice: The use and impact of graded lesson observations in further education colleges. *Journal of Further and Higher Education* 37(5), 694–714.

O'Leary, M., 2020. *Classroom Observation: A Guide to the Effective Observation of Teaching and Learning* (Second Edition). London: Routledge.

O'Leary, M. and Price, D., 2016. Peer Observation as a Springboard for Teacher Learning. In M. O'Leary, (ed.) *Reclaiming Lesson Observation: Supporting Excellence in Teacher Learning*. Abingdon: Routledge, 114–123.

O'Leary, M. and Wood, P., 2017. Performance over professional learning and the complexity puzzle: Lesson observation in England's further education sector, *Professional Development in Education*, 43(4), 573–591.

O'Leary, M., Cui, V. and French, A. 2019. *Understanding, Recognising and Rewarding Teaching Quality in Higher Education: An Exploration of the Impact and Implications of the Teaching Excellence and Student Outcomes Framework*, UCU Project Report.

Parker, J., 2008. Comparing research and teaching in university promotion criteria. *Higher Education Quarterly* 62(3), 237–251.

Parker, P., Kram, K. and Hall, D. T., 2013. Exploring risk factors in peer coaching: A multilevel approach. *The Journal of Applied Behavioral Science* 49(3), 361–387.

Parsloe, E. and Leedham, M., 2009. *Coaching and Mentoring: Practical conversations to improve learning* (2nd Edition). London: Kogan Page.

Pleschová, G. and McAlpine, L., 2015. Enhancing university teaching and learning through mentoring. *International Journal of Mentoring and Coaching in Education* 4(2), 107–125.

Robson, C., 2002. *Real World Research* (2nd Edition). Oxford: Blackwell.

Sachs, J. and Parsell, M., 2014. *Peer Review of Learning and Teaching in Higher Education – International Perspectives*. London, New York & Dordrecht: Springer.

Shortland, S., 2004. Peer Observation: A tool for staff development or compliance? *Journal of Further and Higher Education* 28(2), 219–228.

Tenenberg, J., 2016. Learning through observing peers in practice. *Studies in Higher Education* 41(4), 756–773.

Thomson, K., Amani, A. and Hendry, G., 2015. Peer observation of teaching: The case for learning just by watching. *Higher Education Research & Development* 34(5), 1060–1062.

Tilstone, C., 2012. *Observing Teaching and Learning* (2nd Edition). Abingdon: Routledge.

University and College Union (UCU). 2013. *Developing a National Framework for the Effective Use of Lesson Observation in Further Education*. Available at: http://www.ucu.org.uk/7105. Accessed 15.09.2018.

Vardi, I. and Quin, R., 2011. Promotion and the scholarship of teaching and learning. *Higher Education Research and Development* 30(1), 39–49.

Western, S., 2012. *Coaching and Mentoring: A Critical Text*. London: SAGE.

Whitmore, J., 2002. *Coaching for Performance: Growing People, Performance and Purpose* (3rd Edition). London: Nicholas Brealey.

Wingrove, D., Hammersley-Fletcher, L., Clarke, A. and Chester, A., 2018. Leading developmental peer observation of teaching in higher education: Perspectives from Australia and England. *British Journal of Educational Studies* 6(3), 365–381.

Žižek, S., 1992. *Looking Awry: An Introduction to Jacques Lacan Through Popular Culture*. Cambridge MA: MIT Press.

7 Developing observation and coaching skills

Introduction

As we have established in the previous chapters of this book, observation is a commonly occurring practice in educational settings across the globe. People regularly observe teaching and learning events synchronously and asynchronously, in person and virtually. Yet rarely do those involved actually spend time discussing what the act of observation involves, how it is best approached and/or what the observer's role is or should be to maximise the benefits for those involved in the process. Possibly, one of the reasons why so little attention is given to the act of observation is because it is assumed that it is a human instinct that anyone working in education can perform effectively, as long as there are no physical and/or psychological impairments preventing them from doing so. As Rooney and Boud (2019, p. 442) remark in relation to their work on noticing, 'noticing itself is generally an implied feature in observation and is often treated as non-problematic'. However, as we argue in this chapter, the observation of teaching and learning is a complex skill that requires dedicated training and practice if its value as a stimulus for developing and advancing educators' thinking and practice is to be maximised fully.

When it comes to the creation and implementation of observation models, too much attention is given to the design of the observation 'instrument' or the 'product' at the expense of the process. That is to say, the focus is disproportionately fixated on the development of the observation

DOI: 10.4324/9780429341908-7

'instrument' rather than the process itself and the roles undertaken by the very people at the centre of that process. This is particularly accentuated in the context of high-stakes, assessment-based models of observation, where detailed assessment criteria and observation report forms are commonplace and act as key drivers for the interaction between observer and observee. One of the consequences of this imbalanced focus is that one of the core skills that underpins the whole process, i.e. the act of observation itself, is often not addressed in any substantive way or is even neglected completely. This chapter seeks to redress that skills gap by discussing in depth the process of observation, along with the role of the observer. It also extends the discussion from the previous chapter about the observer undertaking the role of peer coach and what this means in an applied HE context.

The importance of noticing in the observation of teaching and learning

In their analysis of data generated as part of a multi-disciplinary peer observation programme at the University of Porto, Torres et al. (2017) found that the most common aspects that observers noticed when undertaking observations of their peers related to student engagement, particularly how academic staff interacted and communicated with their students. The authors acknowledge that the emphasis on these aspects may have been because this is a common point of reference that maps across all disciplines, regardless of the difference between subjects and/or subject pedagogy, rather than it emerging as a generalisable finding that can be applied beyond their study. Nonetheless, the fact that this emerged consistently as the most noticeable aspect identified by observers collectively across different subject areas raises some interesting questions regarding what we notice when observing teaching and learning, why we notice what we notice and if we notice what matters most when it comes to informing and enhancing teaching and learning.

In his work on the discipline of noticing, Mason (2002) argues that in order to develop our professional practice, we must first develop our awareness. To do so requires us to be 'present and sensitive in the moment' (p. 1). Mason defines noticing as to 'make a distinction, to create foreground and background, to distinguish a "thing" from its surroundings' (2002, p. 33). Mason extends his discussion of noticing to link it more specifically to learning, as he sees noticing as an important learning tool for educators to use to support their professional learning and to research their practice from the inside. He refers to this as *professional noticing*, which he explains as something,

> ... we do when we watch someone else acting professionally (teaching a lesson, working with a client, leading a workshop, delivering a lecture or training session) and become aware of something that they do (a task they set, a pattern of speech they employ, a gesture they use, a question they ask) which we think we could use ourselves.
>
> (2002, p. 30)

For Barnes and Solomon (2013, p. 261), noticing involves 'drawing back from immediate practice to see what one has previously overlooked or become habituated to see'. van Es and Sherin (2002, p. 573) propose three key components of noticing:

> (a) identifying what is important or noteworthy about a classroom situation; (b) making connections between the specifics of classroom interactions and the broader principles of teaching and learning they represent; and (c) using what one knows about the context to reason about classroom interactions.

As discussed in Chapter 3, teaching-learning sites are complex environments with multiple elements occurring and interacting with each other simultaneously at any given time. The complexity of such environments, therefore, means that it is impossible for an observer to notice everything that is going on, even for those experienced practitioners. In discussing their research on developing noticing skills in pre-service teachers in training, Star, Lynch and Perova (2011, p. 132) argue that unless specific training is given to help teachers to differentiate between important and less important aspects then their 'attention will be attracted by whatever is most visually salient, obvious, or personally compelling – independent of its importance in the lesson'. van Es and Sherrin (2002, p. 575) highlight the importance of *interpreting* classroom interactions in their discussion of noticing, as they assert that 'how individuals analyze what they notice is as important as what they notice'. Being able to make sense of the busyness and complexity of events and interactions that occur in teaching and learning events during observations in classrooms is therefore a high-level skill that requires a lot of practice and training. In an similar vein to Mason (2002), Blomberg, Stürmer, and Seidel (2011) refer to this as 'professional vision'.

The term 'professional vision' was originally coined by Charles Goodwin, who defined it as 'socially organized ways of seeing and understanding events that are answerable to the distinctive interests of a particular social group' (1994, p. 606). Although Goodwin worked in the field of anthropology, it is not difficult to see how his definition of professional vision has relevance to teaching and has since been applied by many researchers working in the field of noticing across disciplines. For Goodwin, professional vision encapsulates how professionals have the ability to make sense of what they observe in their day-to-day practice and then use their understanding of what they have observed to make informed decisions. In short, professional vision denotes the ability to notice what is important in any profession. It is not an inherent ability, but one that is cultivated from contextualised, discursive interaction between professionals. In other words, collaborative interaction is essential for professional vision to be developed as colleagues/peers need to work together to identify and discuss those phenomena that are of interest and/or importance to them in their profession. As we saw in Chapter 6 when discussing our cycle of peer observation (CoPO), and will see again in Chapters 8 and 9, incorporating sufficient time both before and after the observation for these discursive interactions to occur is not only instrumental to collaborative sensemaking but a key factor is the overall effectiveness of these models of observation.

In the case of teaching, noticing or professional vision is 'characterized by selective attention and by reasoning processes' (Seidel et al. 2011, p. 261). It requires the ability to recognise and identify significant or critical incidents in the classroom and to home in on such incidents. Being able to recognise such critical incidents can, for example, help to detect potential student difficulties or misunderstandings, which, if left unidentified, could result in more long-term problems that can impact on learning outcomes. While the self-reflection of academic teaching staff undoubtedly has a central part to play in this process, including dedicated spaces in an observation cycle for academics to engage in reflexive dialogue with each other is also important in helping to build shared understanding and to identify these critical incidents. This is where the support of experienced colleagues, particularly acting in a coaching role, can be instrumental in helping more novice teachers to make sense of what they see. Without such support, teachers' learning can remain restricted by their limited experience and inevitably ends up drawing on the same frames of reference, as ultimately this is dependent on what they have or have not done or seen in their professional lives. Rooney and Boud (2019, pp. 441–442) argue that,

> Experienced professionals, regardless of their field of practice, have in common a capacity to 'read' the practice domain along with a capacity for informed decision making within it. Underpinning these capacities is the notion of noticing, which often manifests in various kinds of observing activities for difference purposes.

Rooney and Boud put forward the case for the development of what they refer to as an 'explicit pedagogy of noticing' in HE, particularly in relation to practice-based courses where they maintain that it is an essential skill to prepare students to enter into their respective professions. In drawing on the work of others such as Billett (2016), Goodwin (1994) and Mason (2002), Rooney and Boud (2019, p. 443) maintain that noticing is 'both an intentional activity that can be learned as well as an activity that promotes learning in itself'. They identify three forms of noticing that they consider as integral to developing professional vision: *noticing in context*, *noticing of significance* and *noticing learning*, each of which need to be included as part of any noticing training or development work. Scaffolding these forms of noticing are the development of a *professional frame* that professionals develop over the course of time to help them to make sense of practice and inform their subsequent decision making, and their engagement in *ongoing reflection*. Rooney and Boud (2019, p. 455) conclude their paper by emphasising the need for noticing 'to be practised and the effects of it reflected upon'. This is an aspect to which we return later in this chapter when discussing observer training but before doing so, we first need to deal with the reorientation of the observer's role in an inquiry-based approach to observation.

Reconceptualising and reorienting the role of the observer as coach

The overriding role of the observer undertaken in most conventional models of observation is that of an assessor or evaluator. In essence, the *observer as assessor* performs a gatekeeper function by judging the (in)effectiveness of the teaching performance they observe and using an accompanying set of assessment criteria to record the outcome of their overall judgement. This is problematic for a multitude of reasons, as highlighted by some of the discussion of the relevant research literature on observation in Chapter 5 and the rationale for the development of CoPO in Chapter 6. In this chapter, it is not our intention to examine these reasons in detail but to focus on *what* the role of the observer entails as part of an exploratory, inquiry-based approach to observation and *how* that differs to conventional models of observation. That said, it is important to understand what some of the counterproductive effects are of the *observer as assessor* role if we are to appreciate fully the rationale for the need to reconceptualise it as part of an approach that is driven by an interest in and commitment to enhancing teacher learning and collegial development.

Firstly, in assessment-based models of observation, the relationship between the observer and observee is demarcated in terms of power and agency, with the former controlling the agenda and the focus of the dialogue. This hierarchical relationship can result in a lack of ownership and sense of disempowerment on the part of the observee, as it is the observer's judgements that take precedence over the observee's self-reflection and interpretation of their teaching. As we discuss in more detail below in relation to the observer acting as peer coach, this is a very different dynamic to that experienced in a coaching relationship where the coach takes a non-directive approach, encouraging the coachee to take ownership of their practice and develop self-responsibility for their own development. This is an aspect of the observer–observee relationship that is also discussed in greater depth in Chapter 9 in relation to the model of unseen observation.

Secondly, assessment-based models of observation conceptualise professional learning as unidirectional insomuch as they are based on the premise that it is only the observee who learns from the observer. This belies what research in the field reveals about the value of observation as a tool for reciprocal learning, where both participants stand to benefit from participating in the process by engaging in collaborative reflection and discussion with each other (e.g. Tenenberg 2016). Following on from this, another counterproductive consequence of the *observer as assessor* role is that it positions the observer as the 'expert'. This can be problematic for both the observer and the observee. For the observer, it assumes that they must be an excellent practitioner in their subject specialism, with a wealth of varied experience and proven excellence in their own teaching to draw on. Yet even if someone is considered an expert or excellent practitioner in their field, it does not follow that they will necessarily make an excellent observer. The *observer as assessor* role is essentially based on a 'training model' of professional learning (Kennedy 2005, p. 237), which positions the observer as the font of all knowledge who has the answer to all the questions or problems that the observee may encounter in their professional practice. This positioning is both unrealistic and unfair for the observer in terms of the expectations of their role and the demands on them. Besides, for the observee, this relationship can place them in a subservient position, taking away their professional agency and responsibility, compelling them to rely on the judgements and interpretations of the observer as to how best to develop their own practice.

The model of observer as coach that we adopt flies in the face of the observer as 'expert' and goes against the grain of many observation approaches to professional learning. As we discussed in the previous chapter when providing an overview of CoPO, the observer's role is twofold. Firstly, during the course of the observation cycle, they act as 'detached awareness raisers' (Whitmore 2017, pp. 73–74). Secondly, in both the pre-observation and post-observation professional dialogues, they undertake the role of peer coach. What both of these roles have in common is that the observer as coach acts as a catalyst for their peers to interrogate their thinking and decision making, with a view to advancing their wider understanding of their practice in a way that will enable them to continue to improve it sustainably.

Whitmore (2017, pp. 12–13) defines coaching as 'unlocking people's potential to maximize their own performance. It is helping them to learn rather than teaching them.' He maintains that a coach does not need to have any experience or technical knowledge in the area in which they are coaching. He argues that the important thing is that the coach is committed to the coachee fulfilling their own potential and their role is to support this process,

> A coach is not a problem solver, a counselor, a teacher, an adviser, an instructor, or even an expert; a coach is a sounding board, a facilitator, an awareness raiser, a supporter.
>
> (p. 66)

As we saw in Chapter 5 when discussing instructional rounds and the role of the observer, maintaining a non-judgemental approach to observation can be a considerable challenge for observers. City et al. (2009, p. 84) acknowledge how this is not an instinctive, natural skill but one that 'must be learned, and some other habits – like using general or judgmental language or jargon – must be unlearned'. What is helpful about this particular quote from City et al. is that it emphasises the dual nature of both the *learning* and *unlearning* that observers need to undertake as part of their preparation for undertaking the role of peer coach, though, as Whitmore (2017, p. 13) says, 'it may be harder to give up instructing than it is to learn to coach'. As we discussed in the previous chapter, one of the biggest challenges in moving away from an assessment-based, performance-oriented model of observation to an exploratory, inquiry-based model is severing the link between observation and assessment. This is both a conceptual and an operational challenge that requires a genuine commitment on the part of observer and observee to the principles of such an approach. The development of the observer's coaching skills is central to being able to make this transition successfully.

As mentioned in Chapter 6, inquiry is identified as a fundamental principle of a coaching approach. This is in contrast to the conceptualisation of the *observer as assessor*, where the observer's role is to explain and evaluate what they see. The inquisitive observer approaches observation with a genuine curiosity, a desire to want to explore, examine and learn about what it is they are observing rather than seeking to evaluate and explain to the observee what they think is happening. In short, the nature of the interaction of the observer as coach compared to the observer as assessor differs conceptually and procedurally, which is manifested in a number of ways. Firstly, the role of the observer as assessor is predominantly that of 'information giver', making a series of evaluative declarations about what they observe and how (in)effective they consider the teaching. In contrast, the focus of the role of the observer as coach is more interrogative in the form of asking questions rather than making evaluative declarations about what they witness. This is a fundamental principle that needs to be established at an early stage in observer training and a message that needs to be repeatedly emphasised throughout. It is a message that we instil in our observers from the outset in our training programme.

One of the ways in which this connects to the observer's role as part of an inquiry-based approach to observation is that they are asked to record what they see in a descriptive, factual way, without imposing their interpretation of what they think about what they see. Thus, they compile a descriptive record of what they witness during the observation, paying careful attention to make a record only of the *actual events* that they notice during the observed session, resisting the temptation to express their views on whether or not they liked what they saw and/or commenting on the quality or effectiveness of the teaching. In addition to their descriptive record, observers are asked to make a note of related questions and/or reflective comments that are triggered during the course of the observation that they wish to explore or follow up on in the post-observation dialogue, an aspect which we explore in more detail below.

In order to facilitate this inquiry-based approach, there are a number of key principles and protocols that need to be established between observer and observee, along with a set of core communications skills that observers need to develop as peer coaches. One of the first key principles is the collaborative and collegial nature of the working relationship between observer and observee. It is a non-evaluative, non-hierarchical partnership of peers working with each other, based on mutual respect and common goals. The partnership is a safe and trusting space for those involved to reflect on and discuss teaching and learning. Another key principle is the recognition of the importance of allowing the coachee to take ownership of and responsibility for their own professional learning. Drawing on the notion of the coachee's 'resourcefulness' (Rogers 2012), the observer–observee relationship is built on the premise that the coachee already brings with them a set of tools in terms of experience, knowledge and skills in their respective field, all of which have an important role to play in informing their professional learning needs and identifying those aspects of their practice that should be prioritised. Running parallel alongside the establishment of these core principles is the development of key communication skills for the observer. These include things such as question asking, active listening, empathic and judicious use of silence etc. So, for example, it is part of the coach's role to develop the coachee's resourcefulness by asking stimulating and challenging questioning in order to encourage them to articulate their reflections.

Question asking is arguably the single most important technique employed by the observer coach. In terms of the observer–observee relationship, this inevitably means adopting an approach to dialogue that is primarily interrogative in nature and which creates the conditions for the coachee to engage actively in reflective thinking rather than being the passive recipient of declarative statements from the observer. An interrogative approach is essential for creating a working ethos of inquiry. As some of the research literature on coaching reveals, the use of questions encourages a deeper engagement with reflection, promoting self-reflection to explore one's thinking, beliefs, and assumptions (e.g. Parsloe and Leedham 2009). As Charteris and Smardon (2014, p. 116) argue,

> Coaching questions can enable teachers to elaborate on their ideas and embed them in the practicality of concrete next steps (Robertson 2005). Questioning promotes thinking that problematises what might be otherwise taken for granted. In leading a dialogic process, peer coaches can stimulate a lack of certainty that can be uncomfortable for teachers who are inquiring into their practice but it can enable them to look more deeply at what they take for granted. Questions can enable teachers to cast a new lens over their landscape, to make the familiar strange. This learning culture can assist peer coaches to activate each other's learning.

The very nature of questions means they are more conducive to stimulating discursive interaction as they open up spaces for dialogue. Some researchers in the field also maintain that the interrogative approach associated with coaching requires the person being coached to take more ownership of their professional learning, leading to greater empowerment and emphasis on self-directed learning (e.g. Costa and Garmston 2016). It is the role of the observer coach to ask open, though-provoking questions that will encourage the observee to interrogate their own pedagogic philosophies and decision-making. Besides, it is by helping the coachee to draw on their existing knowledge and skills, along with getting them to reflect on any gaps, that the coach can nurture a greater sense of self-sufficiency and confidence in the coachee. The role of the observer is thus to steer the observee to discover their own solutions rather than prescribe them.

Preparing for observation

In order to prepare observers for their role, it is essential that they undertake a tailored training programme. The extent to which a developmental model of observation is experienced as a meaningful, valuable practice depends heavily on the clarity of purpose, the way in which this is communicated and the support given to participants to undertake this practice. Staff training is not only a crucial component of the overall effectiveness of an institution's approach to observation in terms of providing skills development but also a fundamental forum in which to communicate its underlying aims, rationale and anticipated outcomes. Our experience has taught us that unless adequate training and ongoing support is provided for staff, whatever model of observation is implemented is likely to lack sustainability and value for those involved.

The training programme that we have developed for our cycle of peer observation (CoPO) is scheduled for a full day and is broadly divided into two halves, consisting of a morning and afternoon session. The first half focuses mainly on the *thinking about* observation, prior experiences and perceptions of it in educational settings. It provides opportunities for participants to engage in reflective discussion about the use of observation as a tool for understanding teaching and learning in HE, along with reflecting on the roles of both observer and observee. The second half focuses largely on the *doing* of observation through a range of interactive tasks that put into practice some of the key principles and theoretical concepts that underpin our approach to applying observation as a powerful tool of collegial and collaborative inquiry to understand and improve teaching and learning. It includes a series of situated learning opportunities for participants to engage in undertaking the roles of observer and observee, as well as putting into action a coaching approach to peer observation. In short, the main aims of the training programme are:

- To critically examine why and how observation is used as a mechanism for informing our understanding of teaching and learning
- To critically reflect on the role of the observer and observee in the observation process
- To reflect on what we observe and notice and how this can be transferred to platforming the post-observation dialogue
- To scaffold observers' approaches to facilitating the professional dialogue during the cycle of peer observation (CoPO) as peer coaches

Our training programme includes several elements to it that can be summarised broadly into three key stages:

- Stage 1 – Awareness raising and reconceptualising the practice of observation
- Stage 2 – Immersion activities
- Stage 3 – Skills practice

This chapter now provides an insight into each of these three stages by including some examples of the activities that are covered during the training. The intention is not to provide comprehensive coverage of all the activities nor to itemise them in chronological order but to give the reader a taster so that they can visualise what each stage involves and how they might wish to use or adapt these according to their local needs and contexts.

Stage 1 – Awareness raising and reconceptualising the practice of observation

The awareness-raising stage of preparation for observation begins with self-reflection and collective discussion about previous experiences and perceptions of observation. At the beginning of our full-day observation training programme, we set the following task for academic staff to reflect on and discuss:

> Write down the first words/thoughts that come into your head when you hear the term 'observation' in an educational context. Now share your words/thoughts with your peer.

Table 7.1 Words Commonly Associated with Observation

Positive Associations	Negative Associations
Reflective	Fear
Learning	Being spied on
Sharing	Judgement
Practice development	Test
Improvement	Under the spotlight
Collaboration	Performance management
	Assessment
	Stress
	Anxiety
	Appraisal
	Surveillance
	Panic
	Lack of trust
	Controlling
	Monitoring
	Inspection
	Artificial snapshot

It can be helpful to make a note of the type of words that emerge during the course of this task, as they can often provide an interesting insight into the background and exposure of the group to observation in past and/or current roles and situations. This task also acts as a good icebreaker to provide an opportunity for peers to compare and share their experiences and reflections on the contexts and cultures of observation. The words generated can generally be divided into 'positive' and 'negative' groupings. While the detail will inevitably differ from one group to another, it is common to find repetition of particular words and phrases across groups. Table 7.1 captures an example of the kind of words and phrases typically generated by this activity from a group of academic staff who undertook the training in the summer of 2022.

In addition to this being a useful starter activity that gets staff thinking and talking about observation right from the outset of the training, it is also an important outlet for some staff to divest themselves of prior experiences and associations with assessment-based models of observation, particularly those that might have been unfavourable. In some cases, these may have been destructive and even traumatic experiences that have significantly shaped the way these staff see observation. As discussed briefly in the previous chapter, we coined the term *conceptual catharsis* to describe the process whereby staff are afforded the opportunity to offload their thoughts and feelings about such experiences of observation. Our experience over the last decade has made us realise that confronting existing beliefs, biases and sharing perceptions and experiences of an emotionally charged issue like observation with peers is integral for them to be able to reconceptualise that issue for professional learning. In summary, if we want to enable academic staff to reconceptualise observation by embracing it as an exploratory tool and detaching it from its association with assessment, it is important that they are given the time and space to allow them to do this as part of their training.

Following on from this starter activity, a key theme that is explored in group discussion during this awareness-raising stage of the training is the contention that the dominant use of observation as a method of assessment in conventional models of observation is the single most significant obstacle to maximising its benefits for developing teachers' thinking and practice globally. We draw on the latest research in the field of observation to illustrate this point, much of which is discussed in Chapter 5. We refer to this phenomenon as the *assessment straitjacket*, which we use as a metaphor to describe the conceptual constraints that shape and influence perceptions of observation and its application. Put simply, what this means is that many people find it difficult to conceptualise observation outside of an assessment paradigm. When faced with observing a teaching–learning event, for example, it can be instinctive for many to adopt an evaluation mode and to make judgements about what they see, even if that is not the purpose of the observation. It is almost as though educators have become instinctively hardwired to see the world through an assessment lens when observing classroom practice. Is this a mindset that has become normalised over the course of time? Is it shaped by organisational cultures and attitudes towards observation? This raises a series of further questions relating to the act of observation, and particularly the role of the observer, that can be explored in Stage 1 of the training (see Table 7.2).

Table 7.2 Reflective Questions on Observation and the Role of the Observer

- What does it mean to observe?
- How do you perceive the role of observer?
- Can observers make a record of what they see during an observation that is free from judgement?
- How might observers safeguard against their current biases of 'effective teaching' influencing their record of observation?
- What is the purpose of the pre- and post-observation dialogues between observer and observee?
- What is the role of the observer and observee in these dialogues?

Table 7.3 Observer Reflections on Their Role

- 'As an observer I have a clear idea of what I'm looking for when it comes to effective teaching and learning. If I don't see it happening, then as a senior member of staff I feel I have a responsibility to tell colleagues where they're going wrong and what they need to do to improve.'
- 'You need to have a good understanding of the context to be able to make informed opinions. What I mean is not just the programme you're observing but who the students are, their progress to date, their strengths and weaknesses …'
- 'I try to avoid letting my own preferences influence the way in which I view what I see and the notes that I make, though that's not always easy to do …'
- 'Essentially it's mainly a matter of watching what takes place and saying what you think about it.'
- 'Being an observer can be difficult sometimes because there's so much to see and write down at the same time. And there are times when I think who am I to be making judgements about this person's teaching?'

Table 7.3 includes a random sample of comments from a group of observers from a national project that were collected in response to a question that that asked them to describe how they perceived the observer's role. These reflections can be used as an additional activity to stimulate discussion about the observer's role and the differences/similarities to an inquiry-based approach to observation.

Finally, another awareness-raising task that is useful for generating discussion among peers involves them thinking about their understanding of teaching and learning. This requires them to think holistically about the relationship between teaching and learning and their roles in this relationship, as we touched on briefly in Chapter 3. Although both of the tasks included in Table 7.4 seem very simple, they can stimulate a wealth of complex responses and discussion that can be revisited throughout the training.

Table 7.4 Defining Teaching and Learning

- Task 1 – How would you define teaching? Write down your definition in a notebook or on your laptop/iPad/tablet. Now write down what you consider to be 'effective teaching'. Once you have finished, exchange it with a peer and explain to each other what you have written and why you wrote what you wrote.
- Task 2 – How would you define learning? Write down your definition in a notebook or on your laptop/iPad/tablet. Now write down what you consider to be 'effective learning'. Once you have finished, exchange it with a peer and explain to each other what you have written and why you wrote what you wrote.

Stage 2 – Immersion activities

One of the first immersion activities that we recommend as part of observation training is to provide your participants with the opportunity to undertake the role of observer by using a sample of video recordings of taught sessions. As part of our training programme, we use two short video clips. It works well if you have an assortment of recorded video clips of taught sessions from your own institution to choose from as it can help to provide a familiar and realistic context for those watching the clips. Of course, it goes without saying that it is important to gain consent for filming colleagues' teaching in the first instance. If you do not have access to recordings of taught sessions from your own institution, it is possible to use recordings that are available in the public domain via platforms such as YouTube, though this requires careful vetting and preparation to ensure that the clips are suitable for your audience and that you have identified the relevant part of the clip that you intend to use in the training. We would suggest that the ideal duration for each clip you intend to use should be approximately 15–20 minutes. In addition, a variety of different HE teaching scenarios to choose from is preferable, as this can help to capture the authenticity of the complexity of what constitutes teaching in the HE sector as well as reinforce that teaching events do not always have to involve large groups of students. So, for example, a lecture to a large group of students, a seminar, a small group task, a tutorial etc are all valid, everyday teaching-learning occurrences.

For the first video clip, participants are simply told that they are going to watch a short recording of a taught session and that they are required to take some notes that they can share with others after they have finished watching the recording. They are not given a template to record their notes, nor do they receive any instructions as to what type of information they are expected to note. The rationale for providing such minimal instructions is deliberate as the intention is to create an immersive experience where participants are given the freedom to approach the observation without a pre-determined agenda. The thinking behind this approach is that by allowing participants a 'blank canvas', it ensures that the notes that they make are authentic and can be very insightful in revealing their 'default' position as observers. As they share their notes with each other, they are encouraged to reflect on the following questions:

- What information have you noted?
- Why did you notice what you noticed? Why did you decide to note these things?

- How did you decide what was important or noteworthy?
- What do you think your notes reveal about you as an observer?
- What have you learnt about observing from doing this?

Once they have shared and discussed their notes in pairs/small groups, the discussion is opened up to the whole group, with a focus on what this reveals about the 'default' position they adopted as observers and the key influences that have shaped their approach. The most common finding to emerge from doing this task with dozens of different groups has been that many participants are surprised at how judgemental they are of others' teaching and how they are largely unaware that they slip into this mode as their default response. In short, this first task can be a very effective means of raising participants' awareness of their intuitive behaviour and the need to embark on a process of *unlearning* to enable them to undertake their role as observer coach.

For the second video clip, we choose a different teaching scenario. However, this time the participants are given specific instructions as to how to record their notes. As discussed earlier, observers are asked to record what they see in a descriptive, factual way, without imposing their interpretation of what they think about what they see. For this second clip, they are required to compile a descriptive record of what they observe during the clip, paying careful attention to make a record only of the *actual events* that they notice during the observed session. They are also asked to make a note of related questions and/or reflective comments that they would wish to explore with the observed teacher if they had the opportunity to do so in the post-observation dialogue.

Stage 3 – Skills practice

Knowing when to ask questions and what type of questions to ask to stimulate the coachee to engage in reflection is a skill that requires conscious practice. Similarly, active listening is an important skill for the coach to develop. As part of our observation training, participants engage in a number of role-play/simulation tasks where they are provided with opportunities to practise some of these skills. Tables 7.5 and 7.6 outline very simple introductory tasks that can be helpful to enable participants to practice some of these skills.

In addition to the introductory insight into the role of coaching in CoPO that we provide in some of the tasks discussed above, we also offer additional coaching skills sessions that allow staff to develop their skills in more depth. The additional coaching training provided allows participants

Table 7.5 Coaching Task 1

Coaching Task 1
- Get into pairs
- One person takes the role of the coach and the other is the coachee
- The coachee thinks of a current challenge they are facing professionally
- The coach uses active listening and open questioning to understand the coachee's challenge and to encourage the coachee to explore this further
- Now reverse roles
- Coaches, were you tempted to give advice?

Table 7.6 Coaching Task 2

Coaching Task 2
- Observee reflects on a recently taught session
- Observee recounts this taught session to their observer
- Observer facilitates professional dialogue (using some of the coaching questions included in Appendix 7.1 as prompts)

to conduct and practise professional conversations in a safe space, using the coaching skills of listening and empathic silence, as well as paraphrasing and questioning. These sessions are important in helping to develop a greater sense of awareness among staff of the skills needed to support the non-judgemental and enquiry-based approach that underpins our model of observation. As part of the training, we explore coaching models such as GROW (Whitmore 2017) and STRIDE (Thomas and Smith 2004), both of which help to provide a structure for setting challenges, recognising the reality of the moment, the goals the individual wants to achieve and the barriers that may be holding them back from achieving these goals.

Part of the rationale for drawing on coaching to inform the ethos and methodology of CoPO was based on the premise that the greater the degree of agency and ownership staff are afforded to identify and shape their professional learning, the more authentic and enduring such learning can become. Coaching works on the basis that individuals can improve their own practice by developing a greater self-awareness, which can in turn trigger a process of deeper delving into their thinking and decision-making. Using the metaphor of an iceberg, coaching offers us the potential to delve beneath the surface, to interrogate those underlying beliefs, feelings and incentives that shape how we think and learn. Coaching is a vehicle that has the potential to allow us to lay bare and unpick our thinking and decision-making. Through the framework provided by CoPO, staff are encouraged to do just this right from the beginning of the cycle, to challenge normalised thinking and behaviours with a view to provoking self-reflection and dialogue that can encourage us to reimagine our practice and to look at it through a different lens. With this enhanced self-awareness comes increased self-efficacy and a renewed confidence that can extend beyond our own teaching and into other areas such as playing a greater role in development work across teams, departments and the institution as a whole.

Our observation training is delivered as an all-inclusive, cross-departmental approach, with members of the team representing a range of schools, departments and roles across the faculty. This inclusive approach reflects a deliberate strategy that aims to promote a culture of collegial collaboration and a greater understanding of some of the commonalities as well as the differences that exist across departments, enhancing the development and support of core values, visions and impact on outcomes across the faculty.

Conclusion

This chapter has focused on the operational aspects of preparing for and adopting an inquiry-based approach to observation. Drawing on relevant literature from the field of professional learning and coaching, it has explored the rationale for this approach as well as its benefits. It has also reflected on the process of observation and the importance of noticing. Recognising the central importance that appropriate training and preparation play in the effective implementation and adaptation of a successful and sustainable model of observation institutionally, the second half of the chapter has focused largely on the *doing* of observation. In order to contextualise this, we have included a range of illustrative examples of practice-based activities that we have used successfully as part of an institutional training programme to prepare staff for engaging meaningfully with our inquiry-based approach to observation.

Appendix 7.1

Observer coaching questions for the observation cycle

Pre-observation discussion questions:

- What would you like to achieve from the observation?
- Which areas of your teaching do you feel most confident with?
- Which areas of your teaching would you most like to develop?
- Is there any particular aspect of the session you would like me to focus on to help you explore further?

- How do you prepare for sessions?
- How do you differentiate for students' needs in sessions?
- What is/are your key aim(s) for the session I will observe? How will you know when you have achieved that/those aims?
- What is the most important part of the sessions I will be observing?

Post-observation discussion questions:

- Did you feel you achieved your key aim?
- What did you feel was the most successful part of the session?
- How does the session relate to work the students have done or will do outside it? How are students made aware of that relationship?
- I noticed X (X = critical incident). What was your aim with that? Did you feel it was successful?

Planning for the future questions:

- If you could teach that session again, what might you do differently?
- Which areas of your teaching would you like to develop? What resources are available to you? What support do you require?
- What will you take away from this observation experience?

Clarification prompts to promote deeper reflection:

- Why?
- How does that work?
- Tell me more.
- Can you elaborate that?
- Can you develop that idea further?
- What other ideas/thoughts do you have about that?
- What resonates for you?
- Are there other options?

References

Barnes, Y. and Solomon, Y., 2013. The discipline of noticing as a path to understanding: Researching from the inside. *International Review of Qualitative Research* 6 (3), 360–375.

Billett, S., 2016. Learning through health care work: Premises, contributions and practices. *Medical Education*, 50, 124–131.

Blomberg, G., K. Stürmer, and Seidel, T., 2011. How pre-service teachers observe teaching on video: Effects of viewers' teaching subject and the subject of the video. *Teaching and Teacher Education* 27, 1131–1140.

Charteris, J. and Smardon, D., 2014. Dialogic peer coaching as teacher leadership for professional inquiry. *International Journal of Mentoring and Coaching in Education* 3(2), 108–124.

City, E. A., Elmore, R. F., Fiarman, S. E. and Teitel, L., 2009. *Instructional Rounds in Education; A Network Approach to Improving Teaching and Learning*. Cambridge MA: Harvard Education Press.

Costa, A. L. and Garmston, R. J., 2016. *Cognitive Coaching* (3rd Edition). London: Rowman and Littlefield.

Goodwin, C., 1994. Professional vision. *American Anthropologist* 96(3), 606–633.

Kennedy, A., 2005. Models of continuing professional development: A framework for analysis. *Journal of In-Service Education* 31(2), 235–250.

Mason, J., 2002. *Researching Your Own Practice: The Discipline of Noticing*. London: Routledge.

Parsloe, E. and Leedham, M., 2009. *Coaching and Mentoring: Practical Conversations to Improve Learning* (2nd Edition). London: Kogan Page.

Rogers, J., 2012. *Coaching Skills: A Handbook* (3rd Edition). Maidenhead: Open University Press.

Rooney, D. and Boud, D., 2019. Toward a pedagogy for professional noticing: Learning through observation. *Vocations and Learning* 12, 441–457.

Seidel, T., Stürmer, K., Blomberg, G., Kobarg, M., and Schwindt, K., 2011. Teacher learning from analysis of videotaped classroom situations: Does it make a difference whether teachers observe their own teaching or that of others? *Teaching and Teacher Education*, 27, 259–267.

Star, J. R., Lynch, K., and Perova, N., 2011. Using video to improve preservice mathematics teachers' abilities to attend to classroom features. In M. G. Sherin, V. R. Jacobs and R.A. Philipp, (eds.) *Mathematics Teacher Noticing: Seeing through Teachers' Eyes*. New York and London: Routledge, 117–133.

Tenenberg, J., 2016. Learning through observing peers in practice. *Studies in Higher Education* 41(4), 756–773.

Thomas, W. and Smith, A., 2004. *Coaching Solutions. Practical Ways to Improve Performance in Education*. Stafford: Network Educational Press Ltd.

Torres, A.C., Lopes, A., Valente, J. M. S. and Mouraz, A., 2017. What catches the eye in class observation? Observers' perspectives in a multidisciplinary peer observation of teaching program. *Teaching in Higher Education* 22(7), 822–838.

van Es, E. A., and Sherin, M. G., 2002. Learning to notice: Scaffolding new teachers' interpretations of classroom interactions. *Journal of Technology and Teacher Education* 10, 571–596.

Whitmore, J., 2017. *Coaching for Performance: The Principles and Practice of Coaching and Leadership* (5th Edition). London: Nicholas Brealey Publishing.

Collaborative observation between students and staff as a catalyst for meaningful improvement*

Introduction

A considerable body of research and development on student–staff collaboration in higher education (HE) has been carried out in the UK, the USA and Australia over the last fifteen years (e.g. Cook-Sather, Bovill and Felten 2014; Healey, Flint and Harrington 2014; Healey and Jenkins 2009; Werder and Otis 2010). In this rich body of work, student–staff collaboration is conceptualised, defined and used in several different ways (see, for example, Healey, Flint and Harrington 2014). In this chapter, we focus on collaboration between students and staff to learn about learning and teaching through the use of observation. It draws on a longitudinal research project funded by the Higher Education Funding Council for England (HEFCE) that involved students and staff working collaboratively as co-observers and co-interrogators of their learning and teaching experiences through the shared lens of observation, with students reconceptualised from passive consumers to active collaborators.

---

* This chapter is based on two articles: O'Leary, M. and Cui, V. 2020. Reconceptualising teaching and learning in higher education: challenging neoliberal narratives of teaching excellence through collaborative observation. *Teaching in Higher Education*, 25(2), 141–156; and Cui, V., O'Leary, M., Pressick, I., Reynolds, S., Roberts, L., Turville, N. and White, N. 2020. Learning about learning and teaching: developing classroom consciousness and reimagining collaboration between students and staff. *PRACTICE: Contemporary Issues in Practitioner Education*, 2(2), 128–144. Included with permission.

DOI: 10.4324/9780429341908-8

The backdrop to the project was the introduction of the Teaching Excellence Framework (TEF) (BIS 2015) in the UK, which has positioned the quality of teaching high on the policy agenda. Although reaction to the TEF has been mixed among the HE academic community to date, its introduction has provoked sector-wide debate about the status and quality of teaching in HE. Some of the latest research (e.g. Cui, French and O'Leary 2019; Vivian et al. 2019) has revealed that HEIs are changing their organisational behaviours, with many of them directly operationalising TEF metrics into their institutional policies and initiatives to satisfy the demands of the TEF assessment framework. Research by O'Leary, Cui and French (2019) shows that many academic staff across UK HEIs are concerned about meaningful learning and teaching practices for both students and staff.

As discussed in Chapter 2, there are many different facets to the neoliberalisation and marketisation of HE that have been promoted by policies like the TEF. A particular aspect that we wish to focus on in this chapter is the commodification of students as 'consumers' and 'evaluators' of teaching. With current government policy choosing to frame HE explicitly in economic terms, recent policy discourse has emphasised students as customers of a commodity and/or service users, as evidenced in the 2016 White Paper with the introduction of the TEF,

> Competition between providers in any market incentivises them to raise their game, offering consumers a greater choice of more innovative and better quality products and services at lower cost. Higher education is no exception…For competition in the HE sector to deliver the best possible outcomes, students must be able to make informed choices…Information, particularly on price and quality, is critical if the higher education market is to perform properly.
>
> (BIS 2016)

The student-consumer conceptualisation and discourse play a key part in HE marketisation and privatisation. It is underpinned by a set of interrelated suppositions where students come to see HE as a right based on the increasingly private nature of their contribution with the value of HE equated to the costs of participating (Tomlinson 2017). Throughout the White Paper and recent outputs from the Office for Students (OfS), *'value for money'* is stressed as a key driver to determining quality in HE participation. Two interlinked conceptualisations of *'value'* articulated in the White Paper are the economic value of the degree to the labour market, measured by graduate employment metrics, and the value of the investment made by students in their HE courses. The core metrics, which include student satisfaction evaluations, are intended to capture institutional outcomes across a range of performance criteria in order to inform prospective students, thus creating a market of differentiated 'quality'. However, many scholars have argued that the flawed ideologies and methodologies of policies such as the TEF provide us with limited situated understandings of teaching and learning and fail to bring about meaningful improvements to HE students and their teachers (e.g. Canning 2019; Gunn 2018). As a counter narrative to the TEF quality regime, the Cycle of Collaborative Observation (CoCO) was created to provide the tools, the resources and the platform for students and staff to engage in collaborative discussions, observations and reflections on situated learning and teaching practices on their courses. We started this journey by asking ourselves:

> How can we create and nurture authentic and sustainable practice that involves students and staff collaboratively generating meaningful learning and teaching experiences?

Learning about learning and teaching: context and complexity

As discussed in Chapter 3, teaching in HE is a multifaceted notion. It can be viewed and understood through different lenses e.g. the performance, the process and the scholarship. This is also reflected in how the relationships between teachers, students and the learning and teaching orient themselves (e.g. Su and Wood 2012; Tubbs 2005). Previous research has identified traits of teaching excellence (e.g. Shephard et al. 2010; Skelton 2004), the most commonly occurring of which include the complex interactions and negotiations between aspects of technical, emotional and ethical deliberations. Teaching excellence also involves consistent negotiations and simultaneous engagement between the personal, collaborative, organisational and societal needs (Wood 2017).

In contrast to the current policy conceptualisation of students as consumers and evaluators and staff as providers, we maintain that students and staff should be considered as members of a course community who have agency and are active participants in understanding and shaping learning and teaching in their subject community. With this in mind, the distinction between learner voice and student voice (i.e. the student-consumer conceptualisation) must be made here. HE students juggle multiple roles within academia, which in turn reflect multiple voices (e.g. Cui 2014; Tomlinson 2017). When we use the term 'learner voice' in this book, we refer specifically to students expressing their experiences, understanding and practices regarding their learning in HE. In short, learner voice embodies their learning experiences and what is meaningful to them, their peers and their tutors.

Work by Bowden and Marton (2004) provided conceptual inspiration and theoretical underpinning to our work. They argue for an understanding between students and staff that is based on a common frame of reference of learning and teaching is fundamental to building a *collective consciousness* of learning in the context of their course,

> Learning from other people means that we become aware of their ways of seeing things, regardless of whether or not we are convinced by, or appropriate, their ways of seeing... this means that not only do students have to learn from teachers but teachers have to learn from students as well... Our views of a certain phenomenon can therefore be shared or they can be complementary. Combining differing views implies richer, more powerful, ways of understanding a phenomenon or a situation and is likely to offer more options for handling varying conditions.
>
> (Bowden and Marton 2004, pp. 14–15)

This concept shares the critical social constructivist stand we adopt, emphasising how teaching and learning should be built on an ethos that challenges our taken-for-granted views and practices in order to develop new understandings. Viewing subject specialist learning through the eyes of others enables us to develop a mutual awareness and understanding, which in turn helps us to appreciate, challenge and further our individual and collective understanding. Teaching and learning are social practices that require the protagonists to engage in a process of reflexivity. Examining our own understanding and experience of teaching and learning by cross-referencing these assumptions and opening them up to dialogic exchange enables us to become aware of the strengths and areas for development in our practices. Instead of disseminating feedback to each other about teaching and learning, we argue that by creating shared spaces in which teachers and students can engage in reflexive dialogue, this leads to collective sense making (Fielding 2004), as exemplified in our detailed discussion of CoCO in this chapter.

The other theoretical tool used in the development of CoCO is Brookfield's (1995) work on the critically reflective practitioner. In order to challenge the hegemonic assumptions that we hold about teaching and learning, Brookfield argues that it is important to draw on both our peers' and our students' perspectives to illuminate different interpretations of our actions and provide different frames of references to understand them. According to Brookfield (1995), student learning is one of four key lenses through which teachers are encouraged to evaluate the effectiveness of their teaching. In CoCO, students and staff all take an active role in critically reflecting on their practices, viewing the shared classroom experience from their perspectives and exchanging their observations and reflections with each other. Our methodology draws individual perspectives together to observe learning and teaching at a course-specific level rather than focusing attention on an individual's practice or a one-off session. Central to our philosophy of improving learning and teaching is the need for students and teaching staff to take shared responsibility for developing mutual understanding, using a shared frame of reference from which to generate new understandings of situated learning and teaching.

Improving Teaching and Learning Through Collaborative Observation project

CoCO was developed as part of the *Improving Teaching and Learning Through Collaborative Observation* project funded by a HEFCE innovation in learning and teaching grant. The project took place at Birmingham City University from 2016 to 2018 and included five case studies undergraduate programmes which were: 1) Adult Nursing; 2) Child Nursing; 3) Early Childhood Studies; 4) Primary Education and 5) Radiotherapy. Each case study involved two academic staff and two student researchers for each observation cycle.

Staff members were recruited on a voluntary basis through a faculty-wide recruitment process. All participating staff were required to complete an observation training programme, delivered by the project team before undertaking CoCO with their peers and students. The project team provided project briefings for students on participating courses. Following an invitation to participate in focus groups exploring their interest in and understanding of learning and teaching, students were invited to submit expressions of interest to take part in the project. Student participants were then selected from these expressions of interest, in consultation with staff teaching on the chosen courses. Although student participants were voluntary, they were paid as research assistants for their time for the duration of the project. Like staff, all student participants completed an observation training programme delivered by the project team.

Bringing students and staff together to collaboratively observe, reflect and investigate their learning and teaching requires careful ethical considerations. As well as following ethical research procedures and practices,[1] our project paid special attention to the ethics of student–staff working relationships, the potential impact on participating staff and students as well as the impact between participants and their peers on the course. Trust between the participants was vital. In our project, the research team acted as a mediator at the beginning to facilitate dialogue and allow the participants to have time and space to develop trust. It was important for the students to recognise this was not an exercise in gathering feedback and evaluating staff performance. Instead, the conversations, observations and reflections were focused on making sense of the connections and intersections between learning and teaching on their programmes. Part of the training sessions[2] focused on the use of non-judgemental statements and questions in conversations for developmental learning. It was important for us to ensure that the participants had ownership of the work and were able to select the focus in their respective case studies. This included the power to decide which aspect(s) of learning and teaching they wished to focus on. We were keen to avoid any prescriptive and/or 'one-size-fits-all' approach, as these contradicted the underpinning principles of CoCO and could potentially jeopardise the opportunities for learning between staff and students.

The relationship between participating staff and students and the rest of the students on the course was a factor that required careful thought and sensitive handling. Staff were required to communicate the project, key findings and any action as a result of the project to their colleagues and their students to ensure transparency. Students were also responsible for ensuring that their work did not compromise any member of staff or peer on their course. So, for example, when reporting their observation notes, staff and students were required to keep the identities of their students/peers anonymous and focus on the aspects of teaching and learning that they observed rather than the individuals.

An overview of the project focus and a question-and-answer session was provided for all staff and students from each of the modules selected for participation. This was an important ethical consideration as we were mindful that any students and staff involved in these modules could become subjects of any of the case studies' collective discussion. Participants from each case study were briefed that in their observation notes, discussions and reflections, the identities of other students and staff should remain anonymous. The majority of case study participants agreed to reveal their identities as the co-researchers and co-observers in the publications and disseminations of this project's work. In cases where participants did not give us their permission, their identities anonymised in all project publications.

Cycle of Collaborative Observation

The Cycle of Collaborative Observation (CoCO) drew on the latest research and practice in the field of observation (e.g. O'Leary and Brooks 2014; O'Leary and Wood 2017), taking much of its inspiration from the Cycle of Peer Observation (CoPO) discussed in previous chapters. The project started with us reconceptualising and reconfiguring the way in which we planned for the project's participants to engage with observation as a method for inquiring and enhancing teaching and learning. Like CoPO, severing the umbilical link between observation and its use as a method of assessing teaching and teacher performance was central to the process we undertook in the creation of CoCO and the training and preparation of the project participants. We were convinced that unless we were able to remove observation from the assessment context, this would jeopardise our efforts to capture situated examples of authentic teaching and learning and in turn to create a safe, trusting and collaborative environment for reflection and dialogue between staff and students.

When it came to student involvement, our approach put learner voice and their active involvement in informing and shaping learning and teaching at the heart of this practice, thus reconceptualising students as members of their HE learning and teaching community. Without assuming students and/or staff were experts of learning and teaching, we decided that the best way to embark on meaningful and sustainable improvements was thus to build a shared understanding of learning and teaching between them in the context of their respective courses.

CoCO began with two separate training sessions for staff and students, each session lasting five hours in total (see Figure 8.1 for an overview of CoCO). Staff training focused on their previous experience of observations, developing an understanding of the project's collaborative approach and discussing the stages of CoCO. They worked collaboratively on a range of immersive exercises to facilitate their familiarisation with the methodology and the activities involved. For example, they practised carrying out non-judgemental observations via a selection of video clips of classroom practice and compared their observation notes and reflections with their peers. This was to help to develop an awareness of what different observers notice when they observe, reflect on their learning and teaching values and how these values inform their observations and reflections. While there were many similarities with the student observer training, there was a shift in focus inasmuch as the students' training workshop was concerned with helping them to think about their position as students through the lens of learning, to reflect on how they engage with learning

Collaborative observation between students and staff as a catalyst

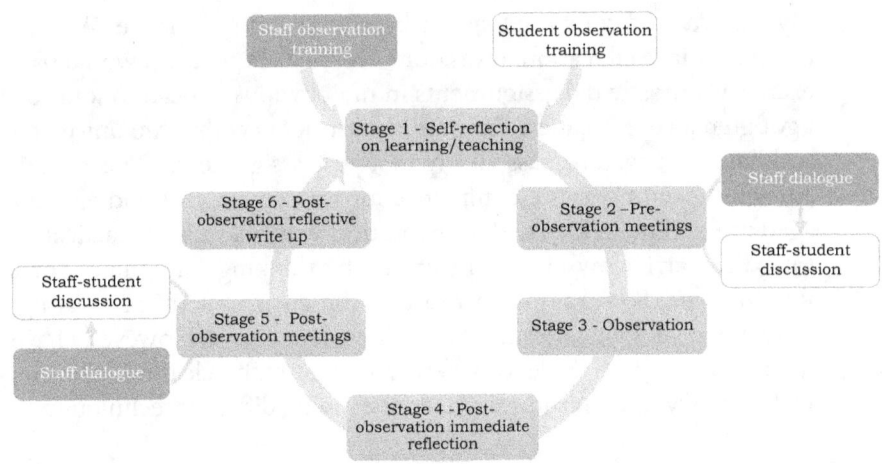

Figure 8.1 Cycle of Collaborative Observation (CoCO)

and teaching, and how that connects to their knowledge and experience as a student on their programme. The core materials developed for student observation training sessions are in Appendix 8.1. These include exercises on reflecting on learning experiences, learning about the role of observation in understanding learning and teaching and practising classroom observation as a method. The materials also outline the CoCO process, tasks for each stage of the cycle and student observers' roles and responsibilities. Our intention here is to provide illustrative examples and a frame of reference for those who are interested in implementing CoCO in their own courses, without being prescriptive to the particular methodology and methods that we adopted.

Stage 1 of the cycle involved staff and students working with a set of prompts to compile individual reflective accounts of their learning/teaching autobiographies. During the training sessions, reflection and models of reflection were discussed with participants but we decided not to prescribe a particular model/method. This was intended to elicit authentic reflections from students and staff about their views and experiences of learning and teaching. Students were prompted to reflect on their prior experiences of learning and how they went about making sense of their experience as learners on their programmes. Their reflective pieces covered a range of topics such as how they go about learning, their understandings of what learning at university means to them and how they overcome challenges to their learning.

Here is an example from an excerpt of a student's reflective account from Child Nursing,

> My first year of child nursing has been quite an experience. When I came back into education, I was quite worried about how I would pass exams as I mostly did assignments in my previous education journey. I got guidance from a few different departments within the university and have managed to pass all my first-year assignments. This experience has given me more confidence for my second year and encouraged me to remain focussed in theoretical work as well as practical … I used to barrier myself from learning by thinking something didn't work for me. For example, it must be the environment, my seating, style of teaching or assessment criteria such as exams. However, I have managed to go into the learning environment with a clear mind frame, willing to try new learning and understanding different techniques.

Staff were prompted to reflect on their teaching and learning journeys by focusing on what their philosophies of teaching were, how these impacted on the preparation, delivery and evaluation of teaching and learning, how these connected to their philosophies of learning, and what they considered to be the relationship between teaching and learning on their respective courses. Here is an example from an excerpt of a reflective account by a member of staff from Child Nursing,

> Historically, as a student I was that student, the one who fell asleep in the back of the classroom. I would attend a session or two and if I found the lecturer indifferent, reading from the PowerPoint and not inspiring me, I would resort to auto-didacticism. The traditional model of teaching whereby the teacher deposits knowledge into the minds of students was not a model I ever aspired to, as I found it to be an ineffective model for me as a student. My inspiration is a result of those lecturers who spoke to me and not at me, the ones who adopted a student-centred approach. Their sessions did not solely rely on PowerPoint but they took an alternative approach, challenging me and engaging me … I believe in teaching approaches that turn students into active participants rather than passive listeners. I favour certain pedagogical philosophies but I think as educators we switch between philosophies to deliver the required educational session depending on the student dynamics and needs. As a relatively new member to higher education, I strive to be dynamic, creative and innovative in my approach, thus I use a range of methods and continually explore new teaching methods. The positive feedback I get from using an approach that make students active participants and using different methods inspires me to continually develop myself.

At the Stage 2 pre-observation meetings, students and staff first met in their peer groups to discuss their individual reflections from Stage 1 and worked together on developing their learning objectives and inquiries for their case study. Aligned with our conceptualisation of learning, we adopted the term 'coaching' and underpinned this with Bokeno's (2009) work, who suggests that organisations focus on 'learning relationships', which are based upon an ethos of inquiry and a willingness to explore unasked questions. Using a coaching ethos and techniques, members in each peer group facilitated each other's development through the use of open and thought-provoking questions. The use of questions aimed to create a working ethos of enquiry and support participants in taking responsibility for their own learning.

After initial discussion in their respective peer groups, staff and students came together to share and discuss their individual reflections and to connect these reflections with teaching and learning on their courses collectively. They identified the areas they wished to investigate together, agreed the focus and dates of the observed sessions, the roles of each member during the course of the cycle and the expectations of both parties. The focus of the discussion was on the processes of teaching and learning rather than on the teachers or students themselves. This was the point at which these two sets of lenses first came together to co-interrogate teaching and learning on their course.

The observation (Stage 3) involved students working in pairs to observe part of the session from their perspective as learners. A lecturer led the session while their peer observed. Students and staff agreed their focus prior to the observations. To ensure that they were able to carry out high-quality observations with limited distractions to their learning during the session, it was recommended that each individual student limit their observation time to 30 minutes. Observers took handwritten notes with no prescribed criteria on what to observe.

Following the observation, immediate reflections (Stage 4) were carried out by all participants individually. Each observer then developed their notes, supplementing them with questions and comments in preparation for their post-observation meetings.

Stage 5 post-observation meetings took a similar format to Stage 2. Students and staff met in their peer groups to discuss their observation experience and relate what they had observed to their own learning/teaching experience on the course. When meeting as a group, all participants brought their notes and reflections to the discussion and linked these back to the Stage 2 discussion and the agreed learning objectives and focus. Each individual's perspective came together to form a collective understanding of the shared classroom learning and teaching they had observed and experienced.

Stage 6 of the cycle culminated in a reflective write-up by each participant independently. The aim was to capture the holistic experience of both parties of the cycle. What's more, each participant was prompted to make connections between this observation experience with their past learning and teaching experiences and their learning and teaching experiences across the course.

Developing classroom consciousness between students and staff

Across the two years of the project, students and staff generated a rich bank of data that included recordings of discussions before and after observations, observation notes, along with reflective accounts about their experiences and learning. When we looked through the data with staff members involved in the project, a key concept emerged across the case studies. In order to capture this concept, we coined the term 'classroom consciousness', inspired by Bowden and Marton's (2004) 'collective consciousness'.

In Cycle 1, each case study focused on understanding the impact of teaching on student learning, exploring key aspects of teaching such as pedagogical approaches, the classroom environment, resources etc. The lecturers decided the focus of the observations and led the discussions during the pre- and post-observation meetings. One of the outcomes to emerge from Cycle 1 across each case study was the development of students' understanding of the relationship between teaching and learning. While Cycle 1 observations focused largely on teaching, the experience of collectively observing, discussing and reflecting on learning and teaching on their respective courses resulted in the unearthing of their classroom consciousness, as the following extract from Katie's (Radiotherapy student) end of cycle reflection illuminates,

> The student observer process so far has been extremely insightful and made me think in more depth why lecturers do things in the way they do. It has made me understand that one technique is not suitable for all aspects of my course; for example being taught anatomy purely through PowerPoints and books would be extremely difficult to absorb and would not put the knowledge in to context. However, the human models and practical tasks gave a more natural way of learning.

Collaborative observation between students and staff as a catalyst

One of the significant developments to occur across all case studies moving from Cycle 1 to Cycle 2 was the collective decision to shift the observation focus from teaching to learning. This shift in focus emerged as a suggestion during a project review day involving staff participants at the end of Cycle 1. After reading and discussing reflections by students, staff were keen to empower their students to take more responsibility for deciding the focus of Cycle 2 observations. This was then later agreed between staff and students in their respective case study meetings before starting Cycle 2. This shift in focus marked a key milestone in the project, leading to a greater depth of reciprocal awareness and understanding of learning and teaching in their classrooms among students and staff compared to Cycle 1. Across the case studies, it gave rise to a more even balance in the discursive interaction between participants. This was not only reflected in an increase in student talking time in Cycle 2 meetings compared to Cycle 1, but also the depth of their critical thinking and reflections on learning and teaching in their classrooms. For example, the extract below, which discusses collaborative group work in Radiotherapy, is illustrative of student reflections across case studies,

> ... we can choose who we want to be in a group with and what time we wish to have the session delivered at ... It was obvious that the students weren't really learning from each other's work as the lecturer had to repeat the same instructions to each participant ... as the session neared its conclusion and the concentration waned, those students who had provided help to other student members before were now not getting the same level of help back from their peers. Thus, it opens the question, why should stronger students help the weaker students if they cannot receive the same level of support back? ... I feel that these observations have shown the need for forming a greater inter-student collaborative effort as we move into the third year to ensure that all students are as successful as possible.

In her work on the scholarship of teaching and teaching excellence, Kreber (2002) refers to a conception of teaching that is 'learning oriented'. We found this a helpful term and concept to explore the significance of this shift in focus from Cycle 1 to Cycle 2. Learning was placed at the forefront of all discussions in Cycle 2 with students encouraged to reflect on their experiences, views and feelings. As Jay (Adult Nursing student) commented,

> This cycle is a lot better, because it's just us, isn't it? So, we can just focus on us, our learning and if everybody individually focuses on themselves, we've got something to put together and collaborate on.

Both Jay and his peer Oliver agreed that focusing on their own learning in Cycle 2 'felt more natural' compared to having to discuss and evaluate their lecturers' teaching (as they did in the Cycle 1 observation), which Jay maintained they were 'not qualified to judge'. Jay's and Oliver's perceptions were representative of their peers in the other case studies inasmuch as the shift to a learning-oriented focus also helped to remove some of the apprehension they felt in their roles as observers of their lecturers' teaching. For the lecturers, because the focus was driven by students in Cycle 2, this provided them with rich and timely insights into their students' learning. For example, in Radiotherapy where the Cycle 2 focus was on classroom dynamics, Nick (lecturer) highlighted how his participation in CoCO had made him reflect on the 'social aspect of the classroom', triggering novel perspectives on his students' learning,

> The most useful thing about this observation project to me is just working out the social aspect of the classroom. I've never had time to stop and think about it before ... I don't remember having conversations about it when I was taught how to teach.

While the observation training for both students and staff emphasised how the observer's role was not to evaluate the teaching but to use observation as a tool of collaborative inquiry through which to explore teaching and learning, the focus on teaching in Cycle 1 meant that discussions often gravitated towards assessing the effectiveness of teaching. With the focus on learning, both parties were able to derive value that fed into their wider classroom consciousness of their learning/teaching and the relationship between the two. Stacey (Child Nursing student) remarked: 'I think that was a good thing because it's made me reflect more on myself and where I'm learning and what my learning is and am I learning?' Nick (Radiotherapy lecturer) commented: 'the feedback I want is "does this make your practice more relevant?" It's not the process of being observed, it's the whole context of being observed.'

Analysis of the transcripts from the meetings across both cycles revealed a development of confidence and fluency among the student participants in their discursive exchanges and the manner in which they were able to articulate themselves. However, it is important to acknowledge that this may also have been partly due to the development of the student–teacher relationship as each quartet got to know each other better over the duration of the project, an aspect discussed further below.

The role of noticing in developing learning and classroom consciousness

Mason (2002, 33) defines noticing as to 'make a distinction, to create foreground and background, to distinguish a "thing" from its surroundings'. As a concept, noticing has been the subject of a wealth of academic research relating to learning and teaching since the 1980s, particularly in the fields of cognitive psychology and second language learning. In relation to the latter, Schmidt (1990, 1993) developed a 'Noticing Hypothesis', the stronger version of which posited that noticing was a necessary condition for learning, whereas the weaker version claimed that noticing was helpful but not a necessity for learning to occur. While the stronger version has been called into question by many researchers (e.g. Truscott 1998), the weaker version still has currency and offers an interesting lens through which to view and make sense of one of the themes to emerge from the project data in relation to the way in which engaging with CoCO impacted on participants' understanding of their respective subjects and the processes of learning and teaching.

The extract below is taken from the Child Nursing end of Cycle 2 evaluation meeting. Here Nathalie (lecturer) and Stacey (student) discuss the notion of building on and moving existing understanding forward. From a teaching perspective, Nathalie draws attention to the importance of presenting students with 'something unknown ... something exceptional' to challenge their existing assumptions but also as a deliberate technique to ensure that the 'new' information stands out enough for them to notice what is different,

> Nathalie – There always needs to be something that gives a bit of a jolt, a bit of surprise, something unknown. Something that challenges something you've taken for granted. It might be something exceptional. So in this session, it was that there was this shocking statistic that really brought things out that was quite unexpected. So it took something that basically challenged an assumption that people had and then turned it on its head. So that very much made a difference as well ... and the understanding and putting something into context as well.

> Researcher – So, do you think that noticing something memorable or different is an important part for you in terms of moving your understanding forward?
>
> Stacey – Yes, for me, for my learning, you think you've got an idea, and then this challenges it, so it sticks with me more because it was different to what I originally assumed because I've stood up and took notice of that fact, it kind of stays in my mind a little bit longer than "this is this, this is that" where I might get distracted. But I go, "What?" and it makes me stop and think, for my learning it will stay there a lot longer.

The 'shocking statistic' that Nathalie refers to that challenged Stacey's knowledge base during the taught session by Ilana concerned the prevalence of the life-threatening condition sepsis and how it was responsible for more deaths in the UK each year than some of the most common forms of cancer. Stacey recognised that the prominent media presence of certain types of cancer was largely why she and her peers had assumed that they must be the leading cause of death. However, her realisation that sepsis was the cause of more deaths than specific types of cancer and that she knew very little about it caused her to reflect on how this had exposed a gap in her knowledge as a student nurse that she needed to fill. When reflecting further on this particular teaching/learning incident, Stacey acknowledged that it was only as a result of being presented with something that had challenged her knowledge base that she was more likely to notice it, which in turn caused her to reflect more deeply on its significance and how this needed to be mapped against her understanding of the subject area as a whole. In noticing and reflecting on the presentation of 'something unknown … something exceptional', Stacey embarked on a process of reflexivity which involved her questioning her existing knowledge and understanding of the topic while simultaneously assimilating the new information presented to her by her lecturers and discussed with her peers.

Viewed through a 'teaching lens', the above exchange provides an important insight into the teacher's 'pedagogical reasoning' (Shulman 1987). As Loughran (2019, 523) argues, it is by examining more closely teachers' pedagogical reasoning that we are able to gain an understanding of 'the complex and sophisticated knowledge of practice that influences what they do, how and why'. In discussions with their students and colleague, lecturers also reveal their extensive bank of professional knowledge and experience on which they draw on when making decisions in the planning and delivery of their teaching. As remarked by some of the student participants in both the previous and following section, participating in CoCO gave them an insight into their lecturers' pedagogical reasoning, which in turn provided them with an opportunity to reflect collaboratively on how this impacted on their learning. Thus, CoCO created the conditions for the iterative development of classroom consciousness to occur between the two parties.

Viewed through a 'learning lens', another aspect of noticing to emerge from the student participants was how focusing on their learning and that of their peers provided them with a space in which to consider their learning behaviours and how these might impact on the effectiveness of their learning. In this next extract, Aneesa talks about taking 'ownership' of her own learning, recognising particular learning habits and behaviours that she believes play an important part in shaping her learning experience:

> Nathalie – That ownership thing, what does that actually mean about taking more ownership?
> Aneesa – So, I think for me, I'm in control of how I learn. So if I walk into a room and I sit at the back, already I'm telling myself, 'Okay I know what this session is on, let's sit at the back because I don't know whether I'm going to engage or not.' The ownership bit comes with, 'I'm here to learn' and every session is important so I have to kind of tell myself, 'No, you are going to sit at the front and you are going to try and take something away from this.' So, for me that's what ownership of my own learning is going to be … There was a session where I knew that this is something I'm going to base my assignments on. But I know it was a session I struggled with, so I thought, 'I'm not going to sit at the back because if I miss say even one point, I'm gone for the whole session.' … Because sometimes when I get lost, I just can't focus on the rest of it. So that session made me sit at the front and I noticed that I actually did stay committed to the session throughout the whole thing. So after Natalie's session, if I reflect, I think sitting more central at the front, it's a bit better for me and my learning.

Building collaborative relationships between students and staff

The relationships between the participants in each case study were critical to their collaborative learning. What brought the participants together, as outlined in each case study description, was their interests in learning and teaching and desire to work together to develop understandings and practices of learning and teaching of their own and on their programme. In a relationship, the link between people defines the sort of connection they have (Duck 1999). It was this shared interest and desire that created a pedagogical relationship link within each case study team. This is different to the link in the neoliberal commodified teaching and learning relationship where the teacher is the 'supplier' and the student the 'consumer'/'evaluator'. Oliver (Adult Nursing student), in his end of Cycle 2 reflection, commented on what this pedagogical connection with his lecturers and a fellow student meant to him,

> The major benefit I have taken away from both cycles is the chance to have an informal meeting with the people providing my education, and have an entire hour set aside to talk about my experience. I was both contributing to and benefiting from the best part of a new model of student-teacher collaboration. It felt like a team-based approach and I had a Jay as my constant peer and colleague to give me a chance to listen to the way other students experience, perceive and evaluate the same things I have. I believe that in practically every situation in life, collaborative problem-solving involving direct interactions between people from different backgrounds is the most comprehensive and usually most successful way to achieve a positive result. I am incredibly happy to have been part of a study that will go on to help show this, and I am grateful for the chance to evaluate my learning experience outside of simply successes and failures.

This pedagogical relationship formed the basis for the collaboration, but, as Baxter and Montgomery's work (1996) illustrated, formal social relationships do not evolve by default but need to be actively developed and the process of developing such relationships is dependent on a dialectic dimension. Through the two cycles of observation, the collaborative learning and the relationship development were intertwined – the collaborative inquiry provided the important context for the relationship and the relationship in term enabled the collaboration to progress. This means the student–staff collaboration involved both an intellectual and a social dimension across the case studies in this project. As discussed above, the intellectual dimension underwent a process of changing focus from teaching to learning in raising classroom consciousness between the participants.

The social relationships across case studies included the formal roles and commitments participants had as students and lecturers in their respective programmes, as well as their personal commitments to their collaborative partnership. Each participant took their formal role and commitment seriously in observing, questioning, critiquing and developing situated pedagogical practices in their classrooms. Besides, the collaborative partnerships brought about renewed personal connections between them. For the students, this was a new and different kind of relationship with their teachers, as Oliver explains during the pre-observation meeting with his lecturers and his fellow student,

> I know that you are obviously human, but when you're a student and you're sitting in front of a lecturer, sometimes it's that barrier of 'I'm a student they're a lecturer' whereas, all of a sudden, when there are personal stories that come into it and their own little phrases and the way that they explain things, that adds to the idea that this is more of a peer relationship. We get more from that relationship than you would from just lecturer and students.

Students and staff across the case studies really valued this personal connection with each other. Here we draw on Carl Rogers' (2002) work on interpersonal relationships in education to explore the details on the quality of such personal connections. Following on from the learning-orientated lens (Kreber 2002) discussed previously, Rogers' conception of learner-centred education allows us to keep our analysis under a coherent conceptual framework in terms of the relationship and orientation between learning and teaching.

From the beginning of CoCO, there was a gradual process of familiarisation between the participants. Cycle 1 interactions between staff and students started by focusing largely on procedural and technical aspects of observation. As the relationships developed, staff participants in each case study began to share their insights on teaching (e.g. their rationale, their approach) and their assumptions on learning more openly. Here is what Nathalie (Nursing lecturer) shared during their pre-observation meeting,

> Some sessions I have delivered and I haven't got through the whole of the content and I have delivered the same lecture to a different group and because there has been no discussion and no feedback and no interaction, we are finished with you know like three quarters of an hour to spare. There is only so much you can do standing at the front saying 'Oh lets discuss this or whatever'.

This openness enabled the establishment of authenticity in the pedagogical relationships between participants. As Rogers (2002) noted, this means that the teacher and the learner come into a direct encounter, they are being themselves and they are aware of their feelings and views, and they are able to communicate them if appropriate. This is clearly reflected in Oliver's comment above, as well as those of the other students who made similar remarks. In particular, this meant students were able to see teaching not just as a job their lecturers do as a 'curriculum instructor' (Rogers 2002) but as decisions and actions carried out consciously and deliberately by an educator who has shared education interests with them. As the lecturers became more open about their practices and views, this was reciprocated by the students who were candid in sharing their opinions and feelings. This authenticity provided a platform for students and staff to engage in an open inquiry of learning and teaching.

As discussed above, one of the principles of CoCO is that participants exchanging their views and listening to others without judgement. Building and maintaining the authenticity of the pedagogical relationship between students and lecturers meant both parties were disposed to exchanging personal feelings and views, acknowledging and respecting different points of perspectives from others and learning from each other, leading to a collective development and enhancement of *classroom consciousness*.

Rogers (2002) observed that this kind of understanding and acceptance is sharply different from the usual evaluative view that focuses on what goes well or badly in teaching and learning. For him, a sensitive empathy grows in a pedagogical relationship that is built on realness and acceptance which then enables learners to feel 'at last someone understands how it feels and seems to be me without wanting to analyse me or judge me. Now I can blossom and grow and learn.' In Rogers' work, the focus was on the impact teaching has on learning and he saw the relationship building and maintenance as being the responsibility of the teacher. In CoCO case studies, both students and lecturers took this responsibility to be conscious about, acknowledging, listening to and reflecting on others' feelings and views. As a result, a shared empathy emerged where students and lecturers were able to see, understand and empathise with each other's actions and reactions, displaying a sensitive awareness of the way the interrelationship between teaching and learning is seen and experienced from each other's point of view. The reflections by Aneesa (student) and Ilana (lecturer) from Child Nursing illustrate the power of such shared understanding in developing their classroom consciousness and pedagogical practices,

> This reflective cycle has enabled me as a student to work in collaboration with Ilana and Nathalie whereby we were all equal participants in research. This relationship has given me an incomparable insight into how much preparation and time goes into teaching and has encouraged me to make the most out of the lectures within my future studies.

> I now have a better understanding on how I can benefit from different methods of teaching and will continue to enhance my own learning through the techniques picked up throughout this project.
>
> (Aneesa)

> Participating in the process has impacted my teaching on a practical level as I will make changes to what I do in the classroom and how I do it. More importantly I've gained a deeper shared understanding about learning and teaching as a result of the collaborative meetings with the students. This observation unlocked the potential for us to understand our students and thereby allowing us to meet their learning needs on a deeper level. However, learning still does depend on the students' willingness to participate in the process. By allowing students to become more aware of their own learning as a result of their participation in observation, this consequently led to them being empowered to overcome self-identified barriers and led to a better and more satisfactory teaching and learning experience for all. By enabling students to participate in the collaborative observation cycle change does not only happen on a one-dimensional level 'teacher growth' but becomes a multi-dimensional change by enabling 'student growth' and 'teacher–student growth'.
>
> (Ilana)

The CoCO model played a critical role in its underpinning principles and its design to facilitate this dialectic relationship development. For each participant, the individual reflections at the beginning and the end of the cycle gave them the space to develop their autonomous voices. In the reflections, each participant openly talked about their experiences of the sessions and reflected on their feelings and views, which then led to their questions on learning and teaching by themselves and in their classrooms. For example, Adult Nursing lecturer Stephanie's Cycle 2 pre-observation reflection (Stage 1 of CoCO, see Figure 8.1) highlighted the areas she wanted to focus on in discussions with students and her colleague Lee,

> I want feedback from my colleague observer on how I made the environment safe, ways to improve, and what to do particularly when students weren't successful in their efforts. It would be good to get both student and staff perspectives on this learning in particular and also gauge whether large groups inhibit the participation or widen the possibility of observation. Another aspect of learning or feedback that would be useful to know is what to do when students don't readily

volunteer as the silence can often be uncomfortable. Should I wait? Should I pick on people or should I do it myself? From a student perspective, I would like to know what learning was achieved from participating and by observing. Could they relate back to the aspects of a health promotion model as they observed and/or reflected on their learning? Would they feel more confident in applying this to their practice and their care planning? To further expand this observation, it would be good if students could reflect how this session has influenced their practice?

In her post-observation reflection (Stage 6 of CoCO), Stephanie wrote, 'I think the big thing for me was that the silence was very uncomfortable!! I felt uncomfortable that I might have put students into too much of a challenging situation, making them feel conscious of their performance in front of many classmates.' She then went into further analysis why she felt students did not engage in the way she intended and evaluated her facilitation of the session. Whereas in their reflection, the students focused on their engagement in the session and reflected on how they participated in the simulations, how they felt at the time when they made the decision to volunteer or not and during the simulation, what they learnt from this experience and what this learning meant to their further development as a student nurse.

Challenges and constraints

It is important to acknowledge that while the collaborative partnerships between students and staff had a tangible impact on enhancing their reciprocal learning about learning and teaching, the project was not without its challenges and constraints. The first, and arguably the most significant, challenge was that of time and timetabling. Coordinating the scheduling of meetings and observations for each quartet over the two cycles of CoCO proved an ongoing challenge for each case study. The complex timetables and heavy teaching loads of participating staff across modules and year groups meant that the opportunities for each quartet to come together were limited. This was exacerbated by the fact that the case studies all involved practice-based courses where students spent a lot of their time outside of the university on placement, thus the window for observing taught sessions and meeting before and after the observation was heavily constrained. That said, the dedication of the project participants, along with the flexibility of the project team in adapting to the local needs and circumstances of participants on a case-by-case basis, enabled us to overcome this challenge.

Preparing students for the act of observing and making clear the remit of their roles was an initial challenge for many of the participants. Both students and staff undertook observation training which emphasised the non-judgmental aspect of their roles as observers and how the purpose of the observations was not to evaluate the teaching but to compile a descriptive log which would act as a stimulus for collective reflection and discussion. The student participants found it difficult at times knowing what to observe, what and how to record what they observed, along with articulating their reflections and experiences in the appropriate discourse. This was partly because they had no pro forma on which to record their observation notes, which was a deliberate intention as the observation was not an evaluation and therefore there were no accompanying assessment criteria. In addition, they had to juggle the dual role of both observer and learner simultaneously. This highlighted how the act of observing and noticing requires the ability to recognise and identify significant incidents in the classroom and to home in on such incidents. However, this challenge was noticeably lessened with the switch in focus from teaching to learning in Cycle 2. Reconfiguring the focus for students to reflect on and discuss with others (i.e. their peers, tutors and researchers) their learning provided an important platform from which to interrogate and unearth tacit practices and processes. By creating discursive spaces in which staff and students could come together with their peers and as a whole group, we found that valuable insights emerged into the processes of learning and teaching that had direct benefit for both parties in developing their understanding and practice.

Engaging in critical reflection initially proved a challenge to some of the student participants, particularly during Cycle 1. With hindsight, this was something that as researchers we failed to anticipate. We had assumed that given reflection was something students on these practice-based courses would be expected to undertake as part of their placement experiences that they would be familiar with the process of reflective writing. However, it was clear that we had underestimated the complexity of the task and how challenging this would prove to be for many of the student participants during Cycle 1 where the focus was on them observing their lecturers' teaching. The switch in focus from observing teaching to their own learning in Cycle 2 seemed to make it easier for the students to engage in reflection. Added to this, as students engaged more with pedagogical discussions with their peers and lecturers, their classroom consciousness developed, which enhanced their understanding of and familiarity with pedagogical concepts and discourse and in turn led to a growth in their confidence in discussing and reflecting on learning and teaching.

Conclusion

Under current neoliberal policy initiatives like the TEF in England, HE teaching and learning have been framed as individual success measured against set criteria based on market values (e.g. Wood 2017). This is counterintuitive to how effective teaching and learning is naturally developed through long-term personal and professional learning that involves critical reflection and the ongoing negotiation of meaning and understanding between those involved. This process is unique to individuals and as such requires a tailored approach. The interrelationship between teaching and learning is inherently qualitative in nature and as such requires appropriate methodologies and methods to explore, interrogate and make sense of these complex phenomena. Bringing students and staff together to engage in co-observation and co-reflection on their shared classroom experience enables them to see learning and teaching from their respective viewpoints and understand the connections and intersections between them. This also supports one of the most effective ways of learning, which involves collaborating with others to see different perspectives and approaches and to question our own practice and beliefs.

An important finding to emerge from the student–staff collaborative observation project is that students and teachers learn about learning and teaching by interacting with their peers and with each other, by sharing their insights and experiences in collaborative and cooperative forums. The case studies in this project have revealed how viewing subject specialist learning through collective eyes can help to develop a mutual awareness and understanding, which in turn can help both parties to appreciate, challenge and further their individual and collective understandings of learning and teaching in their classrooms.

Teaching and learning at course level are two sides of the same coin. It therefore makes sense that any attempt to enhance understanding of and improve these practices is best served by allowing its key participants to be part of a collective community in which they are encouraged to engage in a process of dialectic pedagogical knowledge and relationship development. Affording students and teachers the opportunity to examine their understanding and experiences of teaching and learning and opening them up to dialogic exchange enables them to become aware of the strengths and areas for development in their practices. In the context of HE teaching and learning, instead of measuring and judging the performance of students and lecturers using national and institutional performance indicators such as the TEF and disseminating feedback on their performance to them, approaches like CoCO create shared spaces in which students and academics can engage in reflexive pedagogical dialogue on their classroom learning and teaching. This leads to collective sensemaking which has meaning to both students and lecturers in understanding and developing their practices.

We began this project with a reconceptualisation of improving HE teaching and learning through a sustainable approach at course level involving the active participation of academics and students. Throughout this project, we have seen how meaningful, authentic collaborations between university teachers and their students can lead to the creation of new knowledge about learning and teaching that can be used to enhance their future learning and practices. Towards the end of the project, Ilana (Child Nursing lecturer) raised an important question: 'If collaborative partnerships between staff and students are fundamental to understanding learning then why are we not involving students more?' Ilana's question hits at the very heart of the reconceptualisation of student identity, responsibility and involvement in HE teaching and learning; it is an essential component that needs to be included if we are to further our understanding of the complex relationships and interactions between teaching and learning. The interpersonal relationships fostered during this project occurred over time in small groups of students and lecturers, both of whom were interested in learning and teaching. The mass participation in HE presents a challenge for educators and students to find and sustain space and time for such meaningful collaborative engagement to occur at scale. Nevertheless, the benefits of such collaborative partnerships mean that it is a challenge worth undertaking.

Appendix 8.1: Student observation training workshop materials

Here, we share some of the exercises we designed and developed as part of the *Improving Teaching and Learning Through Collaborative Observation* project. We have also included materials produced by students as part of the workshops (see Figures 8.2 and 8.3 for these materials). Our intention here is to provide illustrative examples and a frame of reference for those who are interested in implementing CoCO in their own courses, without being prescriptive to the particular methodology and methods that we adopted.

Key aims of student observation training sessions:

- To reflect on and discuss learning
- To reflect on and discuss observing

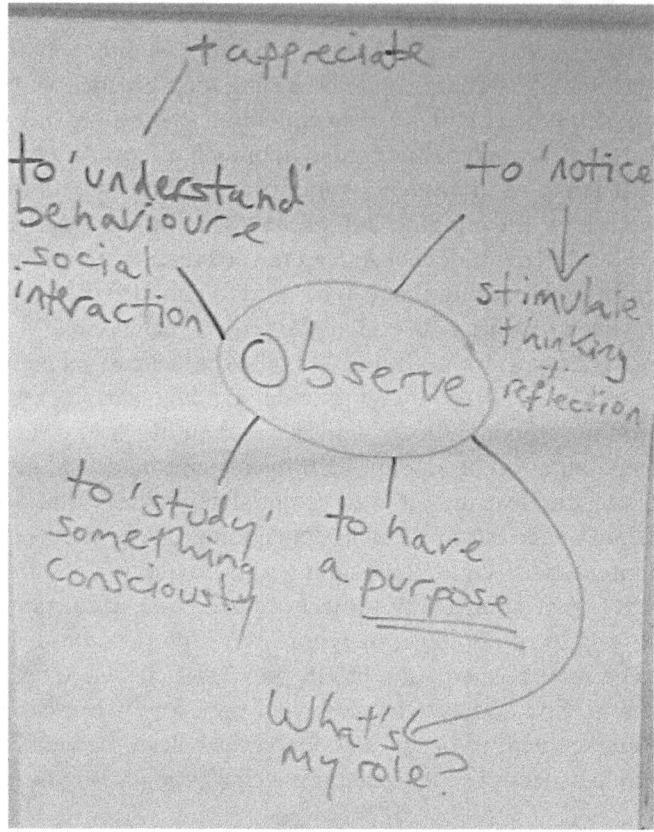

Figure 8.2 Students' ideas on what it means to 'observe' something

- To discuss what your role is as a student observer
- To explain what the role is of your lecturers as part of the collaborative observation and what you can expect from them
- To discuss the practicalities of the work e.g. time commitment, schedules, etc.

Exercise 1: Reflecting on your learning experience

1. Think about your First-Year learning experience:
   - What was it like?
   - How do you feel about your experiences of learning up to now?
   - What has made you feel this way?
   - What do you realise about yourself as a learner?
   - What have you learnt during your first year?

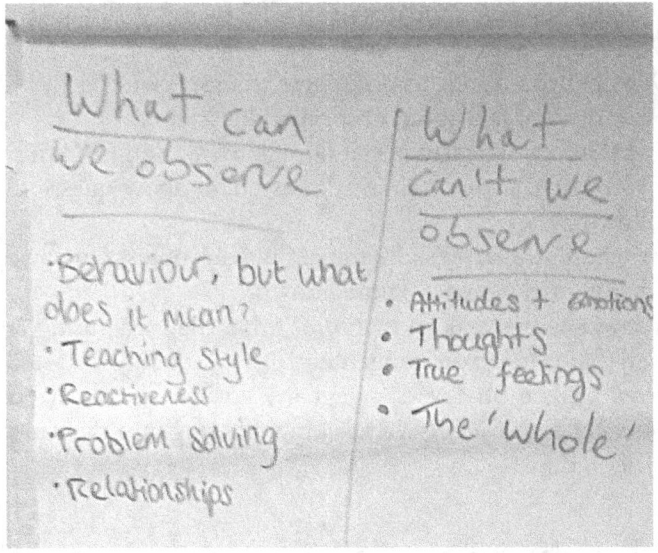

Figure 8.3 Students' suggestions on what can/cannot be observed in an educational environment

2. Write a short learner biography using these prompts after the workshop and use it to inform what you would like to focus on during collaborative observation.
3. Share your reflection and your observation focus with your fellow observers (peer and tutors) in the pre-observation discussion.

Exercise 2: Role of observation in understanding learning and teaching

1. Reflect and discuss:
   - What do you understand by what it means to 'observe' something?
   - What does it mean to observe in the context of a classroom or lecture theatre for example?
   - Can you make a list of what you *can* and *can't* observe in an educational environment?

Exercise 3: Practice-based observing

1. You are now going to watch a short video clip of a learning and teaching scenario in your subject area. Imagine you were a student in the classroom and make notes of what you notice during the video.

2. Now share your notes and discuss the following:
   - What information have you noted?
   - Why did you decide to note these things?
   - How did you feel about observing the session?
   - What have you learnt about doing observation from this exercise?
3. After you shared your notes and discussed the above questions, consider the following:
   - Are there similarities/differences in your notes? Do you agree with what your classmate(s) noted down?
   - Can observers make a record of what they see during an observation that is free from judgement?
   - How might observers safeguard against their current conceptions/biases of 'effective teaching' filtering into their record of the observation?

Informing students about CoCO and their role as student observers

As part of the CoCO project, student observers had specific roles and responsibilities which we discussed with them and their lecturers prior to the start of the project. We found that it was very critical to make it clear to student observers what they were expected to do and what they were NOT going to do as part of the collaborative observation. When implementing CoCO, you might want to use the criteria we developed (listed below) or you might want to create the criteria for student observers' role based on what you plan to achieve. Nevertheless, the role and responsibilities of student observers must reflect the underpinning ethos of student and staff collaboratively learning about learning and teaching as co-investigators.

1. What you WILL be doing as a student observer:
   - Writing a reflective account of your experience as a learner
   - Participating in a pre-observation discussion with your peer(s) and lecturers where you:
     - Share your learning experience
     - Discuss the focus for the observations
     - Arrange who will be observing what during the session[3]
   - Co-observing two of your classes and make notes
   - Reflecting on what you have observed with each other
   - Discussing your observation and reflection with your lecturers
   - Writing a reflective account of your observation and learning

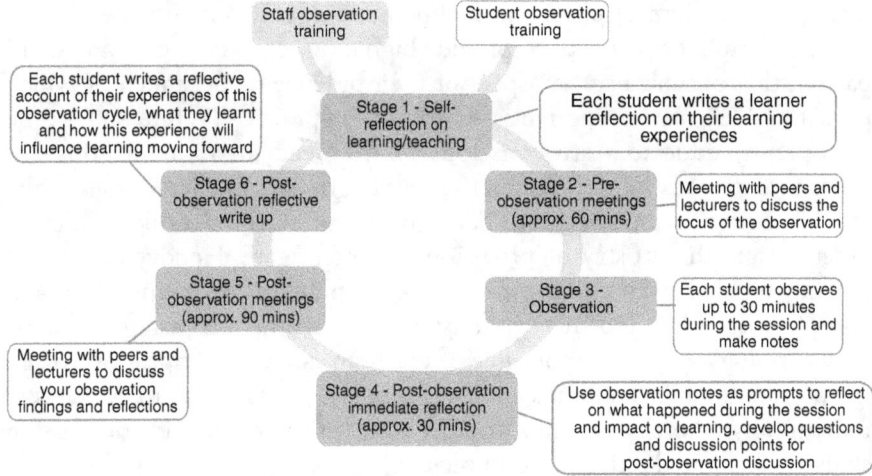

Figure 8.4 CoCO annotated with student observer activities

2. What you WON'T be doing as a student observer:
   - Planning or preparing resources for the class
   - Evaluating or assessing the class/your peers on their learning
   - Evaluating or assessing your lecturer on their teaching
   - Focusing your attention solely on the lecturer or the 'teaching'
   - Using the discussions/reflections as an opportunity to make judgements about the teaching/lecturer
   - Using this as a means of gathering student feedback on your course in general

We also found it was imperative to outline the tasks for each stage of CoCO clearly to student observers. We developed an annotated version of the CoCO model for student observers (Figure 8.4), which we used during the workshops to explain the tasks and what were expected of them. This provided clarity to student observers from the beginning. This annotated version of CoCO was also used as a helpful reminder to student observers of their role and tasks throughout the two years of our project.

Appendix 8.2: An illustrative case study experience – therapeutic radiography

Nick White and Vanessa Cui

Therapeutic radiography requires the practitioner to discharge technical skill that sits squarely within a scientific paradigm that ordinarily constitutes 'hard' science (namely physics and human biology). Contiguous with this, the radiographer also needs to provide high levels of patient care and compassion that occupy a softer aspect of their practice scope, much of which is tacit and learnt via experiential reflection-on-practice (White 2003). The radiography educators are conscious of the need to overcome this dissonance between the two competing paradigms of practice – that is, the conflict between technical-rationality of the medico-scientific model of practice, and the artistry of provision of patient care. Hendry (2019) has recently highlighted that there are competing practice requirements in radiography education and there is tension between the increasing emphasis on technology and the importance of teaching care and compassion within the curriculum. This requires a reassessment of pedagogical approaches in radiography whereby students are able to enact their care and compassion skills via facilitated reflection-on-practice.

Too often students compartmentalise their learning into 'university' and 'practice' and inadvertently locate the 'science' into university and the 'artistry' into practice-based learning, whereas in practice a more equitable approach is seen, with qualified staff discharging both aspects of professional knowledge routinely whilst undertaking their clinical duties. The collaborative observation provides an initial opportunity to review the current approaches to teaching and learning and to explore whether students are truly 'practice-focussed' and ultimately 'practice-ready' as they navigate towards qualification. In particular, the team was initially interested to explore whether university-situated learning was perceived as being practice-focussed, relevant and in fact useful from students via their perspective.

Cycle 1

In the first cycle of collaborative observation the team was keen to reflect the varied ways in which teaching and learning takes place within their curriculum. Training of health professionals more generally lends itself to strategies which allow a focus on knowledge and skills associated with a defined role. To this end the drive to establish the students' developing sense of their professional identity specifically as *therapeutic radiographer* was paramount. In particular, the team sought to consider the relevance of teaching that is applied to clinical practice and how this articulates with the students' own responsibilities as a professional.

The first cycle was therefore derived from these contextual considerations, and the focus was decided by the tutors, namely to gauge some measure of how effective they were at providing information to students which showed alignment of theory to clinical practice. The observations included two taught sessions with a different tutor in each. These were a practical anatomy training session using a workshop/work station design with the tutor acting as instructor.

The second learning and teaching activity involved small group tutorial within a virtual radiotherapy environment, which was student-led discussion activity with the tutor supporting students as they worked through preparatory tasks relating to clinical practice. For both, the aim was to use the cycle of collaborative observation to gauge the effectiveness of moving away from passive relaying of information to that of active learning. Most importantly, the observation cycle provided a legitimate sense of whether the tutors were actually 'getting it right' and to reflect on their current practice – that is, as educators are they making assumptions about their teaching and learning simply as it is viewed through a narrow perspective as teachers or do students' views provide a differing narrative to the teachers' (Brookfield 1995). In addition, the use of two tutors (one acting as teacher and one as observer) also provided a perspective to reframe their own practice.

The collaborative observation procedure was discharged as per the project process outlined – the students and tutors each holding their own reflective discussion, with the tutors subsequently convening a debrief meeting between themselves. The whole group then came together to reflect and discuss on the observations made within the context of the previously agreed focus and aims.

The tutors' meeting elucidated outcomes that validated their clinically-facing pedagogical approach. This included observations of teaching practices that were patient-focussed and problem-based. Interestingly, and rather unexpectedly, post-observation dialogue included reflection on the use of informal 'pause and check' approaches to ensure tutors were gauging understanding and as way-markers as to the level of understanding gained in the sessions. Both tutors described 'knowing' their students (with respect to gauging knowledge and understanding) and that the reception of the session was relaxed and delivered with humour. It is interesting that this effective trait is possibly a reflection of their small-group teaching, although this may be usefully to be applied nationally given that similar cohort sizes are seen at other universities within similar programmes of study.

As part of the post-observation reflective meeting (tutor–tutor), there was useful dialogue which they felt was helped validate their approaches to teaching and learning. In particular, the use of observation was done in the true spirit of the collaborative observation model in the sense that non-judgmental dialogue helped analysis of what was taking place in teaching sessions and to identify areas of effective practice. Figure 8.5 provides an example of the observation notes recorded by one of the academic tutors.

Session 1 small group work (2 students) 9.00-10.00AM

Student lead presentation preparation - focused practical session in preparation for assessment.

Hands on session - although student lead Mark was particularly careful to establish the level of progress/understanding of the students

Discussion amongst student regarding their preparation of the presentation. Mark was keen to constantly return the students to their clinical work.

Throughout the session students reflected on their clinical experiences and tried to relate the image assessment to real world practice experience

Although the session was not designed to address student presentation skills per se Mark was able to offer reassurance to the participating students regarding the content of their work and how to produce a 'coherent flow'

Some highly technical information was covered - both relating to the teaching aid VERT and clinical practice such as radiotherapy treatment techniques etc.

Clear evidence of 'ground rules' being used- Mark permitted the students to participate fully with tactful termination of discussion with students who were 'taking over' the session. Similarly polite and encouraging questioning of students who were less involved

In terms of the success of the session I would say students found this extremely useful and would have gained greater confidence. A real strength of the design of the session is a constant focus on clinical practice throughout- I gained a sense students were not just 'at university in a classroom' learning but were reflecting on practice- this was greatly helped that the session was delivered within an immersive environment for practice.

Peer support was also evidence-for example during a discussion surrounding treatment dose and side effects expected from radiotherapy treatment. I noted peer teaching between the more able students and a colleague struggling with the practical use of the VERT system- this was supportive and helpful. Mark was careful to informally moderate peer support and to disallow overly dominant peer contributions.

A successful session but as with our other areas of delivery Mark was fortunate by virtue of the sense that this is a small group of students for whom close personal supervision of their skills acquisition and learning progress can be made. It's really clear from the interaction of Mark and the students that he 'knows' the personality and needs of each students- this is evidenced through reflection of their placement experience and previous classroom sessions. There was a relaxed and reassuring atmosphere throughout including plenty of humour to keep the students engaged.

Figure 8.5 Radiotherapy CoCO Cycle 1 tutor observation notes excerpt

A significant factor was the use of clearly identified scope and focus for the process, and both tutors felt that pre-observation discussion and agreed negotiated aims lead to clarity in respect of discharging the observation process and subsequent debrief. Without this it was felt that the observer would become overwhelmed with the often-complex and 'messy' dynamic of classroom learning. The focus for Cycle 1 (assessment of theory-to-practice teaching) was discussed and debated; however, if the observations had been done 'blind', the observer may have adopted the more judgmental stance of scoping and assessing teaching sessions and tutor 'competence', without recourse to consideration of the wider context within which that teaching take place. In this respect the collaboration model works effectively

Collaborative observation between students and staff as a catalyst 189

for those programmes of study in which students working towards a professional qualification (such as therapeutic radiography), and where the learning journey also includes development of professional identity and values.

In tandem with this, students also provided their valuable insights as collaborative observers of teaching and learning. Their reflections tended to focus on aspects related to group dynamics and the manner in which learning takes place whilst working alongside their student peers. Figure 8.6 captures the observation notes of one of the student observers in the first cycle.

The VERT session was extremely interesting to observe as it is a very non-traditional lecture. We were in groups of 4 which we were able to book on the Moodle website to allocate our own timed sessions and also who we will be in the sessions with. This worked extremely well as we were able to tactically choose who we want to work with based on who we would be comfortable with, who's strengths we may learn off of and also see each other's ideas that makes us think outside the box to make our presentations more interesting. Within the hour session we had 15 minutes each to work independently but voice our ideas if we wished to, due to the presentation being part of our final module assessment the lecturer was not able to share knowledge based on content, however he was extremely insightful on how to make the most of the VERT technology. The lecturer would also challenge students to make hints and guide as much as he could; for example by asking what we see while on our clinical placements and to bring that routine and knowledge in to our academic studies as part of our presentation. The lecturer also gave hand-outs of a breakdown of the marking criteria providing further support on what sort of things we should be including in our presentation but also what we should be thinking about when planning a treatment which we will be required to do in our profession. Some students were clearly more confident in their ideas and contextualising their knowledge, however those who were not so confident the lecturer could recognise and would accommodate for this by working at a slower pace and breaking down ideas into 'bite-sized' pieces. Again, the session as a whole was very relaxed and infomal with jokes and laughter throughout, relieving stress of the upcoming assessment but had a good balance of the importance of the work.

The student observer process so far has been extremely insightful and made me think in more depth why lecturers do things in the techniques they do. It has made me understand that one technique is not suitable for all aspects of my course; for example being taught anatomy purely through powerpoints and books would be extremely difficult to absorb and would not put the knowledge in to context however the human models and practical tasks gave a more natural way of learning. Observing my peers has also made me appreciate the different ways students learn and how group work can benefit education in the sense that a student may understand a task better if a peer explains it to them rather than a lecturer. I am looking forward to see how the second academic year differs in the way lecturers may present a lecture or how students may obtain information; I believe dynamics may change due to second year being more in depth and a step-up from the first academic year as we are now in full swing of university.

Figure 8.6 Radiotherapy CoCO Cycle 1 student observer reflection excerpt

In particular, one student observer described how she made judgments regarding the variance amongst the student group with regards to their willingness to participate and the attendant differing levels of engagement. Reflections also identified the perceived importance of social interaction between the students whilst working on allocated learning tasks – and students commented that this was an important aspect of their own learning. This is interesting as this stance is supported in work by Bleiker et al. (2011), who identify the importance of the use of shared problem-solving tasks as a pedagogical tool within radiography programmes. This is argued to be more relevant to clinical situations that students will go on to experience upon qualification and better prepares them for the 'complexity of the psychology of patient–practitioner interaction'. Beck (2008) argues that fundamentally all radiography students are training in an area of practice that might be described as a 'people profession' and identifies the need to foreground the development of interpersonal skills within all aspect of teaching and learning, alongside the need for effective professional socialisation.

Cycle 2

The second cycle of collaborative observation took place following the transition of student co-researchers into their second year of study. This was a helpful aspect of the overall project design as it permitted the inclusion of dialogue with students who had cemented their approaches to their own learning, and who had developed a broader range of clinical experiences to form a developing perspective in their role as an emergent radiographer practitioner. Arguably this second cycle afforded to opportunity to interrogate pedagogies associated with their more 'expert' perspective of the field of radiotherapy.

The team's explorative stance differed in this second cycle in that the overarching focus of the cycle was decided upon by the students themselves. In discussion, student researchers agreed a focus looking at the impact of group dynamics and the social interaction amongst members of their peer group. This was made since they previously had felt they had not previously worked as effectively with their peers as they had liked. They were interested to see the varying ways in which students interacted with the tutor and the effect of these relationships had on their own learning. The student's initial pre-observation discussion indicates their interest in discovering less about how the teaching was to be delivered (or its effectiveness), but rather students were more interested in how their own learning takes place amongst the learning going on around them.

With this as the contextual framework two further sessions were undertaken that included the students acting as observers together with an additional tutor performing their own independent observation. In this cycle it was felt that the observations should take place in teaching sessions employing differing formats to those employed during Cycle 1 in order to reflect the range and variety of methods we engage with within our curriculum. Observations were situated firstly in a more traditional lecture-room setting (delivered to a small group of about 20 students) that addressed delivery of aspects of human anatomy and physiology. The second round of observations took place within a smaller workshop-style session which was a tutor-led discussion group. Observations proceeded as per Cycle 1 with students then meeting for peer-to-peer reflective dialogue, with the tutors undertaking a similar dialogue between themselves. Finally, a summary discussion was held with all members present.

Students' reflective writing from the initial lecture session provided some intriguing data. This tended to focus on differing level of participation (i.e. via vocalisation through questioning and answering) as their perceived measure of the effectiveness of learning taking place. One student was critical of her colleagues' reticence to vocalise answers during class discussion and suggested that this 'prohibits ability to learn or remember information'. The student also tried to situate this within the social dynamic of the cohort and attempted to explore the impact of friendship groups, suggesting that teachers should be mindful of these aspects since 'a happy friendly environment contributes to learning dramatically'. Arguably, these perspectives are lost through more traditional established forms of observation or teaching evaluation. More rigid judgements of teaching assessment through observation are likely to omit such nuanced perspectives. As described above, there are aspects of teaching and learning which articulate with successful preparation for practice, and social interaction is an important facet of this. Certainly, this finding is of use when considering how new students are inducted into higher education and emphasises the importance of aims such as establishing student identity and instilling a sense of belonging amongst students (Society and College of Radiographers 2009). This is useful within the context of recent work to improve the student experience and reduce attrition from radiography programmes though reflective enquiry into the pedagogies employed (Nightingale et al. 2019).

Discussion with the students during the debrief meeting furthered the tutors' understanding of what was taking place. Students explained that they had a sense of how they interpreted that the cohort's friendship groups were 'mapped' to the teaching space and that there was a sense of each student trying to associate with a 'student like me'. This is something the tutors were not aware of. Students described that they felt there was a lack of cohesion amongst their group which stemmed from students associating more readily with their own ethnic and social groups, and/or academic ability, and this was felt more acutely given the small cohort size. What also became apparent was that one of student observers used the opportunity to be afforded time and space to critically reflect on teaching and learning within this collaborative project enabled a deeper period of self-analysis. In her reflections and in post-observation dialogue, she clearly attempted to identify her own approach and style to learning within the context of the differing styles seen amongst her peer group. Whilst not a specific aim of the project aim per se, a consequence of her involvement for this student was that her self-reflections resulted in some considered reflective analysis of her own learning (such as her favoured use of self-directed independent approach to learning).

Within the second cycle students were also eager to deliver feedback with regards their practical lived experience as observers and their emerging roles as co-researchers. In particular, students explored the process of acting as an observer whilst trying to engage with the planned teaching and learning activities. Students described that at times they struggled to manage both the observation (including some note-taking) alongside understanding the taught materials. This was apparent to both tutors who were conscious of the students attempting to identify what was taking place within the teaching space. One student described that whilst this was frustrating (with respect to her own learning) that she was prepared for this in view of the previously agreed focus of this cycle of observation. However, her fellow observer expressed some concerns regarding a potential negative impact on his own learning due to distraction within managing the dual role of observer and learner (and he consequently sought additional tutorial support). Post-observation dialogue between student observers and tutors led to some further suggestions for process development. This included the proposal of purposefully identifying the type and suitability of teaching sessions only once the cycle aims had been clearly defined and documented. This might better ensure the observation was more easily facilitated and could be readily analysed with respect to the pre-selected observation focus.

General reflections on the use of collaborative co-observation by tutors

The tutors approached this new approach with some trepidation as historically their experiences of teaching observations had been formalised and judgemental as part of more rigid appraisal schema. Identification of student partners as co-researchers was made via an open invitation to therapeutic radiography cohort; however, the selection of students to eventually act as observers ideally requires individuals committed to their role and who are tied in to the overarching philosophy of the process (i.e. a non-judgmental and developmental ethos). To this end, the tutors were grateful for some involvement in their recruitment and therefore suggest a strategy of careful participant selection and avoid ad hoc use of volunteers whose motivation to participate is uncertain. Additionally, it was clear that training of all involved in the process of collaborative observation is key to its success – the team's first steps into the process went relatively smoothly as they had been provided with a procedural and practical model for guidance.

The team was grateful for the opportunity to provide data that extended beyond the provision of written reports, both students and staff being cautious of creating additional work within an already congested curriculum. Multiple practical data generation methods were used including audio-recorded discussion content, observations captured via photo journalling and handwritten notes, reflective diaries and website blogs. As a whole, the team's experience corroborates recent work (O'Leary and Savage 2020), which identifies the benefit of control of peer observation within the core domains of choice of observer, focus of observation, form and method of feedback, data flow and consideration of the improvement of practice.

The tutors have benefitted enormously from this new approach to teaching observation. In particular, the collegiate approach using negotiated aims has enabled helpful and focussed evaluation of approaches to aspects of teaching and learning within their programme. The students who have now graduated and secured employment as practitioner therapeutic radiographers have been grateful for their involvement with this project work, and have benefited from gaining some emergent experience as novice researchers and investigators of learning and teaching. They also gained some useful transferable skills applicable to their new clinical roles such as collaborative working and focused reflective practice.

Notes

1 The research adhered to the British Educational Research Association (BERA) ethical guidelines for educational research (BERA 2011) and gained ethical approval through the ethics committee at the university where the research team was based.
2 See Appendix 8.1.

3 In our project, we decided with students and staff that each student observer would observe up to 30 minutes in a given session. We were mindful that the observation should not interrupt student learning on their course and any more than 30 minutes might distract them from learning in their class. The students made prior arrangements with their lecturers to ensure the content of the session they planned to observe was covered sufficiently during their pre-observation discussion and the students were supported to revisit the content in the post-observation discussion.

References

Baxter, L. A. and Montgomery, B. M., 1996. *Relating: Dialogues and Dialectics*. New York NY: Guilford.

Beck, J., 2008. Those who can, teach. *Synergy*, April, 4–6.

Bleiker, J., Knapp, K.M. and Frampton, I., 2011. Teaching patient care to students: A blended learning approach in radiography education. *Radiography* 17, 235–240.

Bokeno, R., 2009. Genus of learning relationships: Mentoring and coaching as communicative interaction. *Development and Learning in Organizations* 23(1), 5–8.

Bowden, J. and Marton, F., 2004. *The University of Learning: Beyond Quality and Competence*. London: Routledge.

British Education Research Associate, 2011. *Ethical Guidelines for Educational Research*. Birmingham: British Education Research Associate. https://www.bera.ac.uk/wp-content/uploads/2014/02/BERA-Ethical-Guidelines-2011.pdf?noredirect=1. Accessed 10.2018.

Brookfield, S. D., 1995. *Becoming a Critically Reflective Teacher*. San Francisco CA: Jossey-Bass.

Canning, J., 2019. The UK Teaching Excellence Framework (TEF) as an illustration of Baudrillard's hyperreality. *Discourse: Studies in the Cultural Politics of Education* 40(3), 319–330.

Cook-Sather, A., Bovill, C. and Felten. P., 2014. *Engaging Students as Partners in Learning and Teaching: A Guide for Faculty*. San Francisco CA: Jossey-Bass.

Cui, V. 2014. *The 'wicked' problem of employability development in HE degree programmes: experiences, understandings and perceptions of lecturers and students*. unpublished PhD Thesis, Liverpool John Moores University: Liverpool.

Cui, V., French, A. and O'Leary, M., 2019. A missed opportunity? How the UK's teaching excellence framework fails to capture the voice of university staff. *Studies in Higher Education*. https://doi.org/10.1080/03075079.2019.1704721.

Department for Business, Innovation and Skills, 2015. *Fulfilling Our Potential: Teaching Excellence, Social Mobility and Student Choice*. London: HMSO.

Department for Business, Innovation and Skills, 2016. *Success as a Knowledge Economy: Teaching Excellence, social mobility and student choice*. Higher Education White Paper.

Duck, S., 1999. *Relating to Others 2e*. Buckingham: Open University Press.

Fielding, M., 2004. "New Wave" student voice and the renewal of civic society. *London Review of Education* 2(3), 197–217.

Gunn, A., 2018. Metrics and methodologies for measuring teaching quality in higher education: Developing the Teaching Excellence Framework (TEF). *Educational Review* 70(2), 129–148.

Healey, M., Flint, A. and Harrington, K., 2014. *Students as partners in learning and teaching in higher education*. York: Higher Education Academy.

Healey, M. and Jenkins, A., 2009. *Developing Undergraduate Research and Inquiry*. York: Higher Education Academy.

Hendry, G. and Oliver, G., 2012. Seeing is believing: the benefits of peer observation. *Higher Education Funding Council For England*. 2017. National Student Survey. Last updated online 21st December 2017. Available at: http://www.hefce.ac.uk/lt/nss/. Accessed 29.01.2018.

Hendry, J., 2019. Promoting Compassionate Care in Radiography – What Might be Suitable Pedagogy? A discussion paper. *Radiography*, https://doi.org/10.1016/j.radi.2019.01.005.

Kreber, C., 2002. Teaching excellence, teaching expertise, and the scholarship of teaching. *Innovative Higher Education* 27, 5–23.

Lave, J., 1988. *Cognition in Practice: Mind, Mathematics and Culture in Everyday Life*. Cambridge: Cambridge University Press.

Lave, J., 1993. The Practice of Learning. In S. Chaiklin and J. Lave, (eds.) *Understanding Practice*. Cambridge: Cambridge University Press, 3–32.

Loughran, J., 2019. Pedagogical reasoning: The foundation of the professional knowledge of teaching. *Teachers and Teaching* 25(5), 523–535.

Lundgren, S. M., Lunden, M. and Andersson, B.T., 2015. Radiography – How do students understand the concept of radiography? *Radiography* 21, 68–73.

Mason, J., 2002. *Researching Your Own Practice: The Discipline of Noticing*. London: Routledge.

Neumann, R., 2001. Disciplinary differences and university teaching. *Studies in Higher Education* 26, 135–146.

Nightingale, J., McNamara, J. and Posnett, J., 2019. Challenges in recruitment and retention: Securing the therapeutic radiography workforce of the future. *Radiography* 25, 1–3.

O'Leary, M., and Brooks, V., 2014. Raising the stakes: Classroom observation in further education sector in England. *Professional Development in Education* 40(4), 530–545.

O'Leary, M., Cui, V. and French, A., 2019. *Understanding, recognising and rewarding teaching quality in higher education: An exploration of the impact and implications of the teaching excellence framework.* University and Colleges Union. https://www.ucu.org.uk/media/10092/Impact-of-TEF-report-Feb-2019/pdf/ImpactofTEFreportFEb2019.

O'Leary, M. and Savage, S., 2020. Breathing new life into the observation of teaching and learning in higher education: Moving from the performative to the informative. *Professional Development in Education* 46(1), 145–159.

O'Leary, M. and Wood, P., 2017. Performance over professional learning and the complexity puzzle: Lesson observation in England's further education sector. *Professional Development in Education* 43(4), 573–591.

Rogers, C., 2002. The interpersonal relationship in the facilitation of learning. In R. Harrison, F. Reeve, A. Hanson and C. Julia, (eds.) *Perspectives on Learning*. London: RoutledgeFalmer, 25–39.

Sachs, J. and Parsell, M., (eds.) 2014. *Peer Review of Learning and Teaching in Higher Education – International Perspectives*. London New York: Springer Dordrecht Heidelberg.

Schmidt, R. W., 1990. The role of consciousness in second language learning. *Applied Linguistics* 11, 129–58.

Schmidt, R. W., 1993. Awareness and second language acquisition. *Annual Review of Applied Linguistics* 13, 206–26.

Shephard, K., Harland, T., Stein, S. and Tidswell, T., 2010. Preparing an application for a higher-education teaching-excellence award: Whose foot fits Cinderella's shoe? *Journal of Higher Education Policy and Management* 33(1), 47–56.

Shulman, L.S., 1987. Knowledge and teaching: Foundations of the new reform. *Harvard Educational Review* 57, 1–22.

Skelton, A., 2004. Understanding teaching excellence in higher education: A critical evaluation of the national teaching fellowships scheme. *Studies in Higher Education* 29(4), 451–468.

Society and College of Radiographers, 2009. *Improving Student Retention: Guidelines and Good Practice*. London: ScoR.

Su, F. and Wood, M., 2012. What makes a good university lecturer? Students' perceptions of teaching excellence. *Journal of Applied Research in Higher Education* 4(2), 142–155.

Tomlinson, M., 2017. Student perceptions of themselves as 'consumers' of higher education. *British Journal of Sociology of Education* 38(4), 450–467.

Truscott, J., 1998. Noticing in second language acquisition: a critical review. *Second Language Research* 14(2), 103–135.

Tubbs, N., 2005. *Philosophy of the Teacher*. Oxford: Blackwell.

Vivian, D., James, A. S., Salamons, D., Hazel, Z., Felton, J. and Whittaker, S., 2019. *Evaluation of Provider-Level TEF 2016–17 (Year 2): Measuring the Initial Impact of the TEF on the Higher Education Landscape Research Report*. London: Department for Education. https://www.gov.uk/government/publications/evaluation-of-provider-level-tef-2016-to-2017-year-2. Accessed 16.12.2022.

Werder, C. and Otis, M., (eds.) 2010. *Engaging Student Voices in the Study of Teaching and Learning*. Sterling, VA: Stylus.

White, N., 2003. *Reflective Practice in Radiotherapy Radiography. Synergy*, June.

Wood, P., 2017. From teaching excellence to emergent pedagogies: A complex process. In Amanda French and Matt O'Leary (eds.) *Teaching Excellence in Higher Education*. Bingley: Emerald Publishing Limited, 39–74.

9 Unseen observation

An alternative approach to thinking about academics' professional learning*

Introduction

The COVID-19 pandemic has left an indelible mark on the educational landscape that is likely to be felt for years to come. When governments across the world announced national lockdowns in March 2020, educational institutions were forced to prepare for a rapid transition from face-to-face teaching to online provision. Variations in resources, support systems and the digital literacy of teachers and students, among other factors, all played a part in determining these alternative online teaching and learning experiences. With the 'new normal' quickly established, it was not long before attention was turned to how best to monitor and assure that the quality and standards of teaching and learning in these new online spaces was being maintained (e.g. Huber and Helm 2020). There was also the issue of how best to support teachers to adapt and maximise the effectiveness of their practice in this new environment, especially given that the overwhelming majority had limited experience of teaching and learning in online spaces (e.g. Darling-Hammond and Hyler 2020). Inevitably, this gave rise to important questions such as: How could/should quality assurance and quality improvement be undertaken remotely in these new online spaces? Could and/or should established approaches from face-to-face practice be

---

* This chapter is based on an article that originally appeared in the journal *Professional Development in Education* and was published open access; O'Leary, M. (2022). Rethinking teachers' professional learning through unseen observation, *Professional Development in Education*, DOI: 10.1080/19415257.2022.2125551.

DOI: 10.4324/9780429341908-9

transferred to the online environment? Or would these new ways of working require alternative approaches?

As we have discussed in Chapter 5, classroom observation has traditionally been the dominant method used for monitoring, assessing and supporting the quality of teaching and the development of teachers' pedagogic practice across educational sectors and contexts. As O'Leary (2020, p. xii) has commented, classroom observation has had a long-standing role in the preparation, assessment and professional learning of teachers in the UK for many years:

> Whether it is in the context of an initial teacher education (ITE) course for new/student teachers or lecturers, a collaborative professional learning project for experienced educators, appraisal or an external inspection, classroom observation is a ubiquitous mechanism that permeates the working lives of all educators from the beginning to the end of their careers.

The application and purpose of classroom observation as a mechanism in the UK education system has been principally concerned with attempting to measure teacher performance for accountability and benchmarking purposes. This has led to the hegemony of observation as a performative tool of managerialist systems. While acknowledging the formative focus of peer-based approaches to classroom observation and the growth in the use of models such as lesson study in recent years (e.g. Wood 2017), these remain on the fringes compared to assessment-based models. Another consequence of the normalisation of this performative focus of observation is how it has constrained its value as a tool for developing teachers' learning and their wider understanding of their pedagogic thinking and decision-making. It is precisely the development of these skills to which unseen observation has the potential to make a valuable contribution in reimagining the way in which observation can be used to support teachers' professional learning, as we argue in this chapter.

The migration to online delivery as a result of lockdown restrictions imposed during the 2020/21 COVID-19 pandemic meant that educational institutions were no longer able to rely on in-person classroom observation to undertake their quality assurance and quality improvement work. Instead, they had to think of alternatives to adapt to this new working environment. In the context of the UK, this presented both challenges and opportunities for colleges' and schools' internal quality work, as it also did for initial teacher education (ITE) providers' support and assessment of their student teachers' practice while on teaching placements. During the pandemic, responses varied widely across different institutions and providers. Some decided to put such work on hold, arguing that the transition to online teaching and learning had already resulted in significant workload challenges for their teaching staff. Others sought to transfer established systems of observation to the virtual environment, with 'virtual drop-ins', 'virtual learning walks' and 'virtual reviews' replacing traditional in-person observations. Yet, at the same time, there were those institutions that chose to use the hiatus created by the pandemic as an opportunity to rethink and explore alternative approaches to using observation to undertake this work. It is against the backdrop of the pandemic and these developments that one such alternative approach to traditional observations and the focus of this chapter emerged: unseen observation.

Contextualising unseen observation as a concept and a model of observation

Unseen observation is not a new concept; rather, it is a model that dates back to the 1980s, originating in language teacher education (Rinvolucri 1988). Relatively unknown and having always been on the periphery of classroom observation approaches, it is only in recent years that there has been renewed interest in its use, and the possibilities which it may offer (e.g. Sherrington and Caviglioli 2020). Originally designed for face-to-face interactions, unseen observation experienced a resurgence of interest during the pandemic, which resulted in its use being extended to remote, virtual environments such as those commonly used for online teaching (O'Leary 2021). This is indicative of its flexibility as a model and how it can be applied to differing forms of interaction, as well as a range of different teaching and learning contexts.

While there are some similarities between the stages of the unseen observation cycle (see Figure 9.1) and conventional models of peer observation, as discussed below, there are equally unique aspects that distinguish it significantly from other models. The most noticeable difference between unseen observation and other models is that it does not involve the observation of a taught lesson by a third party. In that sense, the term *observation* may seem like a contradiction. The removal of the physical or virtual presence of a third-party observer confronts the long-standing issue of the Hawthorne effect associated with observation, arguably allowing teachers to behave more naturally and authentically. This is particularly pertinent when considering how performance-management-driven models of observation can lead to increased levels of inauthenticity in teachers' practice, especially when observation is used as a form of high-stakes assessment (Gitomer et al. 2014). Instead of an observer visiting the class to carry out a 'live observation', unseen observation can be defined as a model of observation that relies on the teacher engaging in a process of self-observation and self-analysis, as well as collaborative reflection and dialogue with their 'collaborator', before and after the taught lesson.

The concept of unseen observation is partly inspired by the fields of therapy and counselling inasmuch as it is standard practice for the therapist or counsellor to listen to a person's account of real-life events/experiences *after* they have occurred, in contrast to witnessing them in real time (e.g. White and Epston 1990). The 'collaborator' is thus dependent on the unobserved teacher's own self-observation and reflections on their teaching as a key stimulus for the post-observation dialogue. Note the use here of the term 'collaborator' rather than observer, a term that is also used in narrative therapy where the therapist is considered as a collaborator. This is an important and deliberate distinction as it reconceptualises and reconfigures the relationship and the roles of the protagonists at the centre of the observation process. In unseen observation, the collaborator takes on the twofold role of what Whitmore (2002) refers to as a 'detached awareness raiser' and a 'coach', which, as we have discussed in previous chapters with the models of CoPO and CoCO, means that rather than making evaluative judgements on the teacher's practice, the collaborator's role is to encourage the teacher to reflect critically on their practice, to delve more deeply into their thinking and decision-making by asking probing questions that encourage them to engage reflexively in their professional learning. The collaborator should be an experienced practitioner who has experience in supporting teachers' professional learning and an understanding of coaching skills. Similarly, the term 'professional dialogue' is used rather than feedback as unseen observation is not an assessment-based model of observation and thus does not use assessment criteria as a shared frame of reference between teacher and collaborator.

Unseen observation places the control and accountability of the observation process in the hands of teachers, as it is built on the premise that they are the best people to decide their own professional needs and those of their students (e.g. Darling-Hammond 2017). It acknowledges the importance of the locus of understanding as something that is internal to the understander, which is a key principle of intersubjectivity discussed in the following section of this chapter. This does not detract from the development of a shared or collective understanding in any way. On the contrary, it recognises the importance of allowing space and time for the teacher

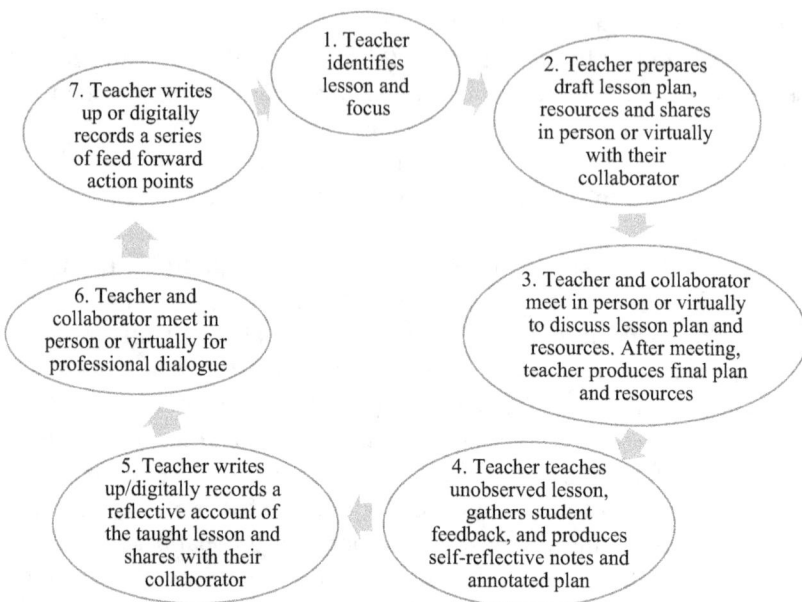

Figure 9.1 An overview of the 7 stages of the unseen observation cycle

to unravel their thinking and decision-making about their professional practice as a necessary stage in the process of shared meaning-making and understanding.

Unseen observation follows a seven-stage cycle (see Figure 9.1) that starts with the teacher identifying a lesson and particular area of practice that they wish to focus on for the duration of the cycle (Stage 1). Unlike many observation models, where the areas of focus are driven by internal or external policy agendas, the teacher is free to choose their own area of focus. The rationale is rooted in the belief that giving teachers the agency to choose their personalised focus not only emphasises their personal responsibility for taking charge of their continuous professional learning, but also invokes an ownership that is likely to be more authentic and sustainable. The only proviso they are given is that they must choose something that emanates from their daily classroom practice that they wish to explore and/or develop in depth with a view to it contributing to the overall improvement of the student learning experience. This typically tends to be an aspect of pedagogy or curriculum that has emerged from individual self-reflection and/or prior reviews of their professional practice by others. It also aligns to Timperley's (2011, p. 7) view that for teachers' professional learning to have meaningful impact, it 'must reference their learning to both themselves and their students'.

In Stage 2, the teacher prepares their lesson plan and resources, sharing them with their collaborator in advance of an in-person/virtual meeting (Stage 3). The pair discuss the rationale for the selected teaching approach(es), tasks and resources planned for the lesson, along with the anticipated impact on the students' learning. The Stage 3 conversation is also an opportunity for the two to develop a shared understanding of some of the contextual factors relating to the chosen lesson and students, as well as exploring more holistic issues about teaching and learning that reveal some of the underlying rationale that informs teachers' thinking and decision-making when preparing a lesson. Examples of typical topics that the two may explore include: how the lesson relates to what students have learnt previously; how the teacher adapts their practice to meet their students' needs; how the teacher intends to monitor students' understanding during the lesson; what the anticipated challenges of the lesson might be etc.

Stages 2 and 3 of the cycle highlight the importance given to the planning and preparation elements of teaching, with the depth of reflection, discussion and articulation of decision-making distinguishing unseen observation from many conventional models of observation, where much of the discussion centres on the post-observation stage. For many teachers, the opportunity to engage in thorough discussions about the thinking and preparation that goes into their planning of a lesson as part of the observation process is rare and largely limited to ITE courses they undertake at the beginning of their careers (Fernandez 2010). Yet the work involved in planning for teaching is an important part of the process and can reveal valuable insights into teachers' professional practice (e.g. Peter 2006). Unseen observation acknowledges this by incorporating a dedicated pre-lesson discussion as a fundamental element of the cycle. It provides a platform for individuals and institutions alike to prioritise and formally recognise the value of in-depth thinking and discussion about teaching and learning in terms of both planning and delivering a lesson. If the collaborator is to develop shared understanding and to make a meaningful contribution to the teacher's learning, then exploring the planning and preparation that has gone into the lesson and what that reveals about the teacher's professional practice and areas for development are essential parts of the process that need to be established as a starting point in the collaborative discussion. Leaving the substantive discussion until the post-observation stage, as is the case with most traditional models of observation, reduces the opportunities to build such shared understanding and, ultimately, makes it more difficult for those involved, as Soslau (2015) found in her research on the use of observation involving ITE tutors and their student teachers.

In Stage 4, the teacher delivers the unobserved lesson and is asked to produce a record of self-reflective notes, along with an annotated lesson plan. They are also encouraged to embed opportunities into the lesson for students to evaluate their learning experience when appropriate. Identifying the most opportune moments in the lesson to incorporate these student evaluations is something that can be discussed during the Stage 3 meeting. These sources of evidence are then used to inform the teacher's subsequent reflections (Stage 5) and professional dialogue with their collaborator (Stage 6). In Stage 5, the teacher writes up and/or digitally records a reflective account of the lesson, which they share with their collaborator prior to meeting. The teacher and collaborator then meet in person/virtually in Stage 6 for a post-lesson dialogue to discuss the lesson, during which they interrogate the assumptions upon which the plan was based and examine the sources of evidence, along with the teacher's perceptions of the lesson's effectiveness in achieving the anticipated outcomes.

In contrast to assessment-based models of observation, where interaction is largely determined by the observer, unseen observation places the locus of control in the hands of the teacher. It is their recounting of the lesson, both in terms of their predictive planning through the lesson plan and their decision-making beforehand, along with their reflective account of the actual taught lesson after the event, that acts as the driving force for professional dialogue between the teacher and their collaborator. Thus, the roles of both parties are transformed, with a greater emphasis on dialogic interaction that is more conducive to participatory sensemaking than the functional transmission of declarative judgements and statements that typifies evaluative approaches. Stage 7 concludes the unseen observation cycle with the teacher writing up or digitally recording a series of feed-forward action points that form the basis of their continuing development on their chosen area of focus. This final feed-forward stage requires the teacher to draw together the insights they have gained on their practice during the unseen observation cycle, with a view to identifying feed-forward action points that they plan to focus on further to improve their practice. For example, have they identified new skills or knowledge they would like to develop? Have they decided to change the way they are doing something? Have they identified any support needs and available resources to meet their changing needs?

Despite the fact that unseen observation has existed as a model of observation for several decades, it has always lacked a supporting theorisation to explain its underlying principles and values, and how it differs to conventional models of observation that are driven by the purposes of assessment.

The next section of this chapter draws on the concept of intersubjectivity to theorise unseen observation in the context of its value as a tool of professional learning.

Intersubjectivity, unseen observation and professional learning

Esterhazy et al. (2021) argue for the need to move beyond what they perceive as the narrow parameters of peer observation of teaching. In their research into teaching in higher education, they propose the alternative term 'collegial faculty development' (CFD) to encompass a more comprehensive and holistic conceptualisation of the range of practices that support teachers to improve the quality of their practice. One of the theoretical tools that they suggest has the potential to make a valuable contribution to our understanding of CFD is intersubjectivity:

> The sociocultural perspective offers the notion of intersubjectivity as a relevant analytical entrance in studying how faculty members learn from – and with – each other through CFD interactions. Intersubjectivity is central in sociocultural thinking (Cooper-White, 2014) and denotes a fundamental reciprocity in interaction. The most basic dyadic relation is two or more actors allowing access to one another's experiences, thereby opening a shared reality. This basic co-constructive notion of reality is deeply dialogic in nature, potentially providing valuable access to the more deeply rooted common feature in all CFD activities.
>
> (Esterhazy et al. 2021, p. 261)

The concept of intersubjectivity was originally developed by the German philosopher Edmund Husserl in the context of the psychology of communication and his wider work on phenomenology. Husserl used the term to refer to the interchange of thoughts and feelings between two people, as facilitated by empathy (Cooper-White 2014). Intersubjectivity can be considered the sharing of one person's experience or perception of reality with another, or, to paraphrase Deetz (1979), the transformation of a personal experience (subjectivity) into an interpersonal experience (intersubjectivity). Fundamental tenets of the interaction between the self and another is the mutual recognition of each other as unique but, at the same time, equal. Intersubjectivity is thus a state of being in which each person recognises and respects that they are social beings who exist as a being with others. Through a series of questions he poses, Deetz (1979, p. 7) captures some of the complex challenges of communication between the self and another that intersubjectivity seeks to tackle in the quest for developing a co-constructed, shared understanding:

> How do I as a communicant get into the other's mind or grasp the other's self so that I can know his/her experience? How do I know that my experience is understood? How can bridges be built between persons so that they understand more completely?

Intersubjectivity has often been used in the social sciences to express shared understanding and meaning-making between two or more people. In discussing Dewey's work on language and communication, Biesta (1995) refutes the idea of it simply involving the transactional transference of information from one person to another. As Merleau-Ponty (2010) notes, 'Language is an act of transcending. Thus, we cannot consider it to simply be a container of thought; we must see in it an instrument of conquest of self through contact with others' (p. 41) as 'language is a manifestation of human intersubjectivity' (p. 63). Biesta (1995) also stresses the importance of understanding intersubjectivity as a collaborative and dialogic process in which meaning is created *through* interaction. As De Jaegher et al. (2017, p. 492) state, 'intersubjectivity is characterised as participatory sensemaking: the embodied, interactive coordination of sensemaking'. This has important implications for teachers' professional learning in the context of observation approaches, especially in terms of how such work is conceptualised and operationalised to create the optimum conditions for meaningful learning to occur.

Firstly, it implies that for effective communication to occur between those involved in the observation process, it is fundamental that a shared understanding is established of whatever the chosen focus is of the professional learning activity between those involved, along with their respective frames of reference. Deetz (1979) argues that intersubjectivity is an a priori condition *for* effective collaborative communication rather than a condition derived *from* communication and must therefore be established as a starting point if meaningful change is to occur. Developing meaningful relationships and effective communication for intersubjective understanding does not occur overnight but over a sustained period of time during which reciprocal trust between those involved is afforded the space and time to develop. Episodic models of observation where observers visit lessons sporadically arguably militate against the development of such meaningful relationships, thus emphasising the importance of embedding intersubjectivity throughout the observation process as a way of being and doing. In her research into the interaction between student teachers and their teacher educators during the post-observation dialogue, Soslau (2015, p. 2) identified this shared understanding as an essential factor for these teacher educators to enable their student teachers to 'learn from their teaching experiences, develop the necessary skills to negotiate and contribute to professional discourse (Smith, 2005), and prepare for engagement in future communities of practice'. Although Soslau's research focused on student teachers, there are parallels to the relevance of the central role that intersubjectivity can play in shaping and coordinating the effectiveness of professional dialogue more widely in the context of observation. It emphasises not only the centrality of collaborative dialogue in sensemaking and shared understanding, but also the need to carefully consider the balance between pre- and post-observation interaction, along with transactional and interactional dialogue, a point which will be explored in more detail below. Furthermore, there are corresponding implications for the dynamics of dialogic interactions, particularly regarding issues of power and control in the context of the relationship between the 'observer' and 'observed'.

Secondly, acknowledging intersubjectivity as an important element of effective professional dialogue raises questions about the extent to which opportunities for collaborative, participatory meaning-making are curtailed in hierarchical, assessment-based models of observation where the observer occupies the principal role of assessor. There is a clear delineation of power and control between the observer and observed in such models which inevitably shapes the nature of the interaction between the two. Typically, the observer leads and often dominates the discussion and knowledge exchange, with the focus and scope of the dialogue largely dependent on what they choose to discuss (e.g. Tilstone 2012). In contrast, the principles and parameters of unseen observation, as discussed earlier, are purposefully designed to maximise the locus of control and ownership of the process for the (un)observed teacher, as it is their teaching that is prioritised as the focus of this professional learning activity. In acknowledging the importance of the locus of understanding as something that is internal to the understander, intersubjectivity in the context of professional learning thus provides a rationale for the need to challenge and reimagine normalised delineations of power and control such as those epitomised by hierarchical models of observation. Furthermore, conventional assessment-based models of observation are typically driven by the 'instrument' rather than the individual. In other words, the accompanying assessment criteria and evaluative outcome underpinning such models play a central role in shaping the focus of the observation as well as the interaction between the observer and the observed teacher. As others have argued, one of the shortcomings of such models is that they tend to adopt a reductionist approach to teaching and learning (e.g. Edgington 2016). An unintended consequence of such reductionist approaches is that they end up failing to address the issue of the teacher as an individual with their own beliefs, values and knowledge systems. Yet all these factors have an important contribution to make in developing a shared understanding of a teacher's professional identity and helping teachers reflect meaningfully on their practice, and as such need to be considered as part of the professional dialogue.

Thirdly, there is the implication that intersubjectivity is an inherently creative and spontaneous process, which makes it difficult to predict and plan for in advance, as these dialogic encounters are contingent on ever-evolving experiences and unique frames of reference. Thus, in the case of using observation as a vehicle for professional learning, it accentuates situated dialogue as the key driver for collaborative sensemaking but also acknowledges the flexible and dynamic nature of such dialogue. This calls into question the appropriateness of conventional assessment-based approaches to observation, for example, as such approaches are invariably underpinned by static criteria that are used as a central point of reference to frame the dialogue between the observer and observed. Arguably, such criteria impose a pre-determined filter or even distort the dialogue between interlocutors, especially given that the observer as assessor draws on these criteria as a key frame of reference when recording their assessment of the observed lesson. Besides, as assessment-based approaches to observation inevitably involve some kind of performance outcome, it could be argued that such conditions lead to the process becoming more 'high stakes' for the observed teacher, which in turn may have counterproductive consequences for the collaborative dialogue between the two. In other words, observations as high-stakes assessments can provoke a guardedness and a reluctance on the part of the observed teacher to lay bare their pedagogic thinking and practice and to engage in honest introspection, dialogue and authentic teacher learning.

Another consideration that is pertinent to optimising the conditions for intersubjectivity to flourish is the creation of trust and respect between those involved. Esterhazy et al. (2021, p. 262) argue that 'trust and respect are closely related to the idea that participants can develop intersubjectivity only when they recognize the relevance of each other's knowledge in their own context'. With regards to the relationship between the observer and the observed, this draws attention to the importance of ensuring that sufficient time and space are built into the observation process to allow participants to move beyond transactional exchanges driven by a performance and accountability agenda, and to focus more on engaging in shared thinking and participatory meaning-making. Building relationships of trust also requires a cultural shift in relinquishing control on the part of the observer to provide the teacher with a greater degree of professional autonomy. As discussed below, this is an underpinning principle of the model of unseen observation and its application in practice.

A final consideration regarding the value of intersubjectivity to our understanding of observation as a tool for teachers' professional learning relates to reflexivity. In his discussion of the American philosopher George Herbert Mead's work on intersubjectivity, Biesta (1998, p. 80) draws attention to Mead's claim that social interaction both precedes and produces reflective consciousness: 'the ability to make oneself the object of one's own attention – an ability which is commonly referred to as reflexivity or self-consciousness – has its origin in the social situation'. In other words, reflexivity is not an inherent characteristic or individual attribute but an effect that emerges because of our social interaction with others, thus implying that social encounters are a precondition for its development. In terms of the relevance of intersubjectivity to the role of reflexivity in observation approaches and to professional learning more widely, there are important considerations for how it can contribute to our understanding of the value of alternative approaches such as unseen observation, along with the implications for how we conceptualise and undertake reflexive practice. Given the central role that reflexivity plays in teachers' professional learning, this is certainly an aspect worthy of further exploration.

In their discussion of the overarching pedagogical principles that inform contemporary education, Thorburn and Stolz (2021, p. 13) argue for the need to improve and modify the way in which we record experiences with tools such as reflective journals. They suggest one way to do this would be to adopt 'a sharper concentration on questions and circumstances that naturally arise through happenings and encounters experienced in lessons'. Although Thorburn and Stolz focus on the experience of school students and their teachers, the principles are transferable to the professional learning of teachers. Just as 'students can come to reflect on their visible and bounded, sense-laden experiences that can yield shared understandings of basic truths from which each student can reflect on and analyse their particular experiences' (Thorburn and Stolz 2021), so too can teachers reflect on and analyse their professional practice through the lens of unseen observation. Working together with their collaborator, whose role it is to provoke discussion and to encourage the teacher to critically reflect on their pedagogic decision-making, teachers are afforded opportunities to interrogate their practice through a methodical, yet personalised approach.

Reflections on the benefits and challenges of unseen observation

Unseen observation shifts the traditional emphasis of assessment-based approaches to observation from a competence-verifying performance to a process of reflexive practice that prioritises deep, meaningful thinking about teaching and learning through collegial conversations and collective reflection. As the description of the cycle above reveals, this takes place through detailed conversations about the teacher's planning, their teaching and analysis of its impact and effectiveness. In removing the performance element traditionally associated with assessment-based models of observation, unseen observation enables practitioners to reconceptualise and reconfigure observation as an educational tool of inquiry to support their professional learning rather than simply to evaluate their performance. Recalibrating the locus of control between the 'observer' and the '(un)observed' is a fundamental factor in creating the conditions for a more equitable working relationship, reducing some of the counterproductive effects often associated with conventional models of observation (O'Leary 2020). Placing the teacher's thinking and decision-making at the centre of the process empowers them to explore and discuss wider aspects of their beliefs about teaching and learning in greater depth, instead of focusing on an isolated observed session. Notwithstanding these perceived advantages of unseen observation, it is important to acknowledge that reconceptualising and reconfiguring observation in such a way is not without its challenges.

Undoubtedly, a commonly identified limitation of unseen observation is the fact that the collaborator hears only one side of the story, as they are reliant on the teacher's self-observation and recollection of the lesson. For some education leaders, the lack of a third-party observation may seem too radical a change to make inasmuch as it relinquishes too much control to teachers and reduces the remit of those who would normally undertake observations as part of their QA role. This loss of control can be unsettling for those who are accustomed to using observation as a tool to evaluate and benchmark teacher performance. Of course, it is conceivable that what teachers say they do in an unseen lesson observation may not necessarily be an accurate reflection of what actually happens. The honesty and reliability of the teacher's introspection, therefore, becomes a linchpin of the potential success and effectiveness of unseen observation and the extent to which teachers are prepared to open themselves up and engage in such reflexivity. However, researchers such as Stolz (2020, p. 1091) have argued that a first-person led recollection of experiences can be 'bound by the same checks-and-balances, or judgements as anyone else when it comes to claims being made about notions of being and associated truth or truths'. This would suggest that honesty may not necessarily be the biggest challenge to the success and effectiveness of models like unseen observation, but rather the extent to which teachers' professional dispositions prepare them for engaging in reflexive practice, a challenge explored further below.

In contrast, the absence of an observer whose primary role is driven by a performance management agenda can arguably have a liberatory effect on some teachers. The removal of the surveillance and performance elements of traditional observations creates a safe space that can encourage teachers to experiment, take risks and be more creative in their teaching without the fear of being judged. As Timperley (2011, p. xviii) argues, 'active inquiry, learning and experimenting have to become teachers' core business of thinking as a professional'. As individual teachers are empowered to decide the focus of their unseen observation, this provides them with increased autonomy to take ownership of their practice, along with the freedom to reflect more meaningfully and deeply on why they do what they do and its impact on their students. That unseen observation is underpinned by a personalised approach means that the professional needs specific to the individual teacher are prioritised and valorised. This lays the foundations for teachers to engage with observation in a more authentic way, which can lead them to experience it as a more meaningful and valuable process. This contrasts with the limited sense of agency that they experience with assessment-based approaches where the focus and terms of reference have been decided for them by others (e.g. UCU 2013).

The ubiquity of observation in education means not only that it is a familiar method to all teachers, but that it is also commonly used as a catalyst for reflective practice in formative models of observation. Reflection and classroom observation have close connections in the context of teachers' professional learning but for such learning to be effective and sustainable, certain conditions need to be established that distinguish formative models such as unseen observation from those associated with performance management. One of the fundamental factors relates to the change in the power differential between participants, with a more collaborative, egalitarian approach characterising the former as opposed to the hierarchical delineations epitomised by the latter. Added to this is the conceptualisation of observation as a tool for reciprocal learning, which is based on the premise that both parties bring knowledge and experience to this discursive relationship, not just the observer, and thus both stand to benefit from participating in the process by engaging in collaborative reflection and discussion with each other.

The centrality of reflexivity to the workings of the unseen observation cycle has implications for both the institution and the individual. It cannot be assumed that staff will already have the necessary skills to undertake these roles effectively. From an institutional perspective, the introduction of a radical approach like unseen observation requires an ongoing investment in time and resources to support the delivery and development of these skills as part of an institutional training programme. Training on self-reflection skills, peer coaching and questioning skills are all examples of the kind of fundamental support that need to be considered and provided to staff before beginning to implement unseen observation across the institution. The reflective skills of the teacher and the coaching skills of their collaborator will undoubtedly play an important part in how successful they are in developing intersubjectivity, along with shaping the quality and depth of their professional dialogue.

Regardless of the differing models, purposes and contexts of observation, opportunities for teachers to review and reflect on their practice and engage in collaborative dialogue with others are commonly identified as the most valuable elements of the process (Martin and Double 1998). Unseen observation provides a framework for practitioners to engage in a structured process of collaborative reflection and sensemaking about their practice. Unlike assessment-based models of observation that individualise teachers' practice, it conceptualises professional learning not as an individual act or the sole responsibility of the teacher but as a process that is socially situated, as it involves colleagues coming together to collaboratively reflect on, analyse and discuss their teaching and their students' learning. Hargreaves and Fullan's (2012) work on 'professional capital' emphasises the importance of collaboration between teachers. Their argument centres on the premise that teachers learn and improve more if they 'are able to work, plan, and make decisions with other teachers rather than having to make everything up or bear every burden by [themselves]' (p. 102). This is the basis of what they refer to as 'social capital' in their conceptualisation of professional capital. As Putnam (2000, p. 19) explains, 'social capital refers to connections among individuals – social networks and the norms of reciprocity and trustworthiness that arise from them'. Visone's (2022) research on 'collegial visits' in a single case study in a US elementary school identified an increase in social capital among those teachers who participated, resulting in a growth in trust, collegial support and a collective commitment to collaborate to improve the student learning experience. Once again, this reinforces the relevance and value of intersubjectivity when considering the effectiveness of observation as a conduit for teachers' professional learning.

Trust is the bedrock of social capital and an essential ingredient of any successful collaboration. As Hargreaves and Fullan maintain, 'groups with purpose that are based on trust also learn more. They get better at their work' (2012, p. 90). Sztompka (1999) suggests that there is a causal link between risk-taking, social capital and trust. By detaching observation from the domain of assessment and empowering practitioners to take control of and responsibility for their own professional learning, unseen observation creates the conditions in which trustworthy interactions and learning relationships can flourish between colleagues. The ethos imbued in unseen observation is that teachers are qualified, trusted professionals whose learning is best supported by being afforded the time and space to engage in participatory sensemaking and reflexive dialogue with their colleagues on their practice, with a view to improving themselves and the learning experiences of their students.

Conclusion

Meaningful and sustainable improvements in teachers' professional learning that feed into improvements in the quality of the teaching and learning experience thrive in organisational cultures where teachers are afforded opportunities to build social capital, develop relationships of collegial trust and engage in reflexive dialogue with their peers. As Darling-Hammond (2014, p. 5) argues, the development of collaborative communities of teacher learning 'will do more to support student achievement than dozens of the most elaborate ranking schemes ever could', thus emphasising the importance of teachers' professional learning as a collective act that is fostered through the development of collegial communities of practice rather than accountability systems that seek to monitor and measure individual teacher performance. Yet the status quo of how the UK education system conceptualises and configures classroom observation as a method in relation to quality improvement and quality assurance continues to rely on an assessment-based approach, which is driven by an individualising performance management agenda that is more concerned with sorting rather than supporting teachers.

Unseen observation imbues an approach to professional learning that challenges normalised policies and practices, particularly the orthodoxies that have shaped the contexts and cultures surrounding educators' engagement with observation and the underlying purposes driving its use in recent decades. In its ontological and methodological reconceptualisation of observation, unseen observation provides a credible alternative for moving beyond the confines of the normalised thinking and practice of performative approaches and allows us to reimagine observation as a genuine tool for supporting rather than sorting teachers.

Unseen observation views teachers as part of a valuable community of qualified, knowledgeable professionals who have earned the right for their work to be trusted. The experience of the pandemic over the last two years has provided us with an opportunity to rethink and reshape our approaches to teaching and learning. It would be an opportunity missed if we were simply to return to relying on normalised, assessment-based models of observation that have limited value to teachers' professional learning. Instead, through further research, with unseen observation we have an opportunity to think about and engage differently with observation as a tool for teacher learning.

References

Biesta, G. J. J., 1995. Pragmatism as a pedagogy of communicative action. In J. Garrison, (ed.) *The New Scholarship on John Dewey*. Dordrecht, Kluwer Academic Publishers, 105–127.

Biesta, G. J. J. 1998. Mead, intersubjectivity, and education: The early writings. *Studies in Philosophy and Education* 17(2), 73–99.

Cooper-White P., 2014. Intersubjectivity. In D. A. Leeming, (eds.) *Encyclopaedia of Psychology and Religion*. Boston MA: Springer. https://doi.org/10.1007/978-1-4614-6086-2_9182.

Darling-Hammond, L., Spring 2014. One piece of the whole: Teacher evaluation as part of a comprehensive system for teaching and learning. *American Educator* 38(1), 4–13.

Darling-Hammond, L., 2017. Teacher education around the world: What can we learn from international practice?', *European Journal of Teacher Education* 40(3), 291–309.

Darling-Hammond, L. and Hyler, M. E., 2020. Preparing educators for the time of COVID ... and beyond. *European Journal of Teacher Education* 43(4), 457–465.

Deetz, S., 1979. Language as dialogic: A look at the problem of intersubjectivity in interpersonal communication (ERIC: ED198580). Retrieved from: https://files.eric.ed.gov/fulltext/ED198580.pdf. Accessed 17.02.2022.

De Jaegher, H., Pieper, B., Clénin, D. and Fuchs, T., 2017. Grasping intersubjectivity: An invitation to embody social interaction research. *Phenomenology and the Cognitive Sciences* 16(3), 491–523.

Edgington, U., 2016. Performativity and the power of shame: Lesson observations, emotional labour and professional habitus. *Sociological Research Online* 21(1), 136–150.

Esterhazy, R., de Lange, T., Bastiansen, S. and Wittek, A. L., 2021. Moving beyond peer review of teaching: A conceptual framework for collegial faculty development. *Review of Educational Research* 91(2), 237–271.

Fernandez, M. L., 2010. Investigating how and what prospective teachers learn through microteaching lesson study. *Teaching and Teacher Education* 26, 351–362.

Gitomer, D., Bell, C., Qi, Y., McCaffrey, D., Hamre, B. K. and Pianta, R. C., 2014. The instructional challenge in improving teaching quality: Lessons from a classroom observation protocol. *Teachers College Record* 116(6), 1–32.

Hargreaves, A. and Fullan, M., 2012. *Professional Capital: Transforming Teaching in Every School*. New York: Teachers' College Press.

Huber, S. G. and Helm, C., 2020. COVID-19 and schooling: Evaluation, assessment and accountability in times of crises-reacting quickly to explore key issues for policy, practice and research with the school barometer. *Educational Assessment, Evaluation and Accountability* 32(2), 237–270.

Martin, G.A. and Double, J.M., 1998. Developing higher education teaching skills through peer observation and collaborative reflection. *Innovations in Education and Training International* 35(2), 161–170.

Merleau-Ponty, M., 2010. *Child Psychology and Pedagogy: The Sorbonne Lectures 1949–1952*. (T. Welsh, trans.). Evanston, Illinois: Northwestern University Press.

O'Leary, M., 2020. *Classroom Observation: A Guide to the Effective Observation of Teaching and Learning* (2nd Edition). London: Routledge.

O'Leary, M., 2021. 'Rethinking the improvement of teaching and learning in a virtual environment through unseen observation', *Future FE Pedagogies*, Volume 1 (Autumn 2021), 7–10. Available at: https://www.et-foundation.co.uk/wp-content/uploads/2021/09/Future-FE-Pedagogies-FINAL-FOR-PUBLICATION.pdf. Accessed 28.02.2022.

Peter, D. J., 2006. Lesson planning and the student teacher: Re-thinking the dominant model. *Journal of Curriculum Studies* 38(4), 483–498.

Putnam, R. D., 2000. *Bowling Alone: The Collapse and Revival of American Community*. New York NY: Simon & Schuster.

Rinvolucri, M., 1988. A role-switching exercise in teacher training. *Modern English Teacher*, Spring 1988.

Sherrington, T. and Caviglioli, O., 2020. *Teaching Walkthrus: Visual step-by-step guides to essential teaching techniques*. Melton, Woodbridge: John Catt Educational Ltd.

Smith, E., 2005. Learning to talk like a teacher: Participation and negotiation in co-planning discourse. *Communication Education* 54, 52–71.

Soslau, E., 2015. Exploring intersubjectivity between student teachers and field instructors in student teaching conferences. *Cogent Education* 2(1), Article 1045219. https://doi.org/10.1080/2331186X.2015.1045219. Accessed 12.02.2022.

Stolz, S. A., 2020. Phenomenology and phenomenography in educational research: A critique. *Educational Philosophy and Theory* 52(10), 1077–1096.

Sztompka, P., 1999. *Trust: A Sociological Theory.* Cambridge: Cambridge University Press.

Thorburn, M. and Steven S.A., 2021. Contemporary education and guiding pedagogical principals: The prospects for an embodied and intersubjective interpretation of phenomenology. *Oxford Review of Education.* https://doi.org/10.1080/03054985.2021.2006171.

Tilstone, C., 2012. *Observing Teaching and Learning* (2nd Edition). Abingdon: Routledge.

Timperley, H., 2011. *Realizing the Power of Professional Learning.* Maidenhead: Open University Press.

University and College Union (UCU), 2013. *Developing a National Framework for the Effective Use of Lesson Observation in Further Education.* Available at: http://www.ucu.org.uk/7105. Accessed 15.02.2022.

Visone, J. D., 2022. What teachers never have time to do: Peer observation as professional learning. *Professional Development in Education* 48(2), 203–217.

White, M. and Epston, D., 1990. *Narrative Means to Therapeutic Ends.* New York NY: W. W. Norton.

Whitmore, J., 2002. *Coaching for Performance: Growing People, Performance and Purpose* (3rd Edition). London: Nicholas Brealey.

Wood, P., 2017. Lesson Study – An Opportunity for Considering the Role of Observation in Practice Development. In M. O'Leary, (ed.) *Reclaiming Lesson Observation: Supporting excellence in teacher learning.* London: Routledge, 103–113.

Concluding comments 10

As we discussed towards the beginning of this book, it is only in recent years that the quality of teaching and learning has emerged as a policy priority and an area of mounting interest in higher education (HE). This interest has intensified the important role that research and scholarly work on teaching and students' learning have to play in informing the policy–practice debate, particularly in terms of how this evidence can be used to support academic teaching staff and their students in better understanding and ultimately improving their teaching and learning experiences. As part of this growing interest and body of work in teaching and learning in HE, observation has come to the fore as an increasingly essential element of institutional policy and practice aimed at developing and evidencing the quality of teaching and learning as well as supporting the pedagogic upskilling of its academic teaching staff.

This book has focused on the improvement of teaching and learning in HE *through* the use of observation. In contrast to conventional approaches to the use of observation in HE that continue to rely on it as a method of assessment with limited value to improving the overall quality of practice, this book has sought to reconceptualise and reposition observation firmly in the domain of educational inquiry. Drawing on a rich bank of applied research involving HE academic teaching staff and students from different disciplinary backgrounds, we have demonstrated how observation can be used to explore and critically reflect on their teaching and learning collegially and collaboratively. In reconceptualising and reconfiguring the use of observation by removing it from an assessment context and transforming it into a method of educational inquiry, new possibilities have emerged

DOI: 10.4324/9780429341908-10

for developing collegial understanding about the reciprocal relationship between teaching and learning. Through the tried-and-tested models we have presented in the second half of this book, we have interrogated the conceptualisation, theory, methodology and application of observation. Conscious of the need to move beyond the theoretical and prescriptive, we have tried to provide the reader with a clear insight into how to maximise the value of observation as a mechanism for promoting authentic scholarly collaboration between academic staff and between staff and students, with a view to enhancing the teaching and learning experiences of both parties.

One of the key lessons that we have learnt from our work over the last decade is that to embark on the kind of change in thinking and practice we advocate takes time and a strong sense of commitment on an individual and institutional level. A commitment to the principles underpinning a scholarly, inquiry-based approach to observation. A commitment to creating safe spaces and opportunities for staff and students to come together to explore and discuss teaching and learning without being monitored or measured. A commitment to investing time and energy in working collaboratively with our peers and students despite the never-ending, competing demands on our time. A commitment to recognising that there will be obstacles along the way but not allowing those obstacles to deter us from achieving our collective goals. As we commented when evaluating the impact and success of CoPO in Chapter 6, it is better to think of it as a long-distance journey rather than a short trip. But our experience tells us that it is a journey worth embarking upon. Findings from our research have continuously supported our original rationale for creating a safe, trusting, collegial space in which academic teaching staff and their students can thrive, as it has opened up new opportunities to engage with observation as a lens to inform and develop collegial understanding of effective teaching and learning.

Meaningful and sustainable improvements in teachers' professional learning that feed into improvements in the quality of the teaching and learning experience thrive in organisational cultures where teachers are afforded opportunities to build social capital, develop relationships of collegial trust and engage in reflexive dialogue with their peers. The findings from our work and that of other researchers in the field emphasise the importance of academics' professional learning as a collective act that is fostered through the development of collegial communities of practice rather than accountability systems that seek to monitor and measure individual teacher performance. With this in mind, it is all the more surprising why many education systems (the UK a case in point!) continue to rely on an assessment-based approaches to observation.

The interrelationship between teaching and learning is fundamentally qualitative in nature and as such requires appropriate methodologies and methods to explore, interrogate and make sense of these complex phenomena. Bringing students and staff together to engage in co-observation and co-reflection on their shared classroom experience enables them to see learning and teaching from their respective viewpoints and understand the connections and intersections between them. This also supports one of the most effective ways of learning, which involves collaborating with others to see different perspectives and approaches and to question our own practice and beliefs.

Providing students and academic teaching staff with opportunities to examine their understanding and experiences of teaching and learning and opening them up to dialogic exchange enables them to become aware of the strengths and areas for development in their practices. In the context of HE teaching and learning, instead of measuring and judging the performance of students and academics using national and institutional performance indicators, approaches like the model of CoCO discussed in Chapter 8 create shared spaces in which students and academics can engage in reflexive pedagogical dialogue on their classroom learning and teaching. This leads to collective sensemaking which has meaning for both students and lecturers in understanding and developing their practices. Scholarly inquiry into teaching and learning needs to be driven by the learning and development interests and goals of the key protagonists rather than a top-down agenda determined by others.

We had two clear aims in mind when we embarked on writing this book. The first was to enable the reader to acquire a comprehensive theoretical, practical and critically informed understanding of observation and how it can be applied as a lens for exploring the complex relationship between teaching and learning in HE. The second was to provide the reader with a suite of structured frameworks and practical resources for developing and applying observation in HE contexts as a means of collaborative inquiry to better understand and improve teaching and learning. We hope that we have managed to achieve this.

Index

Pages in *italics* refer figures and **bold** refer tables.

academics 25, 27, 32, 38, 44–46, 48–49, 54, **58**, 59–60, 63–65, 69, 93, 101, 110, 117–118, **132**, 141, 180; in HE 10, 36, 103; professional learning 7, 55, 198–214; and students 181; and teaching staff 8
academic teaching 65; staff 2, 4, 8, 54–56, 61–64, 66–70, 141, 217–219; students 2
Andresen, L. W 53
assessment-based models of observation 41–43, 75, 109, 120, 139, 143, 149, 199, 201, 204, 207, 210, 212, 214
authenticity 6, 32, 46–49, 56–61, 63–65, 69, 152, 175–176, 205
auto-didacticism 166

Ball, S. J. 16, 18, 27
Bamber, V. 63
Barnes, Y. 140
Barnett, R. 56, 59, 65, 67, 103
Bastiansen, S. 92, 205, 208
Baxter, L. A. 174
Becher, T. 63, 64
Biesta, G. 39, 42, 43, 62, 206

Billett, S. 142
Blomberg, G. 140
Bokeno, R. M. 104, 167
Boud, D. 138, 141–142
Bowden, J. 68, 161, 168
Boyer, E. L. 9, 10, 17, 47, 52, 53, 55, 59, 63
Brookfield, S. D. 64, 93, 161
Buskist, W. 103, 117

Cajkler, W. 45, 48
Campbell, J. 75
Carroll, C. 92, 102
Centres of Excellence in Teaching and Learning (CETL) 23–24, 26
Charteris, J. 146
Chester, A. 101
Cilliers, P. 39, 43
City, E. A. 144
Clarke, A. 101
classroom consciousness 7, 174, 176, 179; role of noticing in 171–173; between students and staff 168–171
Clénin, D. 62, 206
coaching: ethos and techniques 167; non-judgmental skills 109; and

observation skills 107–108, 138–156; in peer observation 103–106; questions 108–109, 130; skills 67, 201
CoCO *see* cycle of collaborative observation
collaboration 12, 48, 149, 174, 176, 181, 188, 212–213, 218; between academic teaching staff and professional support staff 55; between academic teaching staff and students 67; in higher education 158; model of student-teacher 174; peers and/or colleagues working together 67; between staff and students 55, 158; between students and academic staff 59; in teaching and learning 26
collaborative learning 173–174
collaborative observation 5; model 7; between students and staff 158–194
collaborative relationships 173–178
collegial faculty development (CFD) 92, 205
Collegial Peer Observation Scheme 6, 92, 100–134
communities of practice (CoP) 88, 207, 213, 218
complex adaptive systems 39, 40, 43, 59, 69
complexity theory 38–39, 49, 59
Compton, M. 92–93
Continuing Professional Development (CPD) 46, 85
CoPO *see* cycle of peer observation
Costa, A. L. 111
COVID-19 pandemic 3, 14, 198–199
Cranton, P. A. 53
critical engagement: with each other 67–69; in learning 62–63; with one's self 65–67; with pedagogical knowledge 63–64; with the socio-political environment 64–65
Cui, V. 93, 159, 185
cycle of collaborative observation (CoCO) 68, 93, 160–161, 164–168, 165; challenges and constraints 178–179; informing students about 184–185

cycle of peer observation (CoPO) 66, 68, 141, 147–148, 201, 218; challenges of change 111–117; double-edged sword of time 115–117; restoring professional agency through 117–119; seven stages of 108–110, *109*

Davies, W 16
Deetz, S. 205–206
De Jaegher, H. 62, 206
de Lange, T. 92, 205, 208
Dewey, J. 60–61
disciplinary: culture and practice 45; and departmental-level cultures 63; domain 44; knowledge 9, 45; stick 87
disciplines: and departments 10, 17, 63; division of academic 8, 17; and educational levels 11; of noticing 139; specialism of academic staff 32; and subjects 33; as traditional boundaries 40

Edgington, U. 86–87
effective teaching 6, 42, 66, 75, 85, 118, 120, 150–151, 180, 184, 218
Elmore, R. F. 144
Elton, L. 64
Emad, A. I. 103, 117
Esterhazy, R. 92, 205, 208

face-to-face teaching 4, 198
Felten, P 53
Fiarman, S. E. 144
French, A. 159
Friesen, M. 66
Fuchs, T. 62, 206
Fullan, M. 212–213
further education (FE) 12, 89; colleges 85; prevailing observation assessment systems 88; role of observation 84; staff 86–87; teaching triangles 88
The Future of Higher Education 12

Garmston, R. J. 111
Goodwin, Charles 141–142
Gosling, D. 91

Green, J. 22
Groccia, J. E. 103, 117
Guinea pigs 22

Hammersley-Fletcher, L. 101
Hardman, J. 85
Hargreaves, A. 212–213
Haynes, G. S. 78
HE *see* higher education
HEA/Advance HE fellowship scheme 25
Hendry, G. 186
higher education (HE): authentic teaching and learning in 56–61; Boyer's conceptualisation of scholarship in 52; distinguishing teaching and learning 34–37; features of 33–34; intersubjectivity in 61–62; peer review of 101–103; prevalence of QA systems in 89; student–staff collaboration in 158; teaching and learning experience in 37, 54–55, 217; teaching and learning in 2, 6, 8; teaching and learning policies 2; use of observation in 89–93; US sector 9, 53
Higher Education Academy (HEA) 5, 13, 19, 23–26
Higher Education Act of 1992 11
Higher Education and Research Act 35
Higher Education Funding Council for England (HEFCE) 14, 23, 93, 158, 162
higher education institutions (HEIs) 2, 7, 73
Higher Education in the Learning Society 12
Higher Education: Teaching Excellence, Social Mobility and Student Choice 14
Husserl, Edmund 205
hyperrealism 20, 56

Independent Review of Higher Education Funding and Student Finance 13
initial teacher education (ITE) 94, 199, 203
Institute for Learning and Teaching in HE (ILT) 12–13
instructional rounds 82–84, 144

International Society for the Scholarship of Teaching and Learning (ISSOTL) 11

Jewett, P 105

Kanuka, H. 91
Klampfleitner, M. 57, 59
Knight, P. 63
Kreber, C. 11, 46–49, 53, 55, 57, 59, 63–64, 169
Kyriakides, L. 75

Lave, J. 45
learning environment 14, 45, 47, 63, 166
learning relationships 103, 164, 174; teaching- 34, 48, 61, 174
learning rounds *see* instructional rounds
Leat, D. 105
Lieberman, J. 81
Lissack, M. 39, 43
Lofthouse, R. 105
Lopes, A. 139
Lynch, K. 140

Macfarlane, B. 22
MacPhee, D. 105
Making Policy in British Higher Education 15
Marriott, G. 77–78
Martinez, F. 76
Marton, F. 68, 161, 168
Mason, J. 139–140, 142
McMahon, T 103
Measures of Effective Teaching (MET) project 75
Merleau-Ponty, M. 206
Montgomery, B. M. 174
Mouraz, A. 139
Muijs, D. 75

National Association of Schoolmasters/Union of Women Teachers (NASUWT) 77
National Committee of Inquiry into Higher Education Report (NCIHE) 12

Index **223**

National Education Union (NEU) 77
National Student Survey (NSS) 21
noticing 138, 155, 179; components of 140; definition 139; in developing learning and classroom consciousness 171–173; explicit pedagogy of noticing 142; forms of 142; *professional noticing* 140; professional vision 141
Noticing Hypothesis 171

Oates, C. 82–84
observation: assessment-based models 41–43, 75, 109, 120, 139, 143, 149, 199, 201, 204, 207, 210, 212, 214; benefits and challenges of unseen 210–213; concept and a model of unseen 200–205; conventional models of 80–81; lesson study 80; observer preparing for 147–156; peer 101–103; pre-determined 83–84; professional learning 205–209; programmes in schools 79; role of coaching in peer 103–106; role of the observer as coach 142–147; student training workshop materials 181–184; of teaching and learning 139–142
observation cycle 80, 112, 119, 130, 134, 141, 144, 155, 162, 177
Office for Standards in Education (OfSTED) 36
Office for Students (OfS) 14, 159
O'Leary, M. 78–79, 85–86, 93, 159, 199
O'Loughlin, D. 92, 102
O'Neill 103

Page, L. 86
Parsell, M. 95
pedagogical content knowledge 63
pedagogical practices 26, 49, 62–65, 67, 69, 103, 174
pedagogical reasoning 172–173
pedagogical relationship 174–176
pedagogy 62, 103, 133, 139, 202; definition 8; development of content and 17; explicit 142; HE 5, 56; intentional discussion of 117

peer-based model of observation 1, 7, 79, 85, 87, 88, 90, 94, 100
peer observation of teaching (POT) 91–92, 106, 205
Perova, N. 140
Pieper, B. 62, 206
policy 2, 43, **58**; education 3, 76, 78; government 10, 100, 159; HE 3, 11–15, 20, 49, 56, 60; institutional 56, 64, 217; internal or external 202; makers 36, 43–44; neoliberal 3, 180; reforms 6, 26, 36; on teaching and learning 20, 73; TEF 19–20
Postgraduate Certificate in HE Teaching and Learning 24, 44
poststructuralist and psychoanalytical approach 87
POT *see* peer observation of teaching
professional frame 142
professional learning 87, 95, 104, 108, 110, 121, 140, 143–144, 146–147, 150, 154, 198–214, 205–209; of academic teaching staff 205–209; improvements in teachers' 218; observation as a formative tool for 94; teacher agency in 84; of teachers 73
professional noticing 140
professional vision 140–142
Prosser, M. 54–55

Rawlings-Smith, E. 80
Research Excellence Framework (REF) 37
Richardson, K.A. 39, 43
Richlin, L. 53–55
rich problem of practice 84
Robinson, W. 75
Rogers, Carl 60, 175–176
Rooney, D. 138, 141–142

Sachs, J. 95
Sadowski, C. 91
Saunders, M. 63
Schaaf, K. 76
Scholarship of Teaching and Learning (SoTL) 3, 6, 9, 27, 32, 38, 44, 46, 52; definitions of 10; literature 55; policy in England 11–15

Scholarship Reconsidered: Priorities of the Professoriate 9, 52
Schön, D. A. 55
Schönwetter, D.J. 66
schools 37, 90, 94, 107, 114, 155, 199; classroom observation systems 76; and colleges 2, 41, 49, 73, 95, 113; grading 77; hierarchical ranking systems 76; instructional rounds 82–84; lesson study 80–81; MET project 75; primary and secondary 74–75, 78; unseen observation 79–80
Seidel, T. 140
Shattock, M. 15
Sherin, M. G. 140
Shulman, L.S. 9, 38, 63–64
Skelton, A. 45
Smardon, D. 146
Sokal, L. 66
Solomon, Y. 140
Star, J. R. 140
Stolz, S.A. 209–210
Student Outcomes and Learning Gain 14
Stürmer, K. 140
Su, F. 32
systematic observation 54
Sztompka, P. 213

Taut, S. 76
Taylor, K. L. 66
teaching and learning: accelerated policy interventions on 11–13; collaborative relationships between students and staff 173–178; as complex systems 37–44; developing classroom consciousness 168–171; learning about 160–162; neoliberalising 16–18; policy impact and implications on 16; professionalising teaching 13–15; rise of 22–27; role of noticing 171–173; scholarship of 44–49; through collaborative observation project 162–163
Teaching and Learning Inquiry 11
teaching excellence 14, 20, 24–26, 90, 160, 169
Teaching Excellence Framework (TEF) 14, 36, 90, 100; at an institutional level 19; criticisms of 18; metrics 19; process and its related activities 20
Teaching Quality Assessment (TQA) 12
Teitel, L. 144
Tenenberg, J. 118
theory of action 84
Thorburn, M. 209
Tilstone, C. 79, 102
Timperley, H. 202, 211
Torres, A.C. 139
Trowler, P. 63–64

UK Professional Standards Framework (UKPSF) 24
University and College Union (UCU) 42, 87; project 88
unseen observation: benefits and challenges of 210–213; as a concept and a model of observation 200–205; COVID-19 pandemic 198–199; initial teacher education 199; and professional learning 205–209; virtual environment 200
use of observation: in higher education 89–93; in schools 74–84; in tertiary colleges and further education providers 84–89

Valente, J. M. S. 139
value for money 14, 20–21, 159
van der Sluis. H. 24
van Es, E. A. 140
virtual teaching and learning 4

Western, S. 105
White, Nick 185
Whitmore, J. 104, 144, 201
Wikeley, F. J. 78
Willetts, David 37
Wingrove, D. 101, 103
Wittek, A. L. 205, 208
Wittek, L. 92
Wood, M. 32
Wood, P. 45, 48, 80
Wragg, C. M. 78
Wragg, E.C. 75–78, 95

Žižek, S. 105

For Product Safety Concerns and Information please contact our EU
representative GPSR@taylorandfrancis.com
Taylor & Francis Verlag GmbH, Kaufingerstraße 24, 80331 München, Germany

www.ingramcontent.com/pod-product-compliance
Lightning Source LLC
Chambersburg PA
CBHW070309230426
43664CB00015B/2685